The Etchings of Jacques Bellange

Lenders to the Exhibition

The Art Institute of Chicago

Bibliothèque Nationale, Paris

Davison Art Center,
Wesleyan University

Des Moines Art Center

Fogg Art Museum,
Harvard University

Los Angeles County
Museum of Art

The Metropolitan Museum
of Art, New York

Museum of Fine Arts, Boston

The National Gallery of
Canada, Ottawa

Philadelphia Museum of Art

The Pierpont Morgan
Library, New York

Mr. and Mrs. Arthur E. Vershbow,
Boston

Yale University Art Gallery

The Etchings of
Jacques Bellange

Amy N. Worthen
and
Sue Welsh Reed

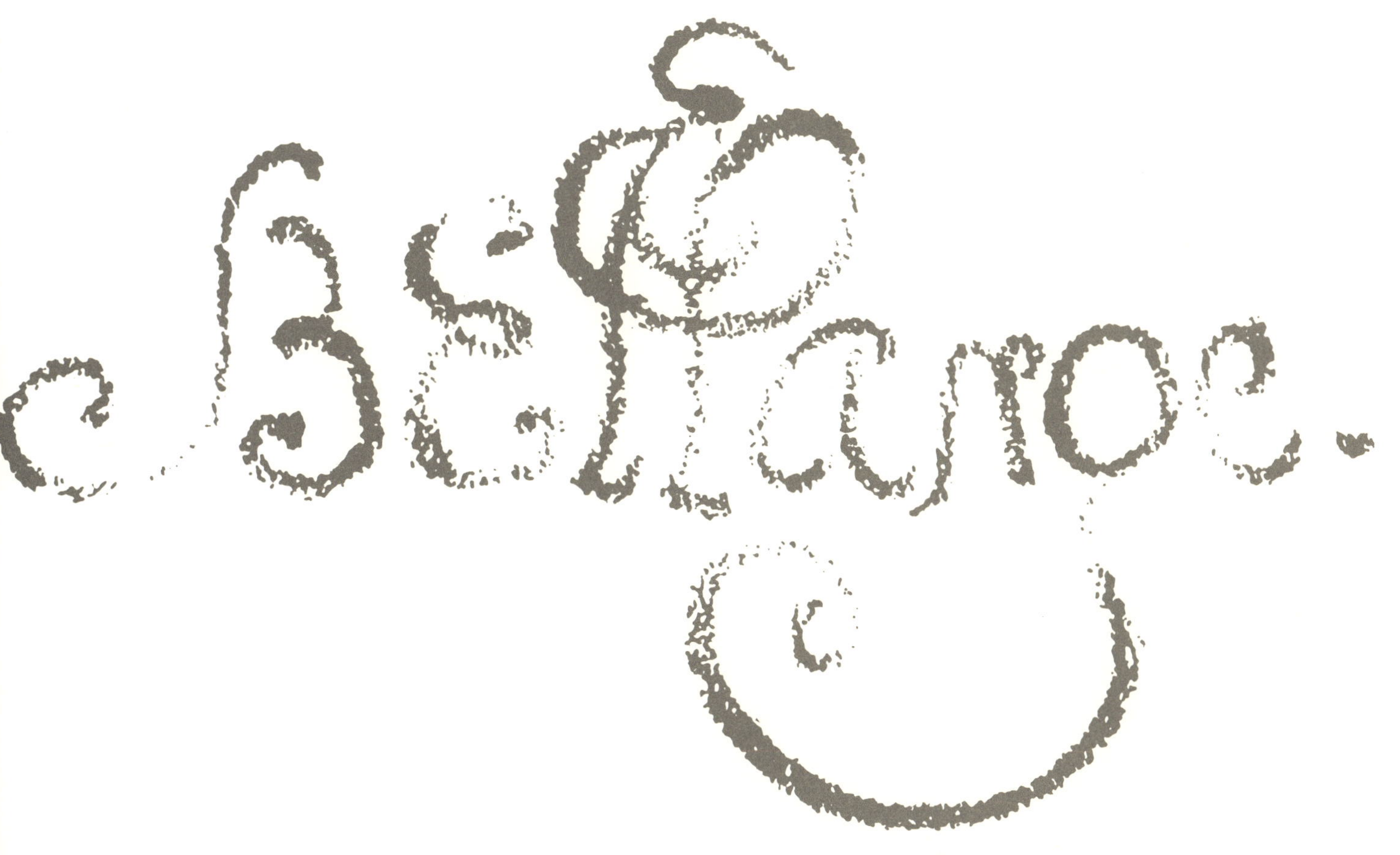

Des Moines Art Center
October 7 - November 16, 1975

Museum of Fine Arts, Boston
December 12, 1975 - February 15, 1976

The Metropolitan Museum of Art
March 23 - May 2, 1976

Table of Contents

Library of Congress catalogue card no. 75-271-77
ISBN 0-87846-094-2
Typeset by Dumar Typesetting, Dayton, Ohio
Printed by The Leether Press, Boston
Designed by Carl F. Zahn

Acknowledgments

THIS EXHIBITION was organized by the Des Moines Art Center, whose director, James T. Demetrion, not only conceived the idea but continued to lend support and assistance in many ways. We are grateful to Merrill C. Rueppel, who as director of the Museum of Fine Arts encouraged a collaboration that has been both profitable and enjoyable. It is a pleasure also to cooperate with the Metropolitan Museum of Art in conjunction with its showing of the exhibition.

An exhibition cannot be held without the cooperation of the lending institutions and their curators. For their generosity and assistance we would like to thank Harold Joachim of the Art Institute of Chicago, Jean Adhémar of the Bibliothèque Nationale, Paris, Richard S. Field of the Davison Art Center, Wesleyan University, Henri Zerner of the Fogg Art Museum, Harvard University, Ebria Feinblatt of the Los Angeles County Museum, the late John McKendry of the Metropolitan Museum of Art, Eleanor A. Sayre of the Museum of Fine Arts, Boston, Douglas Druick of the National Gallery of Canada, Kneeland McNulty of the Philadelphia Museum of Art, Felice Stampfle of the Pierpont Morgan Library, and James D. Burke of the Yale University Art Gallery. We are indebted to Etienne Dennery, Director of the Bibliothèque Nationale and to Pierre Tabatoni of the French Embassy Cultural Services, New York, for their help in arranging the loans from France.

Individuals at other institutions have also been most helpful, and we are grateful to Suzanne Boorsch, Colta Ives, Ruth Lehrer, Anthony Rosati, and Elizabeth Roth. Robert M. Light, Hubert Prouté, Frederick Schab, and David Tunick have been generous with information.

Fellow staff members have helped us in many ways, and we would especially thank Euphemia Conner, Peggy Patrick, and Grace Owens of the Des Moines Art Center, and Clifford S. Ackley, Kathryn Carey, Adolph S. Cavallo, Francis W. Dolloff, Allison Gulick, Lynn Salerno, Barbara Shapiro, Kate Steinway, Stephanie Stepanek, Linda Thomas, and Carl Zahn at the Museum of Fine Arts, as well as Cynthia Strauss, a most able volunteer.

Research in Iowa was facilitated by the help of Minnie Wilson of the Drake University Library and by Harlan Sifford and the staff of Special Collections at the University of Iowa Library. Pierre Gérard and the staff of the Archives de Meurthe-et-Moselle, Nancy, were most accommodating both by mail and in person.

Very special thanks are due Thomas F. Worthen for his constant interest and editorial assistance.

One could not so readily undertake a study of Bellange without the past publications of two European scholars. François-Georges Pariset's numerous articles brought to light much visual and documentary evidence about Bellange and related artists. We are deeply indebted to Nicole Walch for her precise chronology, and for her careful study of Bellange's stylistic development. We also appreciate her personal interest and support.

The exhibition and catalogue are supported in part by a grant from the National Endowment for the Arts, Washington, D.C., a federal agency, with additional support from the Anna K. Meredith Endowment Fund.

AMY N. WORTHEN
SUE WELSH REED

Point of View of the Exhibition

BECAUSE impressions are relatively rare, Bellange's etchings cannot easily be seen. There has been a recent surge in the appreciation of mannerist art, evidenced by numerous publications and exhibitions. It seemed appropriate to gather together all available etchings by Bellange and make them visible to a larger audience. To the best of our knowledge such an exhibition has never before been held. Moreover, the catalogue provides an opportunity to reproduce all the prints and to make available in English information from Nicole Walch's excellent German publication, as well as to publish the results of new research.

Bellange's prints are surprisingly well represented in American collections, and especially in the Museum of Fine Arts, Boston. Its sixty-six impressions from forty-three plates are rivaled only by the Bibliothèque Nationale's fifty-three impressions from forty-two plates. The Metropolitan Museum of Art in New York has a strong, representative group of prints, while other American and Canadian collections own one or more excellent impressions. The finest impressions available have been chosen from these collections in order to show Bellange at his best, something that no one collection in Europe or America can do alone. The exhibition lacks only two unique prints, the *St. Matthew* from Berlin, and the *Ex-Libris* from the Musée Lorrain; both are illustrated.

A number of prints that were important as sources of technique or motif for Bellange have been included in the exhibition, as well as some prints after his designs, and several by artists who were influenced by his work. A critical study of Bellange's drawings does not fall within the scope of this exhibition and is still to be made. However, it has been possible to include several examples of his delightful and masterful draughtsmanship, two of which relate directly to prints.

Introduction

Jacques Bellange worked as court painter at Nancy, the capital of the independent Duchy of Lorraine. His activity at the court is recorded from 1602 to 1616, during the reign of the dukes Charles III and Henri II. Bellange's art, along with that of El Greco in Spain, Fréminet in France, and Bloemaert in Utrecht, is one of the last manifestations of the international style known as mannerism. Until recently a pejorative term, mannerism is derived from the Italian word *maniera*, which had a positive connotation in the sixteenth century. It usually referred to the grace or elegance with which an action was performed or an image was depicted. Many of the complexities and refinements of mannerist art were paralleled in the literature and music of the period.

The stylistic similarities among artists working hundreds of miles away from each other can be explained by the fact that artists all over Europe looked toward the same sources of inspiration—primarily the art of Michelangelo, Raphael, and some of their followers, such as Parmigianino—and also because they interpreted these artists according to similar principles of style, or *maniera*. Since the primary sources of mannerist style were to be found in Italy, many artists went south to study the works of Michelangelo and Raphael, as well as to see the classical ruins preserved in Rome. For those who could not make the journey, engraved reproductions could be obtained, and these quickly circulated images and styles throughout Europe.

Mannerism rejected Renaissance ideals of clarity and logic in favor of a style based on exaggerated form, distortion of space, and the use of sumptuous color. Mannerist art was made for a learned, courtly audience which was, in part, the product of the extraordinary intellectual revolution brought about by the new availability of printed books to a literate public. This readership delighted not only in classical literature but in humanist fantasies and complex allegories as well. Contemporary epics such as Tasso's *Gerusalemme liberata* as well as classical works such as Ovid's *Metamorphoses* provided literary themes for the visual arts. The sixteenth century was a time when vast new wealth flowed into Europe as a consequence of world exploration and conquest. This exploration stimulated a taste for the exotic, and collectors, maintaining cabinets of curiosities, could obtain rare and precious natural and man-made objects from around the world.

In contrast to the scientific and humanistic concerns of Renaissance painting, or the political, didactic, and edifying concerns of the baroque, the aim of much mannerist art was, primarily, to entertain the viewer, who delighted in attempting to puzzle out the hidden allegories, classical themes, obscure meanings, and references to other works of art. Often decorative and witty, mannerist paintings had formal qualities of precious and perfect finish, brilliant passages of color and color contrasts, depiction of luxurious contemporary clothing and fantastic or exotic costume, masterful rendition of textures, metals, and gems, and a strong underlying eroticism—even in religious painting—all of which contributed to the viewer's pleasure.

The leading centers of mannerism were Florence, Parma, Rome, Fontainebleau, Prague, Antwerp, Utrecht, and Haarlem. Parmigianino and Barocci in Italy, Spranger in Prague, and Goltzius in Haarlem were probably the immediate stylistic models for Bellange, whose formative years were in the last decades of the sixteenth century.

The Milieu

LORRAINE, ancient Lotharingia, was the kingdom, then duchy, in the lands allotted to the Emperor Lothair I in 843 by the Treaty of Verdun. By the eleventh century the original, extensive territory had been reduced to that of present-day Lorraine in northeast France. The capital of the duchy was Nancy, whose sole advantage was its central location. The principal fiefs of the dukes of Lorraine included the countship of Bar, and the three bishoprics of Metz, Toul, and Verdun.

The modern history of Lorraine begins with Duke Charles III (reigned 1545-1608),[1] who was raised in France by King Henri II and was married to Claude de France, daughter of the king and Catherine de'Medici. Charles and Claude's children included Henri, Duc de Bar, the future Duke of Lorraine; the Cardinal Charles of Lorraine; and Christine, who became duchess of Tuscany as the wife of Ferdinand I de'Medici. In contrast to his predecessors, who occupied themselves with foreign expeditions and titular claims, Charles devoted his long reign to improving administration and to stimulating commerce and industry, which was based on mining and saltworks. Lorraine was continually disturbed by German troops passing through to help French Protestants and by the agitation of Calvinists in the three bishoprics. In 1572 Charles established a university at Pont-à-Mousson, which he gave to the Jesuits as part of an effort to combat Calvinism. Charles enlarged and fortified Nancy, which until this time was a small, relatively insignificant town, lacking even a bishopric.

Charles III died in 1608 and was succeeded by Henri. The magnificence of Charles' funeral and of Henri's ceremonial entry into Nancy in 1610 were recorded in the extraordinary book *Pompe funèbre de Charles III,* published by the secretary of state, Claude de la Ruelle (see cat. no. 1).

Duke Henri II (reigned 1608-24) succeeded in getting rid of the German bands, and although religious tension continued to be a problem, Henri's convictions were not so absolute as to prevent him while still Duc de Bar, from having a Protestant wife, Catherine de Bourbon, the sister of King Henri IV of France. It was she who introduced ballet to the court of Lorraine in 1600, with costumes, sets, and props designed and constructed by the court sculptors, architects, and painters.[2] The ballet was a great success and was repeated in 1603 on two occasions, one of which was the visit of Henri IV to Nancy. Catherine brought the painter Jacques Danglus with her from Paris in 1601; the following year he and Bellange were engaged in painting the *cabinet* of Catherine de Bourbon with scenes from the lives of virtuous ancient women (see cat. no. 5). Catherine died in 1604, and in 1606 Henri married Margherita Gonzaga, the daughter of Vincenzo Gonzaga, duke of Mantua, and Eleanora de'Medici, sister of Marie de'Medici. The wedding festivities of Henri and Margherita were recorded by Jean de Rosieres.[3] Pariset has described Bellange's participation in the wedding festivities.[4] He repainted the Galerie des Cerfs in the palace, and he designed props and other ephemera both for Margherita's entry into Nancy and for the ballet performed in her honor. Bellange's costume drawings and figure studies in the Louvre and in Stockholm may be related to his plans for such a pageant, and these figure types are frequently echoed or repeated in his etchings.

Margherita had been raised at the brilliant Gonzaga court, which in her lifetime was host to the poet Tasso and employed the composer Monteverdi and the painter Rubens. Exiled in provincial Nancy, Margherita wrote letters to Mantua that reflect her feelings of loneliness. It had been anticipated that Nicole, the daughter born to Henri and

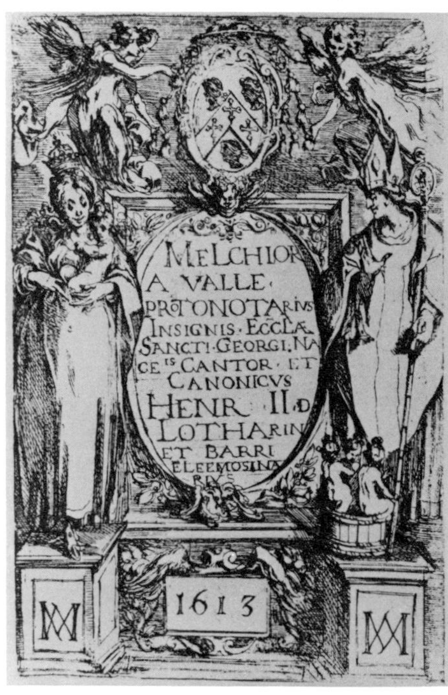

Fig. 1. BELLANGE. *Ex-Libris of Melchior de la Vallée,* etching, 1613. Musée Historique Lorrain (from a facsimile)

1. Much has been written about daily life at at the court of Lorraine at the beginning of the seventeenth century. The reader who is interested in learning about the prices of everything from pen quills to toothpaste is referred to the exhaustive documentary works of Hippolyte Roy and Henri Lepage. H. Roy, *La Vie à la cour de Lorraine souse le duc Henri II (1608-1624),* Paris-Nancy, 1914. H. Lepage, "Le Palais Ducal de Nancy," in *Bulletin de la Société d'archéologie Lorraine,* 1852, pp. 5 ff. A genealogical chart of the House of Lorraine 1489-1675 and other historical background pertinent to Bellange's time may be found in H. Diane Russell, *Jacques Callot, Prints and Related Drawings,* exhibition catalogue, National Gallery of Art, Washington, D.C., 1975.

2. Pariset wrote of Catherine: *"Raised at the Court of Valois . . . the sister of the king felt it was possible to reconcile the pleasures of life with faith, and that one should accept beauty as a gift from the Creator. Cultivated, well-read, a musician and artist, she loved ballet with a passion."* F.-G. Pariset, "Les Fêtes et le témoignage de Jacques de Bellange," *Les Fêtes de la Renaissance,* Paris, 1956, p. 164.

3. Jean de Rosières, *Notables observations, sur le mariage de Monseigneur Henry Prince de Lorraine, Duc de Bar, etc. avec Madame Marguerite de Gonsague, Princesse de Mantoue,* Pont-à-Mousson, 1606.

4. Pariset, *Les Fêtes de la Renaissance.*

Margherita, would be betrothed to the Dauphin of France. With King Henri IV's assassination in 1610, his wife, Marie de'Medici (Margherita's aunt), shifted alliances, and the dauphin (Louis XIII) was engaged to the daughter of the king of Spain. The disappointment resulting from this diplomatic failure substantially reduced Margherita's political influence in Lorraine. In addition, her only children were girls. She is said to have grown old, ignored, ignorant, and superstitious. Yet she must have maintained an active role in the court festivities, for in 1616 she arranged a ballet for which Bellange designed the decorations.

During the reigns of Charles III and Henri II, the construction of the *ville neuve* of Nancy was begun outside the walls of the old town. From 1592 there was a great deal of city planning and building, with many religious groups sponsoring new construction. This was a time of active patronage for the architects, sculptors, and painters of Nancy. Through marital and political connections, the court of Lorraine was in close touch with and fell under the direct cultural influence of the courts of Florence, Mantua, and Fontainebleau. The Florentine court, over which Henri's sister, Christine of Lorraine, the Duchess of Tuscany, ruled, was at this time involved in the planning and construction of the huge Capella dei Principi, or Medici rotunda, in San Lorenzo. Duke Ferdinand I sponsored a competition for the chapel's design in 1602. Don Giovanni de'Medici's octagonal plan, modified by Buontalenti, Nigetti, and others, was to inspire the ducal chapel in the Church of the Cordeliers in Nancy. The construction of this chapel was begun in 1609 under Henri II. It was designed and built by Jean Richier, J. B. Stabili, and Pierre Michel, and its octagonal plan and trompe l'oeil dome is clearly derived from the Florentine structure.

The Italianization of the ducal palace complex proceeded with the construction of a new garden between 1609 and 1612. Rare plants were imported to stock the garden, which was designed by Métezeau, architect to the French king. Simon Drouin designed statues of fourteen classical gods and goddesses to occupy niches along one of the walls of the garden. In 1611, a gallery opening onto the new garden was decorated by Jacques Bellange with themes from Ovid's *Metamorphoses.* Callot's etching of 1625 (Lieure 566) shows the appearance of the Italianate garden during the reign of the Duchess Nicole.

Messengers and ambassadors were continually coming to and from Mantua, Florence, and Rome, and documents attest to a lively exchange of gifts and works of art. Two of Bellange's paintings were sent to Mantua in 1608, and paintings by Pourbus were received. Bellange was paid on several occasions for gilding frames or borders of pictures sent from Italy. One cannot merely state that Renaissance culture had finally arrived in Nancy. The splendid funerals, the entry of Henri II, the funeral book, the ballets, the Italian garden, the Florentine rotunda, and the new town all clearly have political as well as cultural import. The dukes of Lorraine began to recognize their significance as a means of augmenting their stature. Henri in particular encouraged the importation not only of wives but of styles of art and building construction that refer to the most powerful courts of Italy and France. In this light it is easier to understand the wording of the commission to Bellange of 1608 to go to France to study paintings so "he might better serve his Duke."

Nancy was taken by the French in 1633 but was restored to the dukes of Lorraine in 1697. The duchy was finally incorporated into France in 1766.

Painting in Nancy, 1600-1620

The Art of early seventeenth century Lorraine has been characterized as depending largely on French and Flemish late mannerist sources, and at least two of the artists working at the court were brought from Paris at the personal request of the sovereigns: Claude Henriet by Charles III in 1590, and Jacques Danglus by Catherine de Bourbon in 1601. Furthermore, Bellange's 1608 study trip to France confirms the importance the court placed on contemporary French art in relation to its own production. Unfortunately, a precise determination of the style of painting at the court of Lorraine in the years 1600-20 can be made only with difficulty, for few works of certain attribution have survived. We know, for example, of no existing works made in Lorraine by Claude Henriet, the leading painter at the court until his death around 1605.[1] The court artists worked on a variety of projects, from major commissions involving the construction and decoration of the halls of the palace to the designing of ephemera for the frequent court festivals. They were also employed in the city, making church decorations, tomb sculptures, and civic statuary.

Most of this artistic production is known only from documents. On the basis of the few surviving painted works of both religious and classical subject matter,[2] one finds

1. Among the painters recorded as working alongside Henriet and Bellange were Jacques Danglus, Rémond Constant, Jean de Wayembourg, Jean Lamant, Jean Contesse, and Moyse Bougault. Court architects and sculptors included Jean de la Hiere, Florent and Simon Drouin, Jean Richier, J. B. Stabili, and members of the Chaligny family. By about 1620, the painters Claude Deruet, Jean le Clerc, and Georges de La Tour were active in Nancy.

2. The surviving paintings upon which these remarks are based include: Jean de Wayembourg, *Family of Charles III Praying to the Madonna of the Rosary,* 1597, Church of the Cordeliers, Nancy; Rémond Constant, *Holy Family with Angels,* after Hans

in the provincial mannerist art of Nancy a clear reliance on foreign sources. The painters seemed to supress background in favor of the figures, eliminating a feeling of deep space. They understood the use of contrast and had a splendid sense of color and light. There is nothing in these School of Lorraine paintings bizarre or extreme, in the conception of the human figure or in the level of emotion. But there are undeniable stylistic connections with Bellange's art, and it is apparent that he was, rather than an anomaly, the brilliant practitioner of a personal art forged from a variety of sources within the court and from the outside world.

Printmaking in Nancy before 1611

Before Claude de la Ruelle's *Pompe funèbre de Charles III* of 1611, the practice of etching and engraving were virtually unknown in Nancy. Book-printing itself came very late to Nancy, and there was barely an illustrated printed book—or even frontispiece—made in any medium before 1602 in Nancy, Metz, Pont-à-Mousson, or San Mihiel, the major printing centers of Lorraine. In the years 1600-10, Blaise André, Jacob Garnich, and Melchior Bernard were the most prolific printers, had the most frequent contact with writers in the court, and published the greatest number of books illustrated with engraved pictures. This means that they had intaglio presses. We know of only a handful of intaglio prints published in Nancy before 1610-11, and they are all engravings.[1] These include engravings by Alexandre Vallée, Thomas de Leu, Leonard Gaultier, and Jean Appier, a native of Nancy. The prints by these artists were almost all frontispieces, book illustrations, or official portraits.

van Aachen, Church of the Cordeliers, Nancy; and "School of Lorraine," *Venus, Pallas*, and *Juno*, Strasbourg. Attributed to Bellange are: *The Stigmatization of St. Francis*, Musée Lorrain, Nancy; *Head of Roman Emperor*, Musée Lorrain, Nancy; the angel in the *Annunciation* diptych, Karlsruhe; *Lamentation*, Leningrad. We are inclined to accent the *Lamentation*, as well as parts at least of the *Saint Francis*.

The funeral of Charles III in 1608, and the subsequent entry of Henri II in 1610 inspired at least eight books which were published in Nancy and Pont-à-Mousson in 1608-10. Claude de la Ruelle, secretary of state to both dukes, conceived and published his *Pompe funèbre de Charles III* in 1611. It differed from all the previous publications in that it was illustrated with etchings. It was, in fact, a picture book with accompanying text. Although nothing like this had ever been produced before in Nancy, festival books were a well-established art form. The publication of this book must have had political implications beyond de la Ruelle's immediate personal situation, for it set the duchy of Lorraine on a par with other major courts of Europe.

To produce a work of such ambitious character, de la Ruelle had to bring in an etcher, for it would have required far more time to engrave the ninety-four plates than to etch them. De la Ruelle needed etchers, and he had to go out of Lorraine to get them. It must be assumed that etching just did not exist in Nancy; and the fact that the young Jacques Callot, whose boyhood dream was to be a printmaker, had to leave Nancy in order to receive his training, supports this conclusion.

In 1610 Frederick Brentel and Hermann de Loye were summoned to Nancy by Claude de la Ruelle. The ducal court had certain contacts with the Strasbourg publisher Jacob van der Heyden, who had published engraved portraits of various members of the court in 1600 and 1606. Claude de la Ruelle may have turned to him for assistance. Van der Heyden, himself unable to leave a flourishing business and come to Lorraine, may have recommended de Loye and Brentel, both of Strasbourg.

1. Previous writers have called some of these prints etchings. We have examined all known illustrated books and most single sheets printed at Nancy, Pont-à-Mousson, and Metz from 1590 to 1610. None of these was executed in etching.

The contracts for the *Pompe funèbre de Charles III*[2] present an account of the problems of printing a book of this degree of lavishness in Nancy in 1610. They document the very beginnings of etching as introduced to the court of Lorraine. The contract between Claude de la Ruelle and Frederick Brentel is dated May 12, 1610, less than one month after the entry of Henri II, but almost two years after the death of Charles III. Hermann de Loye acted as a translator for Brentel, who did not speak French. The terms stated that Brentel, painter and etcher, and burger of Strasbourg, should within three weeks come to Nancy, to a house owned by de la Ruelle, in order to etch specified pictures of the funeral, including the frontispiece, of which Brentel had already seen the drawings. There follows a list of sums to be paid to Brentel, in addition to which de la Ruelle would be responsible for providing board and lodging and not only transportation expenses for Brentel and "his lad's" move to Nancy and return to Strasbourg but also his expenses in coming to make the present agreement. Further, "*the said Sieur de la Ruelle shall furnish at his expense the plates of copper for the said etching, shall buy the ingredients for the varnish and the acid and for all the other things which concern the said work without the said Master Frederick being obliged to contribute anything to the work except his labors, and if it should happen that one or several of the said six plates are ruined by the said Master Frederick, he shall then be responsible to re-do them at his expense, except for the food and*

2. P. Marot, "Contrats passés pour la gravure et l'impression des planches de la pompe funèbre de Charles III, Duc de Lorraine," in *Gutenburg-Jahrbuch*, 1951, pp. 140 ff.

lodging, for which the said Sieur de la Ruelle shall be responsible during the time of the said work. Moreover it has been agreed between the said parties that for each of the pictures of the said funeral which the said Sieur de la Ruelle will have made by the painters of Nancy, Master Frederick will be responsible for applying the ground on the copper plates and etch the plates after they have been drawn upon."
This excerpt clearly shows that the local artists were to participate in the project, by drawing, presumably with etching needles, on grounded plates which would then be etched by Brentel.

One of the problems presented by the *Pompe funèbre de Charles III* is how to explain the presence of Bellange's "self-portrait" (cat. no. 1) as well as many other Bellange-like faces and costumes that seem to be scattered throughout the twelve plates of section III of the book. If, as indicated by the contract, there was a group effort taking place in the house owned by de la Ruelle where Brentel was working, one can well imagine that the etchers allowed Bellange to put in his own portrait.

On July 6, 1610, a contract was made between Claude de la Ruelle and Hermann de Loye, printer of copper-plate engravings, for the printing of "1000 proofs of the pictures of the funeral rites of the burial of His Late Highness." It provided for the lodging of de Loye, his wife, and one small lad (if they came along), plus the expenses of travel, including food and a carriage. De Loye, for his part, promises that he will: *"do the said work and will furnish the black [pigment] and while staying here will work diligently in order to print, and because it is necessary to obtain large quantities of copper plates, for which the said Sieur de la Ruelle has given to the said Sieur Hermant the patterns and models in paper for their size, the said Sieur Hermant has promised to furnish in this city of Nancy the required quantity beaten and polished, @ 18 gros the pound, which the said Sieur de la Ruelle will be responsible for paying him for . . ."*
This contract was witnessed by Jean Callot, herald of arms of the duke, and the father of Jacques Callot. It should be noted that, between the first and second contracts, certain work had been added. De la Ruelle's conception of the project seems to have grown and changed in the presence of Brentel and de Loye. A receipt terminating the contract at the conclusion of the project, dated July 2, 1611, indicates that de la Ruelle was also responsible for providing the printing paper.

The most important omission in the contracts has to do with the printing press. Did de Loye bring his own from Strasbourg, for which the carriage mentioned in the contract was required, or did he build one, or have one put at his disposal by some printer in Nancy? Further, one finds no mention of Matthaeus Merian in the contracts.[3] It is possible that Merian, then 17, was the "garçon" mentioned as Brentel's assistant in the May 12 contract. Wüthrich[4] contends that they worked as equals, which is supported by Merian's signature on the frontispiece. Although we do not have a precise understanding of Merian's role in Nancy in 1611, it is evident that his stay there was important both for himself and for Bellange. For in 1615-16 we find Merian working for Jacob van der Heyden of Strasbourg, making etched copies of eleven of Bellange's etchings (see cat. nos. 25, 35, 37, and 39).

The printed funeral books were distributed by de la Ruelle. The *Pompe funèbre de Charles III* must have made a great impression on the people of Lorraine, for it has been continuously admired there. Numerous copies have survived, including a hand-colored copy in the Nationalbibliothek in Vienna.

3. Marot suggests that additional contracts have yet to be found.

4. L. H. Wüthrich, *Das druckgraphische Werk von Matthäus Merian d. Ae.*, vol. 1, Basel, 1966.

Everyone of any importance at court or in Lorraine was represented, and hundreds were identified by name. The publication of this book must have had a substantial effect in stimulating the spectacular development of etching in Nancy. After 1611 the concept of patronage of the graphic arts must have occurred to others at the court and in Lorraine, which resulted in the printmaking activity of many of the artists associated with the court, including Bellange and, later, Callot, Israël Henriet, and Claude Deruet.

Bellange as a Printmaker

It appears that Bellange's career as a printmaker, which resulted in an oeuvre of at least forty-eight etchings, involved a time span from approximately 1610/11 to 1617/20, which can be divided into three phases.[1] In the first, represented by *The Entry of Henri II* (cat. no. 1), Bellange learned the rudiments of etching from a professional etcher. We assume that his instruction came from either Matthaeus Merian or Frederick Brentel, who, despite his commercial background, etched with a fine line and in a delicate and subtle manner that differs considerably from the coarse single-etch method virtually universal at that time among commercial printmakers. Bellange's etching in the funeral book, and his other early independent etchings dating from about 1613, including the *Ex-Libris* and the Prémontré prints (cat. nos. 2-4), reflect Brentel's etching technique. The *Vision of Saint Norbert* reveals the difficulties of the novice Bellange in obtaining a controlled bite.

In the second phase (spanning cat. nos. 5-26, 28-40), Bellange studied a wide range of "Old Master" and modern engravings and etchings,

1. This discussion is based on a slightly modified version of Walch's chronology.

most significantly those of Parmigianino and Barocci. In the prints he not only found figures and compositions to use in his prints and drawings but discovered more complex methods of enriching his etching technique. Studying the methods of various artists, he saw prints that used multiple biting, drypoint, and engraving combined with etching. Bellange came to see the etching plate as an object to be elaborated and corrected if necessary, not predetermined by the original drawing but subject to the as in the *Virgin with a Spindle,* (cat. artist's changing will. Sometimes, no. 8), his borrowed methods were used to excess, as in his compulsive use of stippling for flesh, borrowed from Barocci. At first, Bellange used this technique discretely, then obsessively, until his faces looked like orange rinds. Later, as in the *Blind Hurdy-Gurdy Player* (cat. no. 27), he learned to use a lighter hand, mixing stippling with other strokes, or stippling cloth as well as flesh.

The prints of Bellange's second period are highly complex in composition and technically very labored, lacking spontaneity. Although in almost every case no working proofs survive, we can still reconstruct the concentrated effort Bellange expended to master new and unorthodox techniques. Sometimes he scraped and burnished out mistakes, leaving an uncraftsmanlike trace (cat. nos. 43 and 50); sometimes he just drew over and re-etched the section that displeased him (cat. no. 8). Many of the plates were poorly bitten (cat. no. 5), or foul-bitten (cat. no. 18). In some prints he found the immediacy and delicacy of drypoint touches suitable for his image (cat. no. 6 and cat. no. 26). He also came to use the burin to make small, dark accents or add stippling (from cat. no. 6 on). These two latter techniques made it possible to avoid a further grounding and re-biting of the plate.

This second phase comprises the bulk of Bellange's work, the most ambitious, crowded, and derivative compositions. The large prints are so filled with work that one feels that Bellange had a more reliable etching ground than was supposed to have existed in France before Callot's return from Italy in 1621. As A. Hyatt Mayor has said, writing about Callot's *Fair at Impruneta* (Lieure 361), until then no etcher would have dared expend so much labor on a plate, for the etching ground might flake off and the acid foul-bite.[2] Yet Bellange's work on the *Saint Lucy* (cat. no. 29), the *Adoration of the Magi* (cat. no. 31), and the *Carrying of the Cross* (cat. no. 40) could hardly have been risked had Bellange lacked reliable materials. It is not known whether Bellange developed these himself or received information from Brentel or Merian, who seem to have had knowledge of good etching grounds. That Bellange himself played some role as a technical innovator was first suggested by Sandrart. He wrote: *"Bellange was the first inventor and practitioner of neat* (zierlich) *etching in all history."*[3] In 1804, Huber-Rost interpreted this to mean that Bellange was the first to use hard varnish. There is evidence in Bellange's prints for Sandrart's statement. Although Sandrart wrote at least half a century after Bellange, and we are not sure of the source of his information, he may have been told this by Merian's son, Matthaeus Merian the Younger, who was Sandrart's student and companion in the 1630's. However, Sandrart, too, was an etcher, and perhaps he based his judgment on his own observations.

In the third phase of his development as an etcher (cat. nos. 27, 42, 43, 45-64), the dense festivity of Bellange's largest plates became more solemn, dramatic, and organized. Bellange continued to adapt figures and compositions from earlier sources, but now his command of the etching medium enabled aesthetic necessity to direct his technique. His etchings of the late period approximate his spontaneous wash drawings. His developing interest in strong, painterly, chiaroscuro effects, which overrode his previous use of abundant detail, is probably due to an influx of Caravaggesque ideas in Nancy. Bellange's *Annunciation,* (cat. no. 42), for example, was very likely inspired by a painting attributed to Caravaggio which arrived in Nancy in 1616.[4] Bellange's desire to render striking light effects led him to the procedure of selectively stopping-out parts of an already bitten image. In two prints from the Apostle series (cat. nos. 55 and 57) we observe Bellange's highly original procedure of showing the actual brushstrokes of the stop-out varnish he used to render the light of the halo.

Bellange was, to adopt Bartsch's terminology, a *peintre-graveur,* a painter-printmaker. Although his mannerist style owed a debt to Spranger and Goltzius, he rejected the mannerist engraver's delight in the virtuoso techniques of swelling, curving, parallel lines. Instead, Bellange found in etching what he needed, and improvised, invented, or borrowed the rest. His attitude pre-dated by only a few years that of Seghers, Rembrandt, and Castiglione.

Bellange's Graphic Style

Although we have little evidence of Bellange's painting style, we can characterize his graphic style. His drawings show an eloquent and spontaneous handling of line and wash to create graceful and elegant decorative forms. The etchings are characterized by a distinctive con-

2. A. Hyatt Mayor, *Prints and People,* New York, Metropolitan Museum of Art, 1971, 455.

3. Joachim von Sandrart, *Teusche Academie der edlen Bau-, Bild-, und Malerey-Künste,* Nuremberg, 1675-79.

4. A recently discovered canvas of the *Lamentation* (Hermitage), attributed to Bellange, utilizes the dramatic light emanating from a single candle, as does its preparatory wash drawing (Dijon). See I. V. Linnik, "Un tableau de Jacques de Bellange nouvellement découvert," *Revue de l'art,* no. 20 (November 1973), 65-70.

ception of the human figure, by highly rhythmic compositions, and a free, inventive use of the etching medium.

Bellange's figures have interesting silhouettes. Their anatomical proportions are frequently distorted for design purposes. Affected, mannequin-like poses and the extravagant gestures of boneless hands give the figures an intense theatricality. Bellange will alter lines already etched to refine the gesture of a hand or the attitude of a head in order to create a more elegant form or expressive pose, and simultaneously, a more striking decorative pattern (see cat. nos. 6 and 50). He delineates a figure with extremely close attention, not only to its contours but also to the negative spaces around it. The area between a gesturing arm and torso or between body and a fluttering bit of drapery assumes an ornamental shape of its own.

Bellange's treatment of costume is wonderfully artificial. Skirts are long and trailing, or gathered up and mysteriously inflated; garments are wet and clinging. In the earlier prints the peculiar spongy texture of stippled flesh suggests a plasticity at variance with drapery that betrays no sense of a body beneath it; later the body, however distorted, is to be perceived through the clothing.

Certain recurring facial types are peculiar to Bellange. The "beautiful," too perfect, oval face, whose shape is echoed by heavy-lidded, oval eyes and high, upswept brows, appears in holy persons, male and female (the Virgin, Child, angels, Saint John), often with an ambiguous smile. It is this bisexual canon of beauty that contributes so much to the sexual ambiguities in Bellange's prints. Note especially Saint John (cat. nos. 57 and 59), who also has the high waist, narrow chest, and shoulders, large abdomen and thighs, more often found in Bellange's women. These proportions are paralleled by the voluminous bloomers and short, tight jackets of contemporary men's fashion such as the noblemen wear in the *Entry of Henri II* (cat. no. 1) or in prints by Callot or by the Dutch artist Willem Buytewech.[1] Several other facial types found repeatedly in Bellange's prints are a feminine profile with clear-cut nose and heavy-lidded eyes, and foreshortened heads with upturned gazes. Ugly, hook-nosed, evil-eyed men recur, like actors in a repertory company, both as tramps and as saints (cat. nos. 28 and 50). In the earlier prints (cat. nos. 1-41) Bellange used pure ornament to enhance his figures: already elaborate costumes are further embellished with embroidery, furs, and jewels; exotic headgear is plumed. Armor and precious vessels are embossed, often with human or satyr-like faces, while shoes based on antique sandals are ornately cut and strapped. Coiffures are complex confections, whether tightly bound in multiple braids or profuse and curly.

Bellange's compositions are pleasingly rhythmic. These stylish but impossibly proportioned creatures strike attitudes for design's sake, so that unbroken contours may undulate from shoulder to fingertips, neck to hemline, or knee to toe. Repeated and opposing curves and angles of heads and limbs lead the eye musically across the image—here stately, full, mellow, there quick, accented, brilliant. Bellange's thematic repetitions, linear and tonal contrasts, and ornamentation can be likened to those of Claudio Monteverdi (1567-1643), his musical counterpart at the Mantuan court.

The figures are arranged in one or more parallel planes, like stage flats, in a space that has been constructed so as to appear limited or undefined. Space is limited by tilting up the ground plane or blocking the view with figures. It is made indefinite by filling an interior with clouds or draperies, or by shading the background with horizontal lines. In Bellange's prints, as in paintings by his contemporaries in Nancy, there is virtually no middle ground. There is a strong consciousness of the format of each print; a figure usually touches at least one border, or is cut off by it.

Bellange's use of light is unnatural. He selectively illuminates those elements that contribute to his conception of beauty of design. The source of the light, however, is quite consistent, falling from in front of the picture plane and usually from the upper right. This frontal lighting tends to negate volume, although its angle divides forms into a light and a dark side. In the earlier prints these light and dark areas are nearly equal and create decorative flat patterns. In the late, more tonal prints, fewer elements are spotlit and these elements project, thus increasing the plasticity of the figures. Although there is rarely any specific description of atmosphere, the transparent shadows and stippled flesh give a suggestion of *sfumato*, the smoky softness of Correggio and Barocci.

In all of his prints Bellange bleaches out patches within the outlines of a form so that there are no interior modeling lines and the area reads as a brilliant flat white shape. It may be a round spot that emphasizes a gardener's balloon-like overskirt (cat. no. 17), but it is more likely to accentuate the slender shape of an arm, as with the Saint John in the *Holy Family* (cat. no. 20) or the right-hand figure in the *Three Women at the Tomb* (cat. no. 62). One can sometimes see marks of burnishing to intensify the white areas, as on the arm and hem of Saint Thomas' robe (cat. no. 51).

Bellange handles the etching medium without rigidity or system. His loose and inventive manner of working contributes to the spontaneity of each line or group of lines.

1. See, for example, Buytewech's European noblemen of 1615 (van Gelder 10-16) and Callot's *Capricci*, etched in Florence about 1617 and repeated in Nancy about 1622 (Lieure 214-263 and 428-477).

Although he uses cross-hatching, it is not consistent or schematic. For a time, stippling is used for flesh only; later it is used more sparingly and for more purposes. The elaborate, "scrolly" calligraphy of Bellange's signatures and inscriptions is similar to that which appears in the inscriptions of the *Entry of Henri II* (cat. no. 1), and in the following decades on Georges de La Tour's paintings. Autograph signatures by Bellange appear on the four *Hortulana*, the *Holy Family with Saint Catherine*, *The Martyrdom of Saint Lucy*, *The Three Magi*, and *Three Holy Women* (cat. nos. 15-18, 20, 29, 33-35, and 38).

As a portraitist Bellange must have painted directly from nature. Most of his prints and drawings, however, are inventions of his imagination, and few seem to have any connection with life studies.[2] His capricious inventions were meant to surprise and delight, and must have appealed to the appetites of bored courtiers. For many artists mannerism was an acquired style, but for Bellange it seems to have been organic to his personality.[3]

His prints, often described in French as *spirituel*, are indeed witty, ingenious, and lively. The myriad shapes and textures Bellange created with his etching needle also touch our senses. We enjoy the contrasting juxtapositions of plain or ornamented surfaces, large or small, dark or light forms, ugly or beautiful faces. Uncertain genders, unattractive facial features and expressions, and grotesque, distorted anatomies simultaneously repel and fascinate us. The tension caused by these unexpected contrasts and conflicts, combined with the liveliness of his technique, invests Bellange's images with a vitality often at odds with their fantasy and artificiality.

2. The red chalk kneeling figure at the Ecole des Beaux-Arts, Paris, is probably a study for the angel in the *Annunciation* (cat. no. 42) and possibly drawn from life.

3. The watercolor miniature of an equestrian at the Musée Condé, Chantilly, records with great precision the actual appearance of the sitter's face, but the body and horse are in the same distinctively personal style of Bellange's etchings.

Bellange's Use of Sources

Throughout this catalogue considerable emphasis is placed on Bellange's use of source material in his etchings. The prints discussed here clearly demonstrate that Jacques Bellange—like his contemporaries—depended to a large extent on the inventions of other artists as the starting point for his own compositions. Although many artists felt that a study trip to Italy was a necessity, it was possible to become familiar with the art of Italy entirely through the study of prints. It is not surprising, therefore, to find an artist like Bellange, living in the isolated provincial capital of Nancy, depending upon them to keep up with current styles, as well as for help in composing certain themes.

Whether Bellange always consciously used sources is difficult to say. The *Virgin with a Spindle*, *Diana and Orion*, and the *Carrying of the Cross*, all have such a degree of correspondence with specific models as to make it likely that Bellange worked with the borrowed image at his side (see cat. nos. 8-9, 10-13, 40-41). On the other hand, prints like the *Martyrdom of Saint Lucy* and the *Three Women at the Tomb* present a complicated overlay of quotations and reminiscences of other artists' work (see cat. nos. 29-30, 62-63). In some of his prints Bellange depended on ornament to integrate borrowed figures with the rest of the composition. In other prints, the compositions or pictorial ideas were themselves borrowed, while the individual figures are of his own invention.

Besides studying prints for their imagery, Bellange looked at the prints of other masters to improve his own etching technique. Parmigianino, Barocci, and very likely Ventura Salimbeni provided him with models.

Appreciation and Influence of Bellange

Bellange's prints and drawings were recognized and admired well into the baroque period, generally disliked in the eighteenth and nineteenth centuries, and appreciated again in recent times. In addition to written criticism from Bellange's own time to the present,[1] one can cite a substantial number of works of art copied from or inspired by Bellange's work.

He is mentioned three times in verses from the seventeenth century. In 1606, Jean de Rosières published a sonnet relating Bellange's experience when painting a portrait of Margherita Gonzaga, a delightful example of courtly flattery.[2] He is named in a verse composed by Balthasar Gerbiers in 1620, a memorial to Goltzius. These lines compare Bellange with the greatest artists of

1. A number of the following examples are drawn from Walch; quotations and complete references may be found on pages 19–29 and notes 34–65.

2. A Madame sur
son portraict
Faict par le peintre de Monseigneur
le duc de Lorraine

SONET
Belange, en ce temps des peintres
l'outrepasse
Voulant par un chef d'oeuvre a la posterite
Faire porter son nom vers l'immortalite
Comme a faict un Appelle, un Zeuxis, un
Parrhase.

Il disoit, a part soy, ie veux peindre la face
De Venus, que l'on teint la parfaicte beaute:
Je veux peindre ses traicts, son teint, sa
gravite
Mais comment sans la voir faudra-t-il que je
fasse?

Tout pensif et perplex s'endort sur tel soucy
Lors Venus sourisant luy parle et dict ainsi:
Belange, si tu veux au naif me despeindre,

Aduise MARGUERITE, au poil, au front,
aux yeux
Au nez, bouche, menton, tasche de la bein
peindre:
Elle est Venus en Terre, et je la suis aux
Cieux.

Quoted from Pariset (1956), p. 185.

other nations.[3] And in the often quoted *Ville de Paris en vers burlesques* of 1652, by Sieur Berthaud, a picture-seller hawks drawings by famous artists, including Bellange.[4]

The first documentary mention we have of specific etchings by Bellange is contained in the inventory of the estate of Claude Deruet, made in Nancy in 1660. Deruet had been apprenticed to Bellange from 1605 to 1609. From 1613 to 1619 he was in Italy, but he returned to Nancy to become court painter in 1620, presumably at Bellange's death. Deruet was a close friend of Jacques Callot and a voracious collector. The inventory and appraisal of the works of art owned by Deruet was made by two artists from Nancy. Their list, which runs some eighty pages in print,[5] usually identifies works by subject matter; but on occasion, the appraisers indicated an artist's name. Deruet owned at least six paintings by Bellange and an undetermined number of Bellange's etchings.[6] His *Carrying of the Cross* was appraised at 2 francs. For the sake of comparison, Callot's *Miseries of War* series was appraised at 1 franc, and the large *Siege of Breda*, 4 francs; Goltzius' *Eight Muses* was valued at 1 franc, 8 gros; and Durer's engraved *Passion* was worth 1 franc.

It is interesting to speculate on the degree of influence that came through Bellange's immediate followers to their students. Among those to be counted in Bellange's circle, either as students or followers, are Deruet, Georges Lallemand (see cat. no. 14), Jean Appier, called Hanzelet, of Nancy and Pont-à-Mousson, and Matthaeus Merian (see cat. no. 25). That any of Bellange's style was passed from Deruet to his student Claude Gellée (le Lorrain) is open to question; however, Lallemand's students in Paris included Büsinck, Vignon, Brebiette, and the young Poussin. At least the first three of these show evidence early in their careers of Bellange's manner as transmitted by Lallemand, and we know little of Poussin's earliest work.

Although there is an observable degree of stylistic influence of Bellange on the artists of Paris and Nancy in the first half of the seventeenth century, his wider contribution may be through the popularization of certain of his secular images. His *Hortulana* figures were reflected in many copies and adaptations, but his *Fighting Tramps* and *Blind Hurdy-Gurdy Player* enjoyed even greater popularity. Weigert has estimated that there were at least thirty prints made in seventeenth century France that derive from Bellange's two etchings.[7] Blunt has shown that Georges de La Tour, who worked in Lorraine, certainly knew Bellange's tramp etchings.[8] Among other descendants of these prints we would signal the blind musicians and beggars of Callot, della Bella, and Rembrandt.

Callot and Bellange

Jacques Callot, etcher and engraver, owes more to Bellange than is generally acknowledged. Born in Nancy in 1592, he was the son of Jean Callot, herald of arms of the court of Lorraine.[9] Jacques Callot's youth has been the subject of much romanticizing, especially in regard to his trips to Italy. The question of his training in Nancy and his exposure to Bellange's art concerns us more here. In 1607 young Callot was apprenticed to Demenge-Dominique Crocq, a goldsmith and engraver of medals and seals, whose family had a long record of service to the court. Biographers tell us that even as a child Callot could think of nothing but learning to engrave. In the first decade of the seventeenth century there were no resident intaglio printmakers in Nancy; Bellange was not to learn to etch until about 1611. Although Crocq was a logical choice as a master for Callot, we have no indication that anything Crocq and his shop engraved was ever printed. Hence, Callot traveled to Italy about 1608 to find a suitable teacher and eventually met up with his childhood friends from Nancy, Claude Deruet and Israel Henriet, at the printmaker Antonio Tempesta's shop in Rome. He worked in Italy, primarily in Florence at the Medici court until his return to Nancy in 1621. He died there in 1635.

3. Balthasar Gerbiers in his *Claght-Dicht*, 1620, a memorial to Goltzius, who died in 1617.
"Prijst, prijst Italia u Raphael en u Angele,
Duyts-Land Albert Durer,
pugt Vranckrijk van Bel Angele . . ."

4. "J'en ay de beaux de Caravage,
Du Titian et du Carage;
J'ay des pieces du Tintoret,
Du Parmaisan, d'Albert Duret;
J'ay la Danae de Farnese,
Deux grands desseins de Veronese,
L'Architecture d'Ondius,
Les nuditez de Goltzius
Quatre crayons faits par Belange,
Et trois autres par Michel-Ange . . ."

5. A. Jacquot, "Notes sur Claude Deruet, peintre et graveur lorrain, 1588-1660," *Réunion des sociétés des beaux-arts des départements*, 18, 1894.

6. Walch published the entry from the inventory as "42 estampes de feu le sieur Bellange" (p. 46). The complete quote should read "42 estampes de feu le sieur Bellange et autres" (Jacquot, "Notes sur Claude Deruet," p. 864.)

7. R.-A. Weigert, "Le Commerce de la gravure au XVIIe siècle en France. Les deux premiers Mariette et François Langlois, dit Ciartres," *Gazette des beaux-arts*, 41 (1953), 168 ff.

8. A. Blunt, "The joueur de vielle of Georges de La Tour," *Burlington Magazine*, 86 (1945), 108ff. More recently, scholars have seen stylistic similarities between de La Tour's earliest paintings and Bellange (Pierre Rosenberg and François Macé de l'Epinay. *Georges de La Tour, vie et oeuvre*, Paris, 1973, pp. 88-89; and Benedict Nicholson and Christopher Wright, *Georges de La Tour*, London, Phaidon, 1974).

9. Jean Callot's name appears in connection with projects with which Bellange was involved, i.e., as a witness of the contract between Claude de la Ruelle and Hermann de Loye for the printing of the *Pompe funèbre de Charles III*, and as a designer of heraldic devices used in the funeral. Jean Callot was also an author of heraldic texts. For much information on Jacques Callot and his time, see H. Diane Russell, *Jacques Callot, Prints and Related Drawings*, exhibition catalogue, National Gallery of Art, Washington, D.C., 1975.

Callot grew up in the milieu of the court; his close friend Deruet was Bellange's apprentice. Callot would have experienced the feasts and pageants for the 1606 marriage of Henri II, and Charles III's funeral in 1608, for which Callot's father designed the heraldic banners, devices, and decorations. Callot's ten etchings of 1627, *Le Combat à la barrière* (Lieure 575-584), help us to visualize the festivals of ten and twenty years earlier, with their fantastic chariots and allegorical costumed figures, while his two versions of the *Temptation of Saint Anthony* (Lieure 188 and 1416) reflect the astonishing scenographic displays of these festivals of the late mannerist period.

Despite Callot's residence in Italy during much of Bellange's career as an etcher, one feels that Callot was aware of at least some of Bellange's graphic work. In addition to official exchanges, Callot could have known Bellange's prints through gifts received from his own family, or through Claude Deruet, who probably remained in contact with Bellange even while he was in Italy, until 1619. In particular, Callot's *Bearing of the Cross* (Lieure 286) reflects Bellange's large print of the same subject. Pariset has suggested that Callot's *La Grande Chasse* (Lieure 353) is related to Bellange's cycle of paintings for the Galerie des Cerfs, and to Bellange's wash drawing, *La Chasse au cerf* in the Musée Lorrain.[10]

Many of Callot's figure types seem to have a source in Bellange's conception of the human figure: the elegantly posed soldiers who make up the human staffage in so many of Callot's etchings, the carefully tattered but never repulsive lower classes, and the vacantly staring oval-faced women. But unlike Bellange, who worked with the extremes of stylization and who is always capable of producing an intense reaction from a twentieth century viewer, Callot was a detached observer of life, whose prints, produced in large quantity, have a decorative, regularized character. Callot was also a superb technician. His preferred etching tool, the *échoppe,* could produce a swelling line like that of the burin and was uniquely suited to portray the swagger and posturing of the soldiers in the diorama-like *Miseries of War* (Lieure 1339-1356). Callot's *Beggars* (Lieure 479-503) are among his more obvious debts to Bellange but evoke neither the horror of Bellange nor the pity of Rembrandt.

Callot's youth and adulthood in Nancy and Florence gave him a fantastic theatrical conception of life. His association with the glamorous courts of Europe encouraged his tendency to invest all living things with a curious and lively elegance, as if he were the choreographer of a continuous graphic ballet.

Later Criticism

In the eighteenth and nineteenth centuries tastes changed, and Bellange's work was viewed by cataloguers and collectors with reactions ranging from curiosity through distaste to condemnation. P.-J. Mariette tells us that Bellange's "licentious" manner merited scorn, yet he had a great vogue. J. Strutt said that Bellange's etching style is "by no means destitute of merit" and explains the "incorrect drawing" as a product of affectation rather than of ignorance. Basan called Bellange "a bad painter and a worse etcher," adding, "one finds much more of bizarreness than of judgment, very little correction and a very bad taste in gravure." Huber-Rost's comment that "this artist had more of genius than of taste" anticipates the criticism of Robert-Dumesnil, who nevertheless owned a significant collection of Bellange's etchings. Robert-Dumesnil wrote: "*Persuaded, with this author [Basan], that it is possible to appreciate the artistic talents of an artist from whom we no longer have paintings, through the prints he has left, we can only agree with his opinion on the bizarreness and lack of correction of the compositions of our master, who if he were alive today, would deserve to be the leader of the Romantic School, of which he anticipated, two centuries in advance, the means, effect and power. As for his prints, we beg the indulgence of a severe public for* [cat. nos. 6, 8, 43] *which seem charming to us. After that, we abandon to all the severity of Basan* [cat. nos. 45-61 Christ and the Apostles] *which are, in effect, detestable . . .*"[11]

The current appreciation of Bellange is a far cry from Robert-Dumesnil's opinions. The Art Nouveau and Symbolist movements of the late nineteenth century gave to the twentieth century the ability to enjoy extravagance in a work of art. Many of the qualities that delight us today in the works of Aubrey Beardsley and Alphonse Mucha are recognizable in Bellange and other late mannerists. An age such as ours, brought up on an art based on the total reworking of notions of form, along with fashion illustrations containing distortions of the human body far more radical than anything any mannerist produced, can hardly object to "defects" of Bellange's draughtsmanship, or his portrayal of the human figure. The rediscovery of El Greco encouraged a positive reevaluation of Bellange. Burchard and Dvorak were among the first to compare El Greco and Bellange. The abandonment of "good taste" or morality as a criterion of fine art and the rise of the formalistic study of the history of art made a new appreciation of mannerism and Bellange possible. Aspects of Bellange's style so frequently condemned in the nineteenth century became fascinating to twentieth century writers conditioned by Freud to discover neuroticism (Blunt) or even perverted sexuality (Tietze-Conrat) in Bellange's art.

10. F.-G. Pariset, "Deux dessins de Jacques Bellange au Musée Lorrain," *Pays Lorrain,* 1951, pp. 3 ff.

11. A.-P.-H. Robert-Dumesnil, *Le Peintre-graveur français,* Paris, 1835-1871, vol. 5 (1841), pp. 82-83.

Recent scholarship has produced a modest number of specialized studies on Bellange. Pariset deserves the credit for having called attention to the many aspects of Bellange's activity and his role in the court of Lorraine. Reed attempted the first major chronological ordering of Bellange's etchings through a careful analysis of his evolving etching technique and style. Nicole Walch's recent monograph combined a revised chronology with a definitive catalogue raisonné and impressive documentation, considered the problems of Bellange's sources, and reproduced, for the first time, all of the etchings.

Types of Impressions and Watermarks

SEVENTEEN of Bellange's etchings appear at first without, and later with, the engraved inscription *Le Blond excud* (published by Le Blond).[1] There were several Le Blonds who published prints in Paris in the seventeenth century, the earliest being Nicolas, who died in 1610.[2] His two sons, Jean (ca. 1590/94-1666) and Rolland (1596-ca. 1651/56), were also publishers.[3] A younger Jean (ca. 1635-1709), well documented as a painter and publisher of prints, was Rolland's son and took over his uncle Jean's business around 1666-67. It is the first Jean who most probably published Bellange's prints and many by Abraham Bosse as well.[4] Although 1633 is the earliest date to appear on prints bearing Le Blond's name, M. Préaud sees no opposition to supposing that he might have entered the business closer to 1610, the year his father died. Those plates of Bellange published by Jean I Le Blond may have been in Paris in the 1620's and almost certainly were by the mid 1630's, for by then Lorraine had become French territory and Paris was a far greater print market than Nancy.

Bellange's prints can be divided into three groups for a consideration of quality. Those plates known both before and with Le Blond's name can be assumed to represent two groups, those printed earlier in Nancy and those printed later in Paris. For those plates not known to have received Le Blond's name, other criteria, such as the presence of plate scratches or watermarks, must be used in order to establish a printing sequence.[5]

In the earliest of Bellange's impressions minor surface scratches and abrasions print more strongly than was later to be the case. Often the plate is not wiped as clean at the corners. Finely bitten lines print sharp and clear, and, where they are closely laid, more subtle tonal transitions are achieved. Besides good contrasts between paper and ink, a well-printed early impression in good condition has a silvery gray patina to its surface that contributes to the effect of the image. Unfortunately, many of the Nancy impressions are poorly preserved, which detracts from their total quality. Moreover, these early impressions are not always very evenly printed and often have large printing creases.

Parisian impressions, those bearing Le Blond's name, can be quite good, that is, carefully inked and wiped and well printed in strong black ink on a good quality paper. However, they are equally likely to show signs of plate wear, with lines no longer holding the requisite amount of ink. Some Le Blond impressions appear on rather poor quality paper and are very pale indeed. Such impressions must date from late in the century and be from plates that had been printed extensively.

The Adoration of the Magi (cat. nos. 31-32) has an extended printing history. Impressions bearing Van Merle's name begin to show signs of wear. The impression of the fifth state (cat. no. 32), with the publisher's name removed, exhibits not only added work but signs of having been reworked overall with the burin to deepen the etched lines.

Counterproofs of Bellange's prints do exist. There is one of the *Blind Hurdy-Gurdy Player* (cat. no. 27) in the Bibliothèque Royale, Brussels, and one of *Christ* (cat. no. 61) in the Museum of Fine Arts, Boston, on an unwatermarked paper.

Since most impressions of Bellange's etchings are mounted down, only a small number of impressions, mostly from American collections, have been studied for watermarks. Although no conclusions can be reached from this study, the information collected can be summarized (see table below).

Several characteristic symbols of Lorraine used in watermarks and found in book paper of the late sixteenth and early seventeenth centuries are the crowned interlaced C's of Charles III and Claude de France ⊂⊃ and the double-barred cross of Lorraine ☨, often found together. In the drawing *The Rest on the Flight* (cat. no. 44) such a watermark appears. These papers were almost certainly of local manufacture, for fine paper was produced in Lorraine during the reigns of Charles III and Henri II. The crowned H or HM of Henri II and Margherita also appears as a watermark. Specifically Lotharingian marks such as those with the ducal monograms have appeared occasionally among Bellange's prints. Far more often one

1. The name appears on Walch 7 iii, 8 ii, 9 iii, 10 iii, 11-13 ii, 14 iii, 15 ii, 17 ii, 18 ii, 21 ii, 25 ii, 26-28 ii, and on R.-D. 10 ii. The subjects comprise four madonnas, two holy families, the *Pietà*, the *Three Magi*, *Two Tramps Fighting*, the *Blind Hurdy-Gurdy Player*, the four *Hortulana*, and one large print, *Diana and Orion*.

2. We are indebted to Maxime Préaud of the Bibliothèque Nationale for the information on the Le Blond family that he most generously provided.

3. As the younger son, Rolland inscribed his publications *Le Blond le jeune*.

4. Bosse's series *Le Mariage à la ville* (Blum 116-121), published by Le Blond, is dated 1633.

5. See, for example, the *Martyrdom of St. Lucy*, where a scratch fades with printing (Walch, p. 174).

finds bunches of grapes, a widespread seventeenth century watermark, prevalent in France as well as in Lorraine.[6] Grape watermarks are difficult to distinguish one from the other, and from the following table it may be seen that the only possible explanation is that these papers were commonly used for printing both in Nancy and in Paris.

6. Lucien Wiener, *Etude sur les filigranes des papiers lorrains*, Nancy, 1893, p. 13.

Watermarks Found on Impressions of Bellange's Etchings

(Quality of impression indicated when known.)

Watermark†	*Title of Etching*
1. Plates that never received Le Blond's name	
Eagle	*Portia*, W. 6
Coat-of-arms	*Portia*, W. 6
Hunting horn in shield (See Briquet 7862)	*The Martyrdom of St. Lucy*, W. 16, fine (cat. no. 29)
CB on a skewer or sword	*The Martyrdom of St. Lucy*, W. 16, poor
Arms of Dachsbourg (Dabo), shield with 8 batons (Wiener, Pl. 13, no. 7)	*Military Scene*, W. 19, fine (cat. no. 28)
Rampant lion with countermark horn (See Heawood 3122)	*Military Scene*, W. 19, 2 impressions
Double-headed eagle	*Military Scene*, W. 19, good
Crossed arrows (Briquet 6283)	*The Adoration of the Magi*, W. 20 i (cat. no. 31)
Double-headed eagle and LEBLOYS (name)	*The Adoration of the Magi*, W. 20 v (cat. no. 32)
Crowned H of Duke Henri II (See Wiener, Pl. 11, no. 5)	*The Annunciation*, W. 24 i *The Three Women at the Tomb*, W. 46 i (cat. no. 62)
Hunting horn surmounted by cross of Lorraine	*The Annunciation*, W. 24 ii, 3 fine impressions
Large grapes*	
with countermark . . . D	*The Annunciation*, W. 24 ii
Like Heawood 2107 except with 5 grapes on a side	*The Raising of Lazarus*, W. 47 impressions (cat. no. 64)
with name — R	*The Raising of Lazarus*, W. 47
Small grapes*	*Apostles*, W. 31, 32, 36, 37, 40, 42, 43, and 44 (see cat. nos. 45-61)
Numeral 4 with letters (found as countermark to interlaced C's. See Wiener pls. 2-4)	*The Three Women at the Tomb*, W. 46 ii
2. Impressions from plates before receiving Le Blond's name	
Small crowned shield with A (?)	*Virgin and Child*, W. 8 i (cat. no. 7)
Numeral 4 with letters (see note above)	*Pietà*, W. 17 i (cat. no. 24)
Grapes*	*Diana and Orion*, W. 10 ii
	Hortulana, W. 12; W. 13 (cat. no. 17)
	Two Tramps Fighting, W. 18 i, 2 fine impressions (cat. no. 26)
	The Three Magi, W. 27 i, W. 28 i
	Holy Family, R.-D. 10 i (cat. no. 23)
with name below	*Diana and Orion*, W. 10 ii
with name below	*Holy Family with Saint Catherine*, W. 15 ii
with countermark (name ?)	*Diana and Orion*, W. 10 ii

†Briquet: C. M. Briquet, *Les Filigranes*, Geneva, 1907.
Heawood: Edward Heawood, *Watermarks*, Hilversum (Holland) 1950.
Wiener: Lucien Wiener, *Etude sur les filigranes des papiers lorrains*, Nancy, 1893.

*Grape watermarks often include a name either under the grapes or as a countermark. None of these names has as yet been deciphered.

3. Impressions from plates bearing Le Blond's name

Grapes*	*Holy Family with Saint Catherine*, W. 15 ii, weak
	Blind Hurdy-Gurdy Player, W. 21 ii
with name below	*The Virgin with a Spindle*, W. 9 iii
with name below	*Pietà*, W. 17 ii, pale
with name below	*The Three Magi*, W. 26 ii, W. 27 ii, W. 28 ii, all good (cat. nos. 33-35)

4. Unknown states of plates that received Le Blond's name

Grapes*	*The Virgin with Child on his Cradle*, W. 7, pale
	Holy Family with Saint Catherine, W. 15

Documentation

BELLANGE'S career as a painter and designer at the court of Lorraine can be traced from approximately thirty records of payment, contracts, and a poem. Occasionally some bit of documentary evidence can be correlated with a particular drawing or a print, but, for the most part, artistic and documentary evidence do not mesh. There is virtually nothing in the records concerning Bellange's activity as a printmaker. Neither his birth nor his death dates are really known, despite the fact that one often sees them in biographical entries and sales catalogues. Some of the most important events and documents relating to Bellange are listed below. Numbers in parentheses indicate the volume number in the Archives départementales de Meurthe-et-Moselle, or Archives municipales of Nancy.

1600-1601
Crispin de Passe published an engraved Passion series, including the *Three Holy Women at the Tomb*, H. 153, designed by Bellange. At least three other engravings designed by Bellange, but undated, were probably published by de Passe at about this time.

1602
Bellange worked on portraits or unspecified decorations in the ducal palace with Jacques Danglus, Jean Contesse, and Jean de Wayembourg (B. 1271). He was paid, together with Danglus, for painting and gilding the *cabinet* of Catherine de Bourbon, which included six paintings of Roman history and six emblematic designs (B. 1278). The paintings by Bellange listed in Deruet's estate inventory of 1660 are probably related to this project.

1604
Bellange was paid 20 écus for a portrait of Mary Stuart (died 1587), daughter of James V and Mary of Lorraine, which was painted for a M. Poincts (B. 1299).

1605
On April 19, Claude Deruet was apprenticed to Bellange for four years, at 200 francs (3 E 1901).

1606
May. Redecoration of the Galerie des Cerfs in the ducal palace. Bellange repainted a cycle of twenty scenes of the hunt as well as decorative figures. The room was popularly known thereafter as the Galerie Bellange. The gallery was destroyed in a fire in 1871. No reproductions of Bellange's paintings exist. (B. 7347, 7348).

Bellange was paid for decorations made for the June wedding festivities of Henri, Duc de Bar, and Margherita Gonzaga. He decorated a triumphal arch and made twelve gilded cupids on cardboard as well as various costumes and decorations for the nuptial ballet (B. 1292; 1295; BB 1; CC 29-31, 36-39).

August. Payment for two full-length portraits of Duke Charles III (B. 1311).

Jean de Rosières' sonnet, inspired by Bellange's portrait of Margherita Gonzaga, published in November.

1607
Payments to Bellange for completion of paintings of a *Magdalen* and a *Saint Francis* (B. 1299, 1302).

1608
In an account book, under a section entitled "other expenses for trips, embassies, and messengers for the service of His Highness" a payment of 135 francs was made to Bellange in March for a trip to the court of France to "study paintings and works of art there, in order to better serve his Duke" (B. 1308, fol. 258).

1609
A payment to Bellange, indicating his return from France

1610
Bellange decorated a new gallery on the front of the palace (B. 1852).

1610-11
Bellange etched a portion of plate 10 of section III, "The Entry of Henry II," in the *Pompe funèbre de Charles III*

1611
Bellange decorated a gallery in the palace facing the newly constructed Italian garden with themes from Ovid's *Metamorphoses* (B. 1335).

1613
Bellange etched the *Ex-libris of Melchior de la Vallée.*

1615-16
Matthaeus Merian etched copies of eleven of Bellange's etchings.

1616
Bellange designed costumes and machinery for a court ballet organized by Margherita Gonzaga (B. 1378). This is the last mention of Bellange's activity in the court documents.

1620
Deruet, returned to Nancy from Italy, became court painter. This implies that Bellange was no longer active and may have died.

1624
Document (B. 7753) refers to the Galerie des Cerfs *"du feu Bellange"* (of the late Bellange).

Catalogue

The two catalogues raisonnés for Bellange's prints are:

R.-D.
A.-P.-H. Robert-Dumesnil, *Le Peintre-graveur français*, vol. 5 (Paris, 1841) and vol. 11 (Paris, 1871)

Walch or W.
Nicole Walch, *Die Radierungen des Jacques Bellange, Chronologie und kritischer Katalog*, Munich, Robert Wölfle, 1971 (extensive bibliography)

In the present catalogue measurements are taken from Walch unless otherwise noted. The irregularity of the plates is notable. When plate measurements are unknown, the dimensions are of the most complete impression.

Bartsch or B.
Adam Bartsch, *Le Peintre-graveur*, Vienna, 1803-1821 (and later editions)

Hollstein or H.
F.W.H. Hollstein, *Dutch and Flemish Etchings, Engravings, and Woodcuts ca. 1450-1700*, Amsterdam, 1949–
—, *German Engravings, Etchings, and Woodcuts ca. 1400-1700*, Amsterdam, 1954–

Lugt
Frits Lugt, *Les Marques de collections de dessins et d'estampes*, Amsterdam, 1921; supplement, The Hague, 1956

1
The Entry of Henri II into Nancy
(Plate 10)
Etching
W.1
183 x 494 mm.
7³⁄₁₆ x 19⁷⁄₁₆ in.
At top: "Les Comtes, Barons, Seigneurs et Gentilz-hommes, Officiers et Ministres de l'Estat . . ." Plate 10 of "L'ordre tenu au marcher, parmy la ville de Nancy capitale de Lorraine, a l'entrée en icelle du sérénissime Prince Henry IIe . . . ," *Pompe funèbre de Charles III*, Nancy, 1611.
Metropolitan Museum of Art, New York. Elisha Whittelsey Fund, 1959

Charles III, 63rd Duke of Lorraine, died on May 14, 1608. His funeral was celebrated from May 15 to July 19, 1608, on which day he was interred in the Franciscan Church of the Cordeliers next to the ducal palace in Nancy. Charles' funeral and the subsequent entry into Nancy on April 20, 1610, of Henri II, his son and successor, were recorded in a lavishly illustrated volume conceived and financed by Claude de la Ruelle, secretary of state and finances. The last page of the work is a map of Nancy dated 1611. The *Pompe funèbre de Charles III* is divided into five sections: (1) a title page and ten illustrations of the funeral; (2) the funeral procession; (3) the entry of Henri II; (4) how Duke Henri II goes to church; (5) the map of Nancy. The whole work comprises ninety-four plates and seventeen text pages.

According to the *Pompe funèbre*, Claude de la Ruelle was the master of ceremonies of the funeral. He was the "inventor," that is, he determined the program of the ten large plates illustrating the funeral. He also wrote captions in French and Latin for the plates. Jean de la Hière, architect of the court, did the perspective renderings. Frederich Brentel and Matthaeus Merian etched the plates. Hermann de Loye printed the copper plates. Blaise André and Jacob Garnich printed the text pages. Père Leonard Périn translated parts of the text into Latin.

The *Pompe funèbre* has been described by Wüthrich,[1] and documentary material relating to its publication has been published by Marot.[2] Nicole Walch has shown that plate 10 of section 3 of the *Pompe funèbre* contains what is certainly a self-portrait by Bellange, that was drawn on the plate among a group of mounted courtiers. In this, albeit unsigned, earliest of his etchings, datable to 1611, the style differs markedly from the other figures on the page, drawn by another hand. In the funeral procession, Bellange, the court painter, rode with the other gentlemen of the court, where he was known as Jacques de Bellange (1605) and Monsieur de Bellange (1606). Bellange signed seven of his etchings *Bellange Eques* (knight), leaving little doubt as to his rank.

A.N.W.

1. L. H. Wüthrich, *Das druckgraphische Werk von Matthäus Merian d. Ae.*, vol. 1. Basel, 1966, pp. 10-18.

2. Pierre Marot, *"Contrats passés pour la gravure et l'impression des planches de la "Pompe Funèbre" de Charles III, Duc de Lorraine,"* in *Gutenberg-Jahrbuch*, 1951, p. 140 ff. See also section on "Printmaking in Nancy before 1611."

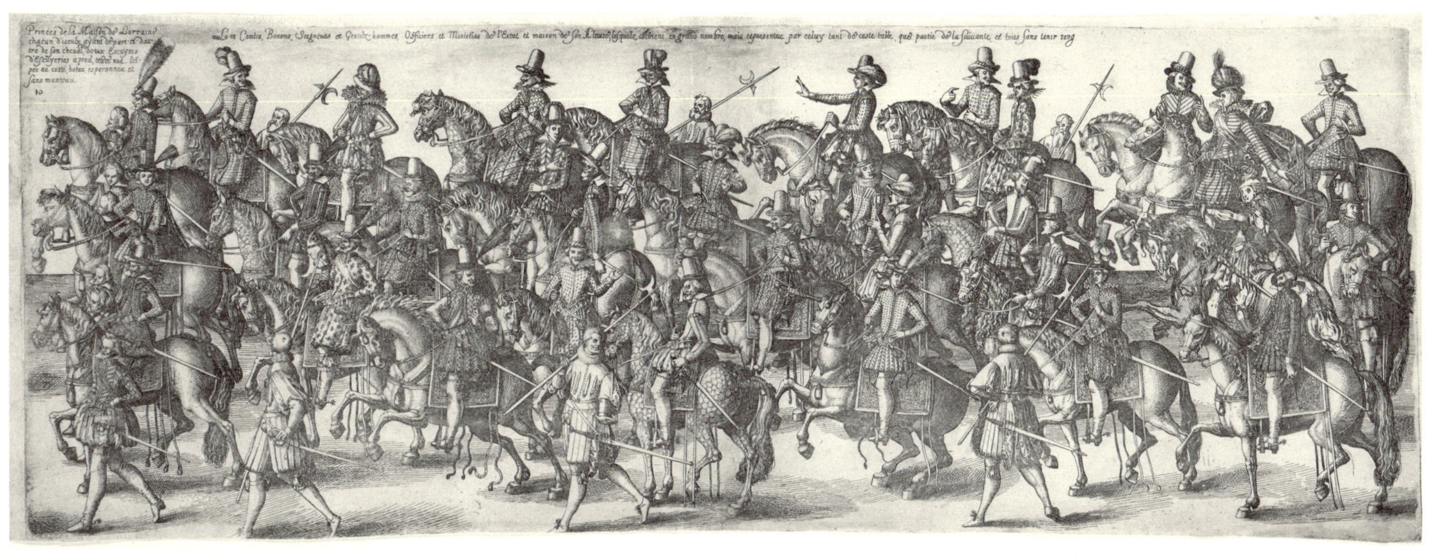
Princes de la Maison de Lorraine chacun d'iceulx ayant de part et d'autre de son cheual deux Escuyers d'Escuyeries a pied, teste nue, l'espée au costé, botez esperonnez et sans manteau.
10
Les Comtes, Barons, Seigneurs et Gentilz hommes, Officiers et Ministres de l'Estat et maison de son Altesse, lesquelz estoient en grand nombre, mais representez par celuy tant de ceste table, que partie de la suivante, et tous sans tenir reng

1

1 (detail)

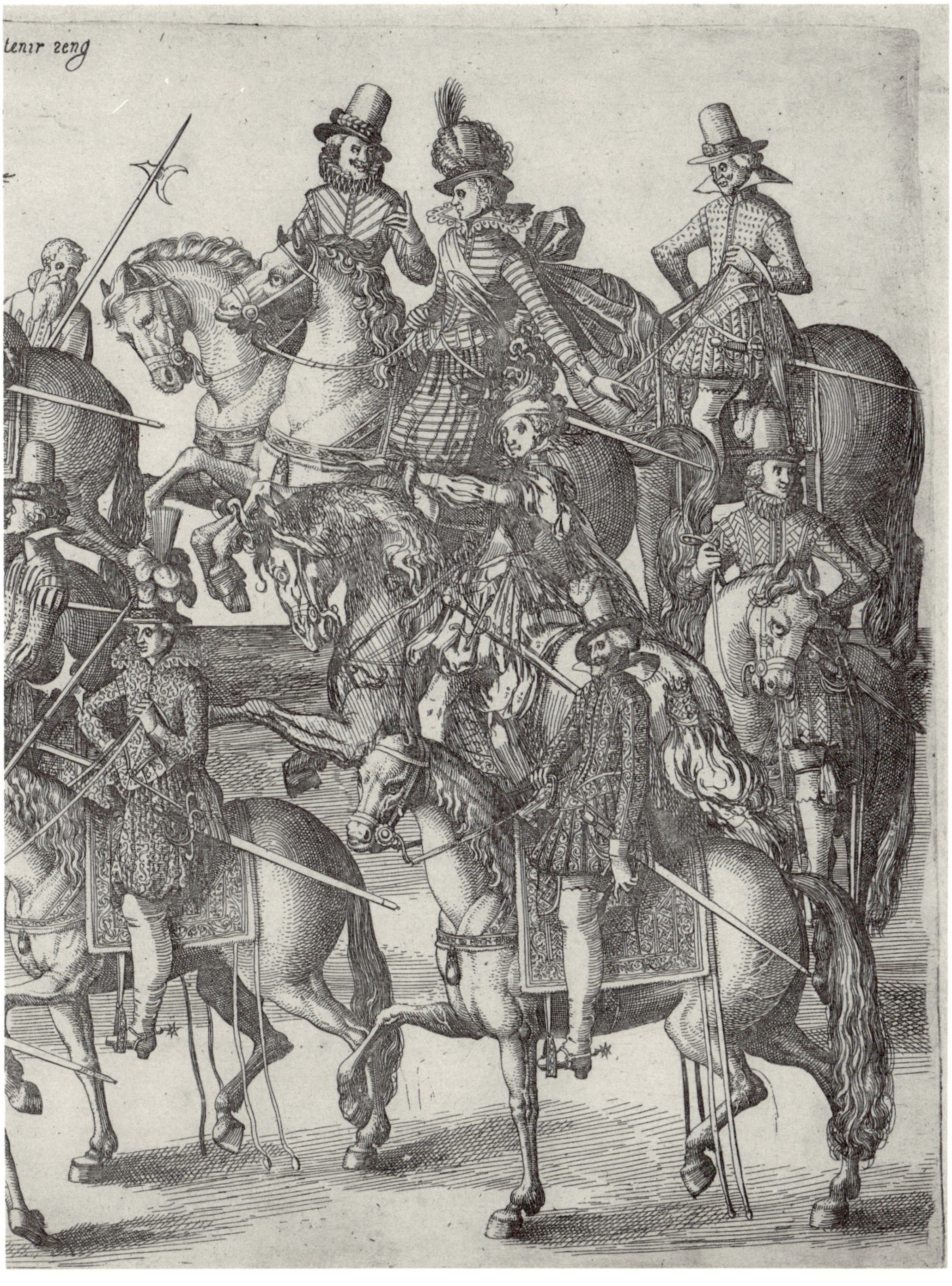

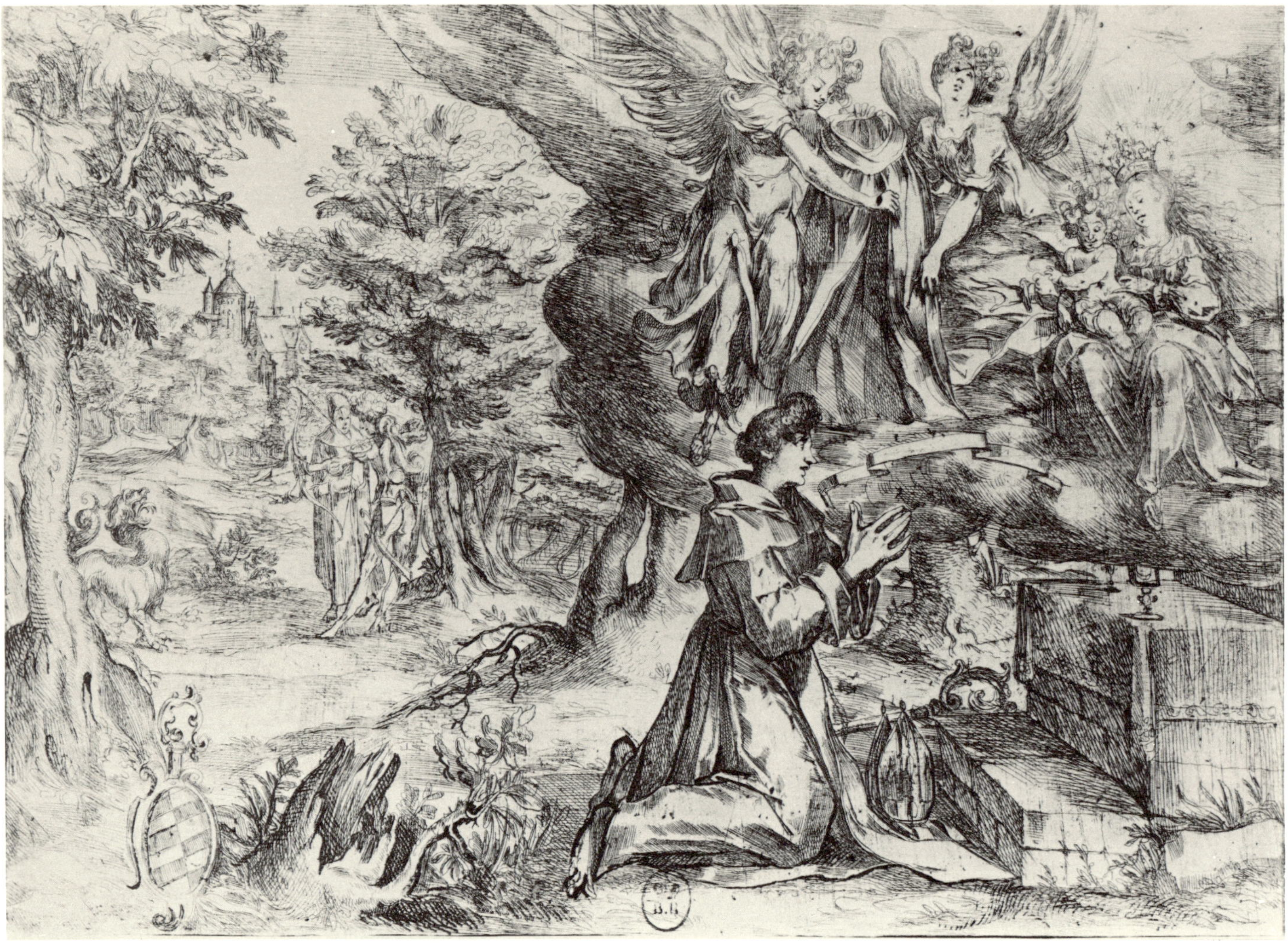

2

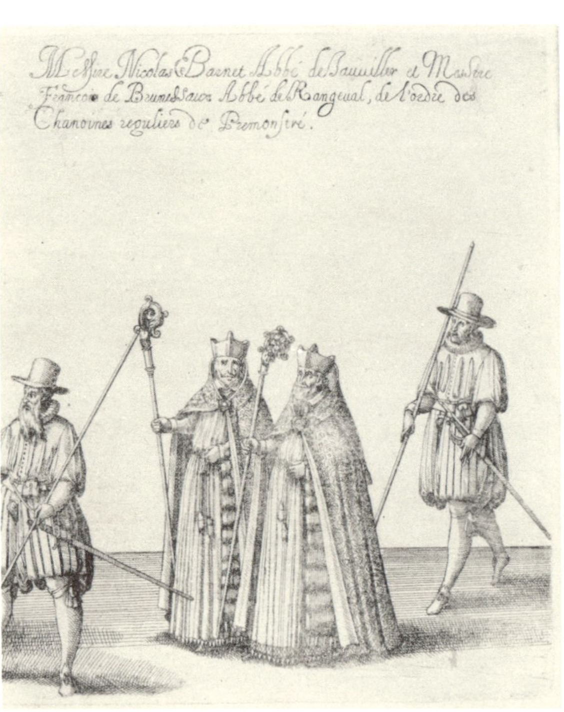

Fig. 2. Brentel, *Nicholas Barnet*, detail of *Pompe funèbre de Charles III* (section II, plate 34), etching, 1610-11. The Metropolitan Museum of Art, Elisha Whittelsey Fund, 1959

2
The Vision of Saint Norbert in Prémontré
Etching
W.3, R.-D. 12
195 x 247-250 mm. (plate)[1]
7⅝ x 9⅞ in.
Bibliothèque Nationale, Paris

Walch has convincingly identified this etching as the *Vision of Saint Norbert in Prémontré*.[1] Saint Norbert was the founder of the Premonstratensian order. He was related to the Holy Roman Emperor Henry IV, and he was an Augustinian until 1119, when he broke with the Augustinians on account of their lax morals. He established a small community at Prémontré in the forest of Coucy, near Laon. The habit of the new order consisted of a white woolen cloak or scapular over a black tunic, and a white four-cornered beret. The Prémontré order was well established and extremely active in Lorraine during the time of Jacques Bellange and had particularly strong ties with the ducal court. In about 1600, under the leadership of Servais de Layruelz, the Prémontré abbeys of Lorraine, of which there were thirty-eight, began a vigorous reform movement.

Representations of Prémontré subjects are uncommon in art. When Saint Norbert is shown, it is most often in his role as the Bishop of Magdeburg. His attributes are a chalice with a spider, or a demon at his feet[2] but this is not the case in the Bellange etching. The foreground scene of Bellange's print represents Saint Norbert in prayer before an altar. His bishop's mitre and crozier are beside him. The Virgin, crowned as Queen of Heaven, with the Child on her lap, appears above the altar. Two angels, almost identical to those in Bellange's *Ex-libris of Melchior de la Vallée* (fig. 1), present a scapular similar to the one worn by Saint Norbert. Although the setting of this event is a forest, the scene is undoubtedly meant to refer to the place where Saint Norbert had his vision. According to a fifteenth century tradition, he was passing the night in the Chapel of Saint John the Baptist at Coucy, when the Queen of Heaven appeared and bestowed the white habit as a symbol of the new order.

In the background, an archer with a companion is slaying a dragon. Walch has demonstrated that this scene, unknown outside of this print, represents a popular interpretation, based on a legend, of the word Prémontré that was current in Bellange's time. A dragon was terrorizing the forest of Coucy. An archer, who was led into the forest by a hermit to kill the monster, shrieked in terror as he realized the dragon was near, "Tu me l'as de près montré"[3] (literally, "you have shown me him [too] close").

In the left foreground of the etching there is a coat of arms surmounted by a crozier, indicating that the owner is the abbot of an abbey of regular canons. This coat of arms, with the heraldic description "Bandé contrebandé d'or et d'azur de six pièces"[4] belonged to the Barnet family of Lorraine, ennobled in 1567. The coat of arms in the *Vision of Saint Norbert* undoubtedly belonged to Nicholas Barnet, who was the twenty-fifth abbot of the Prémontré of Jovilliers from 1592 to 1617.[5] Nicholas Barnet marched in Charles III's funeral procession in Nancy, in 1608, and his portrait is recorded in Claude de la Ruelle's *Pompe funèbre de Charles III* (fig. 2). Barnet died in 1624.

How did Barnet know Jacques Bellange? The most likely explanation is that Nicholas Barnet was a close relative, possibly the brother, of Louis Barnet, counselor-secretary to Henri II. Two other members of the Barnet family, Balthasar and Jean (Louis' father),[6] were active in the political and intellectual life of the court of Lorraine in the late sixteenth century. Despite these facts about the Barnet family, one can only speculate on the circumstances surrounding the execution of the Saint Norbert etching. The *Vision of Saint Norbert* and the *Ex-libris of Melchior de la Vallée* (fig. 1), which bears the date 1613, are the only two prints in Bellange's oeuvre with coats of arms (see also cat. no. 43). The etching quality of these two prints, as well as the positions of the angels, are so similar that it is very likely the two prints were executed at nearly the same time. It is possible that Barnet knew Melchior de la Vallée, who was canon of the Collegiate Church of Saint George in Nancy[7] and who could have put Barnet in touch with Bellange. Other possibilities are that Barnet, who was probably related to Claude de la Ruelle, became interested in etching during the work on the *Pompe funèbre de Charles III* in which his own portrait appeared. Finally, the Barnet family had received a monopoly from the duke for the beating of copper[8] and may have had contact with printmakers because of this.

If Bellange was making his etchings for the clergy, and most of his subjects are religious, he was probably doing them as an informal gesture of friendship. Had the prints been commissioned, they would have been inscribed with dedications. The informality of Bellange's etching projects would account for the lack of documentation concerning his activity as a printmaker.

A.N.W.

1. Only one impression of this etching was known to Walch. A second, untrimmed impression has recently appeared in a European collection with the dimensions given here. The complete plate has a sizable space below the image for an inscription.

2. See, for example, Callot's *Saint Norbert*, Lieure 998.

3. Walch, p. 66.

4. J. B. Riestap, *Armorial Général*, reproduced from 2nd ed., 1884, New York, Barnes and Noble, 1965, p. 118.

5. Barnet restored the abbey and monastery, near Staineville and Saint Dizier in western Lorraine, for it had been devastated by Protestants, and he obtained an important relic of Saint Rufine for the abbey.

6. Jean Barnet, secretary to Duke Charles III, died in 1591. He was a seigneur of Pulligny. Documents show that his sons included Louis, Jean, and René Barnet. If Nicholas was a son of Jean Barnet, then he was related to the de la Ruelle family, for Jean Barnet's second wife was Marie de la Ruelle. The *Pompe funèbre* contracts state that Claude de la Ruelle had the plates etched at one of the houses owned by him in Pulligny (near Nancy). Thus it is possible that, through family connections, Nicholas Barnet came to have an interest in etching.

7. Jean Barnet (son of the above-mentioned Jean Barnet, secretary to Charles III) had a prebend or stipend in the church of Saint George. If Nicholas Barnet was his brother, this would have been another link between Nicholas Barnet and Melchior de la Vallée, the two known patrons of Bellange's etchings.

8. In 1608 Louis' widow and heirs received a monopoly from the duke for the beating of copper in their shop in Nancy.

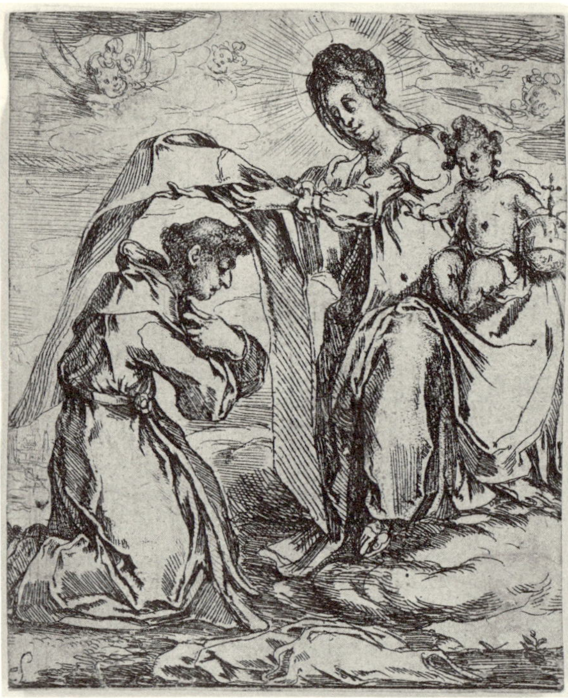

3

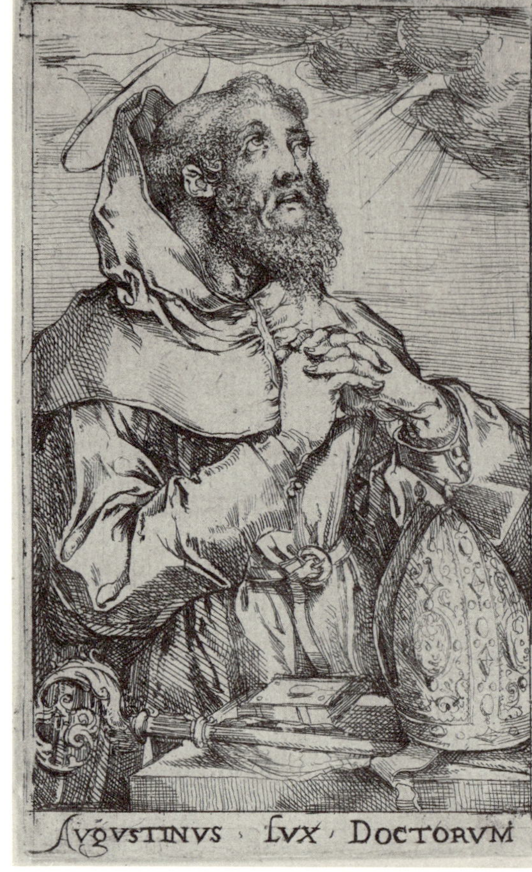

4

3
The Virgin Bestowing a Scapular on a Monk
Etching
W.4 (unique)
90 x 75 mm.
3⁹⁄₁₆ x 2¹⁵⁄₁₆ in.
Lower left: [B] *el*
Philadelphia Museum of Art. The Academy Collection

The small etching of a monk receiving a scapular is perhaps an alternate version of the *Vision of Saint Norbert* (cat. no. 2). In this image the Virgin herself is bestowing the scapular. She is not crowned, but has a halo. The image is trimmed, as can be seen by the cut-off signature. Until another untrimmed impression of the plate is discovered, we will not know how much of the image is missing. All of Bellange's other prints have an etched borderline inside the plate mark; this seems to have been a standard part of his procedure. The *Virgin Bestowing a Scapular on a Monk* has a black border only along the bottom edge, which indicates that the print is missing three of its original edges.

A.N.W.

4
Saint Augustine
Etching
W.5, R.-D. 16 (unique)
114 x 65 mm.
4¼ x 2⁹⁄₁₆ in.
Lower margin: *Augustinus Lux Doctorum*
Coll.: Robert-Dusmesnil (Lugt 2200)
Museum of Fine Arts, Boston. Otis Norcross Fund. 40.131

Images of Saint Augustine are frequently found in series of the patristic Doctors of the Church, as for example in paintings located on the piers of a crossing of a church, where Saints Ambrose, Augustine, Jerome, and Gregory are literally supporting the structure of the church. Single images of Saint Augustine are uncommon. Since we do not know of any other Doctor of the Church etchings by Bellange, it seems probable that this *Saint Augustine* is part of a rather casual Prémontré group (with cat. nos. 2 and 3) in which Saint Augustine is shown in his capacity as founder of the order from which the Prémontrés are descended. The frontispieces of at least three seventeenth century books published in Lorraine show Saints Norbert and Augustine paired on their title pages.[1]

The iconographical connections, the stylistic and the technical similarities among the *Vision of Saint Norbert*, the *Madonna Bestowing a Scapular on a Monk*, and the *Saint Augustine* lend credence to the idea that these three prints belong to the early phase of Bellange's etching career and that they are contemporary with the *Ex-Libris of Melchior de la Vallée of 1613*.[2]

A.N.W.

1. These books, whose title pages are reproduced in Justin Favier, *Trésor du bibliophile lorraine*, are (Favier, pl. 1) Pierre Desbans, *Psalterium Davidicum secondum vitum . . . ordinis Praemonstratensis*, Pont-à-Mousson, DuBois, 1629. Illustrated by J. A. Hanzelet (Favier, pl. 14) Jean Midot, *Vindiciae communitatis Norbertinae antiqui rigoris*, G. Bernard, 1632.
(Favier, pl. 56, fig. 2) *Histoire de Notre-Dame de Benoitevaux*, Verdun, 1644.

2. See Walch, pp. 64-69, and Sue W. Reed, "The Etchings of Jacques Bellange," in *Prints*, New York, Print Council of America, 1962, pp. 131 ff.

5

The Death of Portia

Etching

W.6, R.-D. 38 (only state)

236-241 x 181-185 mm. (plate)

9½ x 7⁵⁄₁₆ in.

Lower margin, in burin: *Bellange Eques in incide*

Fogg Art Museum, Harvard University

This and the following three prints (cat. nos. 5-8) have common stylistic characteristics which place them close in time and show technical advances from the earliest independent prints (see cat. nos. 2-4).

Portia was the wife of Marcus Brutus, who assassinated Julius Caesar. At the news of her husband's suicide, she herself committed suicide by swallowing live coals. Although the subject was uncommon, a painting by this title by Bellange was listed in the 1660 inventory of Claude Deruet, Bellange's successor as court painter to the duke of Lorraine.[1] In 1602, one of Bellange's earliest recorded commissions, with Jacques Danglus, had been to paint six scenes from Roman history for a room of Catherine de Bourbon at the ducal palace. The subjects were not recorded, but Portia, a loyal wife, would have been appropriate.

Portia is presented as having an elegant, but anatomically impossible silhouette, long necked, high waisted, and exaggeratedly attenuated below the waist. The type relies ultimately on a canon of female proportions set forth by the North Italian painter, draughtsman, and etcher, Francesco Mazzola (il Parmigianino, 1502-1540). (Variations on this figure type are found in cat. nos. 6 and 8.) The artificiality of Portia's gestures, her motionless pose, and the ornamentality of costume, hairdo, and brazier, contribute to the theatrical effect of this image.

As Walch has pointed out, although the stippled head and neck suggest volume, the remainder of the figure is described in two dimensions, the drapery folds having virtually no plasticity. That this was intentional seems borne out by the fact that there is evidence of burnishing on Portia's skirt and on the tablecloth below the brazier, to eliminate the interior modeling.

S.W.R.

1. Walch, p. 77, and notes 15 and 131.

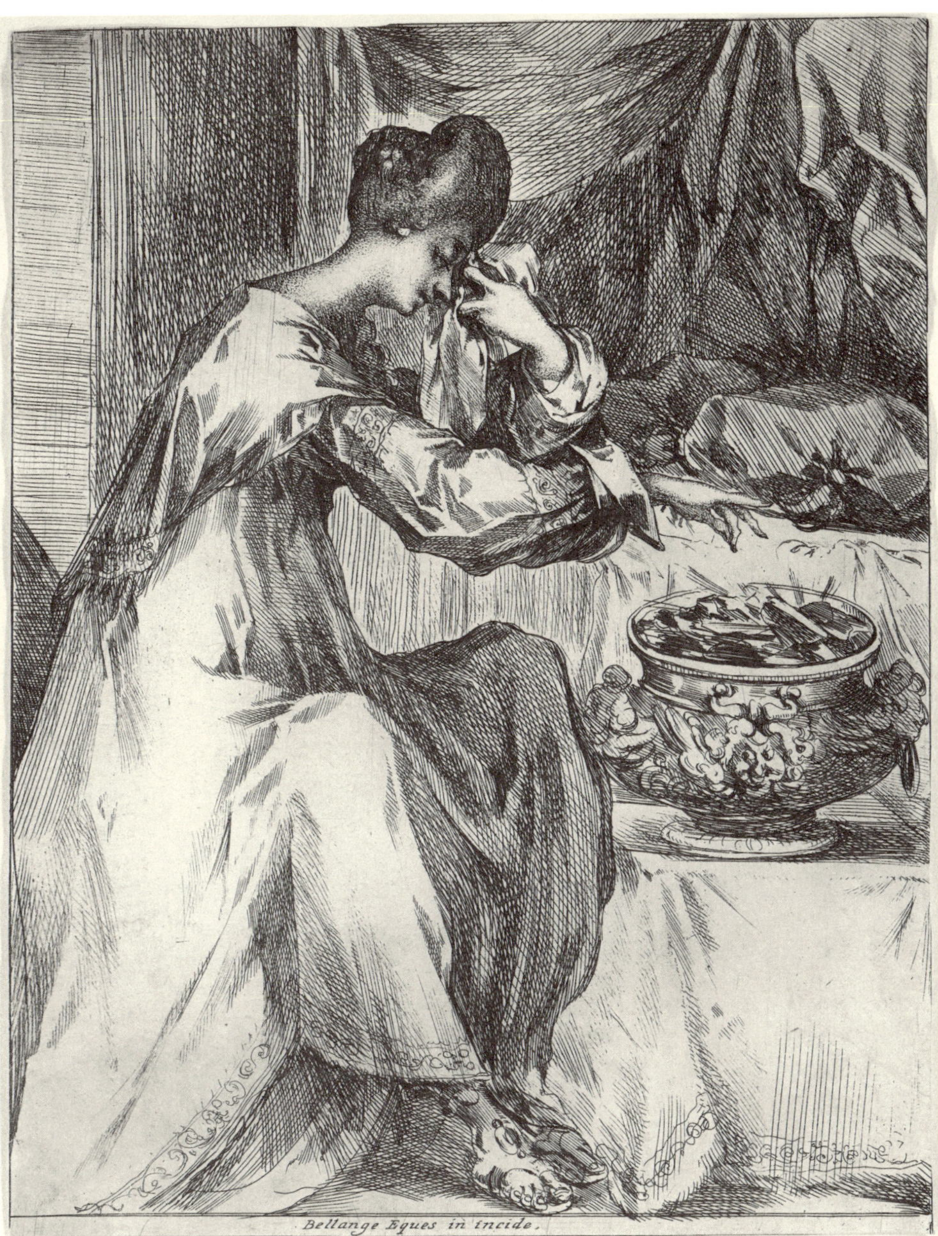

5

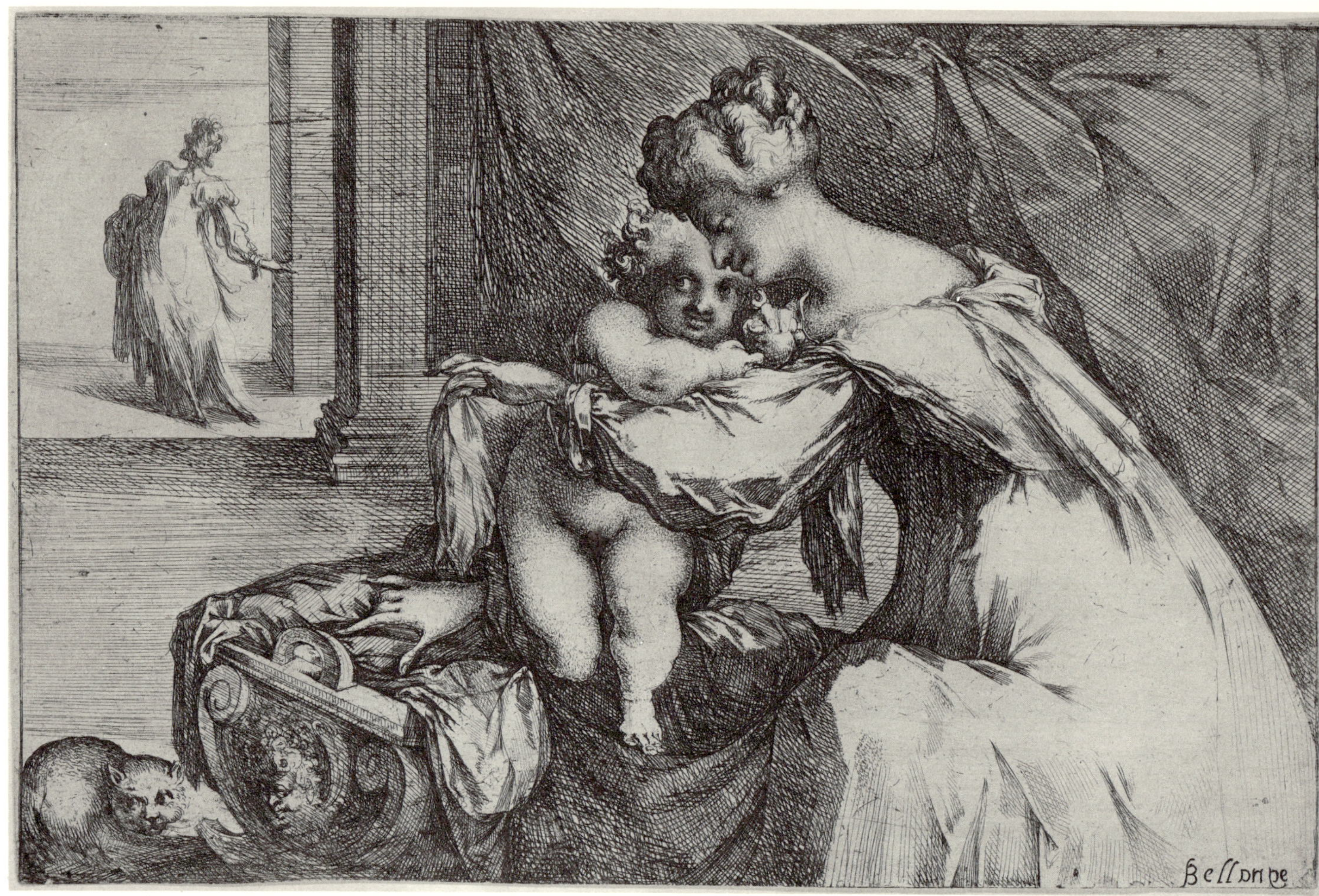

6

6
The Virgin with the Child Standing on His Cradle
Etching and drypoint, touched with burin
W.7, R.-D. 5 (second state)
141-147 x 211-218 mm. (plate)
5¾ x 8⅝ in.
Lower right, etched: *Bellange* (*ang* reversed)
Coll.: Robert-Dumesnil (Lugt 2200)
Museum of Fine Arts, Boston. Otis Norcross Fund. 40.113

The three-quarter length figure of the Virgin repeats almost exactly the pose of Portia (cat. no. 5). Walch notes that the composition is closely related to a *Madonna and Child* etched by Ventura Salimbeni (ca. 1568-1613, Bartsch 6), the Sienese painter whose prints have been cited frequently in relation to Bellange.[1]

An unfinished proof of Bellange's print, known only through a photograph,[2] makes it possible to comment on Bellange's etching procedure, here more advanced in its technique than in *The Death of Portia* or those that preceded it. In the proof, the composition is outlined in its entirety and lightly shaded. The finished state, comprising one or more additional bitings, exhibits further etched hatching and cross-hatching to darken the drapery of the background and that of the figures. The play of dark against light is stronger than in *The Death of Portia.* All of the stippling that models the flesh was executed at this time, some of it with the burin. The drypoint was employed to shade the floor and the "sky" seen outside the doorway. The Virgin's left hand, which holds up a fold of bedding, was partially erased by burnishing and re-etched as a slimmer form and with a more elegant gesture. The profile of her nose was altered as well, perhaps intentionally, but more likely as a result of the adjacent burnishing on the child's brow.

Although the physical proximity of mother and child implies an emotional relationship, they are as cool and as removed psychologically as is Portia, while, perversely, the ogling cat and leering mask on the cradle have more vitality. The retreating background figure has no identity, and is only decorative, theatrical staffage.

S.W.R.

1. Walch, p. 80, note 134.
2. Repr. Walch, p. 161.

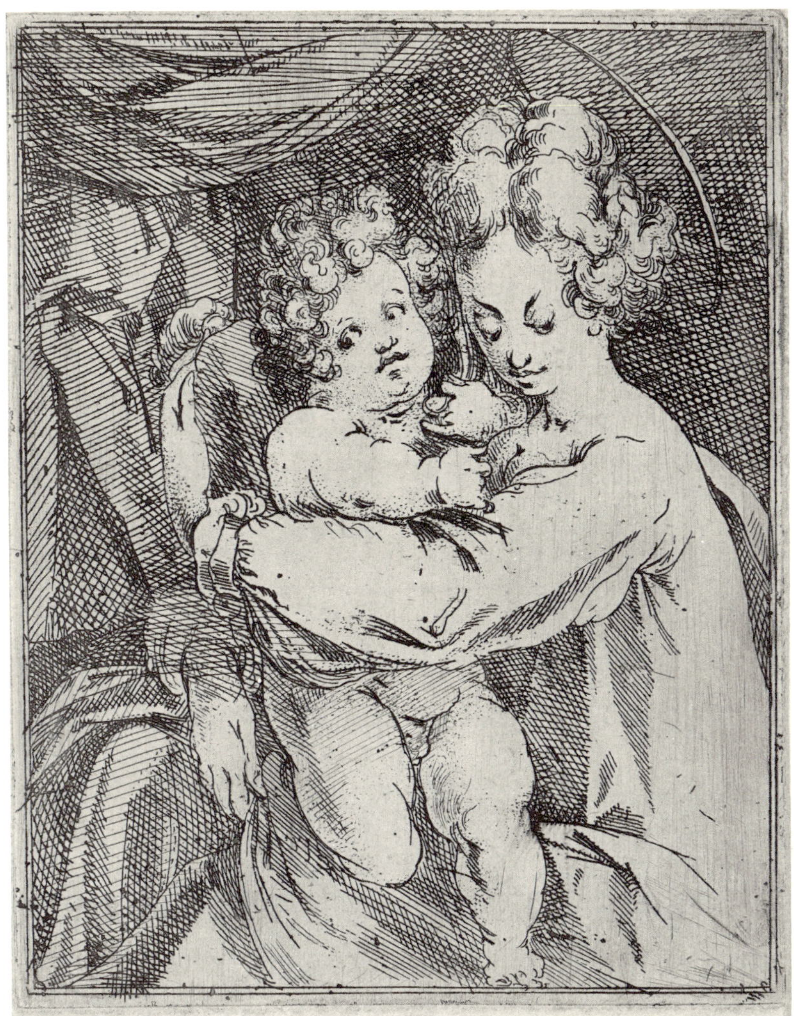

7

7
The Virgin and Child
Etching
W.8, R.-D. 2 (first state)
129-131 x 100-102 mm. (plate)
$5\frac{1}{8}$ x 4 in.
Watermark: small shield
Museum of Fine Arts, Boston. Otis Norcross Fund. 40.167

For a discussion of this print see *The Madonna with the Rose* (cat. no. 43).

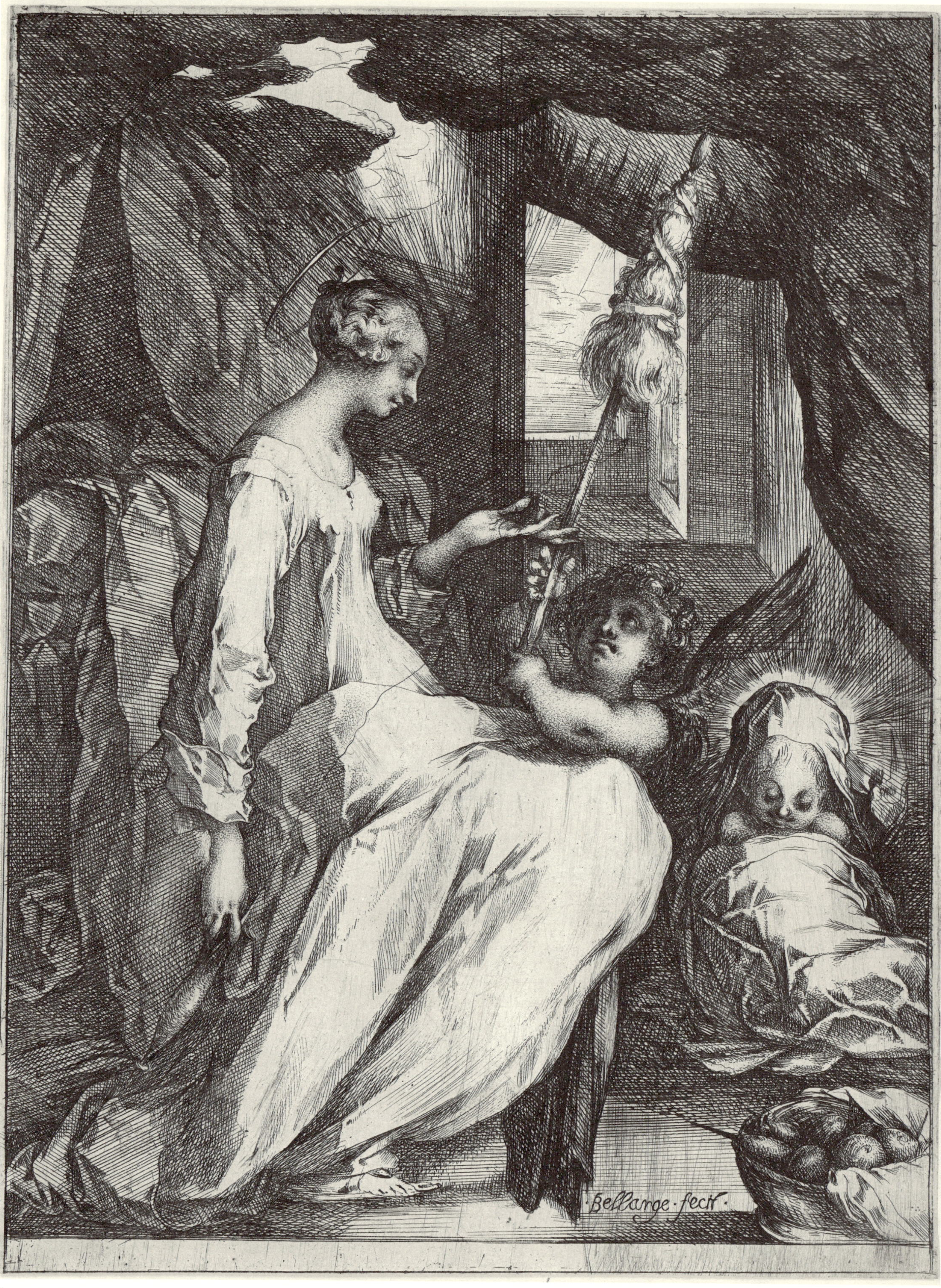

8

8

The Virgin with a Spindle

Etching, touched with burin
W.9, R.-D. 3 (second state)
253-259 x 186-190 mm. (plate)
10 3/16 x 7 1/2 in.
Lower right, etched: *Bellange.fecit.*
Museum of Fine Arts, Boston. Otis Norcross Fund. 40.107

9

FEDERICO BAROCCI
Italian, 1526-1612

The Annunciation

Etching, touched with burin
After a painting of 1582-84
Bartsch 1
435 x 314 mm. (plate)
17 1/8 x 12 3/8 in.
Museum of Fine Arts, Boston. Gift of Miss Ellen T. Bullard. M30773

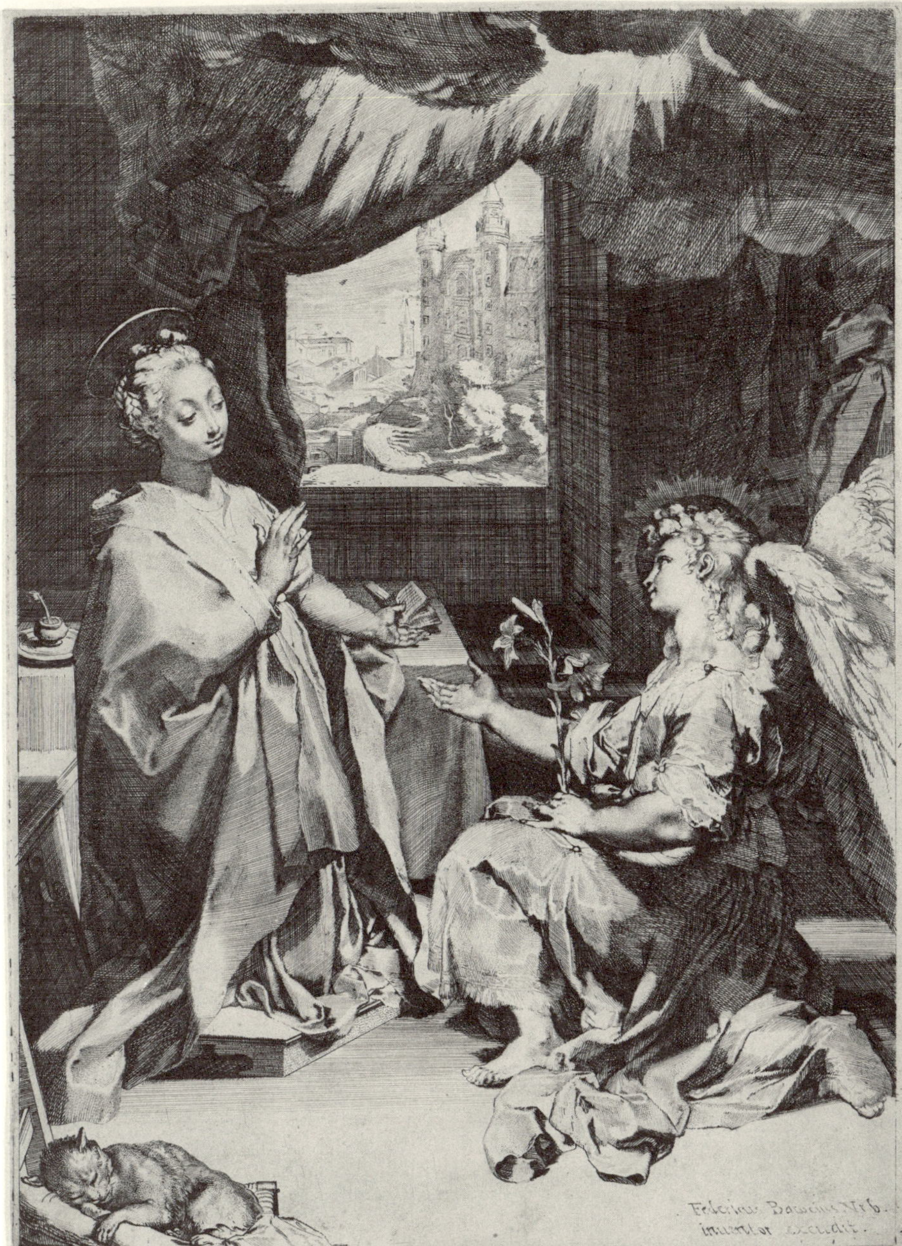

9

Bellange's print (cat. no. 8) relates in figure type and technique to others (cat. nos. 5 and 6), but a more complex setting has been introduced. Additional layers of space are suggested by the heavenly light breaking through the dark cloud and by the daylight perceived through the angel's transparent wing.

Federico Barocci's *Annunciation* provided the source for Bellange's background, which is reversed. Bellange also narrowed the window opening by adding vertical hatching at the left. The Virgin and angel in Barocci's etching are well defined, volumetric figures, occupying a logical interior space, whereas Bellange's treatment is mannerist and irrational. Bellange's Virgin has a more plastic upper torso than Portia's but her lower body is even more two dimensional, some of the striated shading having been burnished to flatten it. Bellange's space is limited and indeterminate; the floor tilts sharply upward; and the interior is filled almost indiscriminately with clouds and drapery. The awkwardly posed body of the Child blocks off any connection between the elements. The parallel lines that shade the bed curtains serve a dual purpose, since they also radiate from the Virgin's body. A similar device is used in the *Pietà* (cat. no. 24).

In both Barocci's and Bellange's etchings the burin was used to make a few well-integrated touches. In Barocci's *Annunciation* incisive strokes deepen the shadow below the platform on which the Virgin kneels, and fine, sharp lines model the angel's right thumb and the curls of his hair. In Bellange's print the burin was used for curved accents in the Virgin's hair, while short, vertical strokes shade the floor at the right of her foot.

Barocci's technique of faceted drapery planes, defined by delicate cross-hatching, flicks, and dots, was adapted by Bellange in subsequent prints (see especially the *Annunciation*, cat. no. 42). Only the beginnings of this technique are visible here, on the swaddling clothes of the Child.

S.W.R.

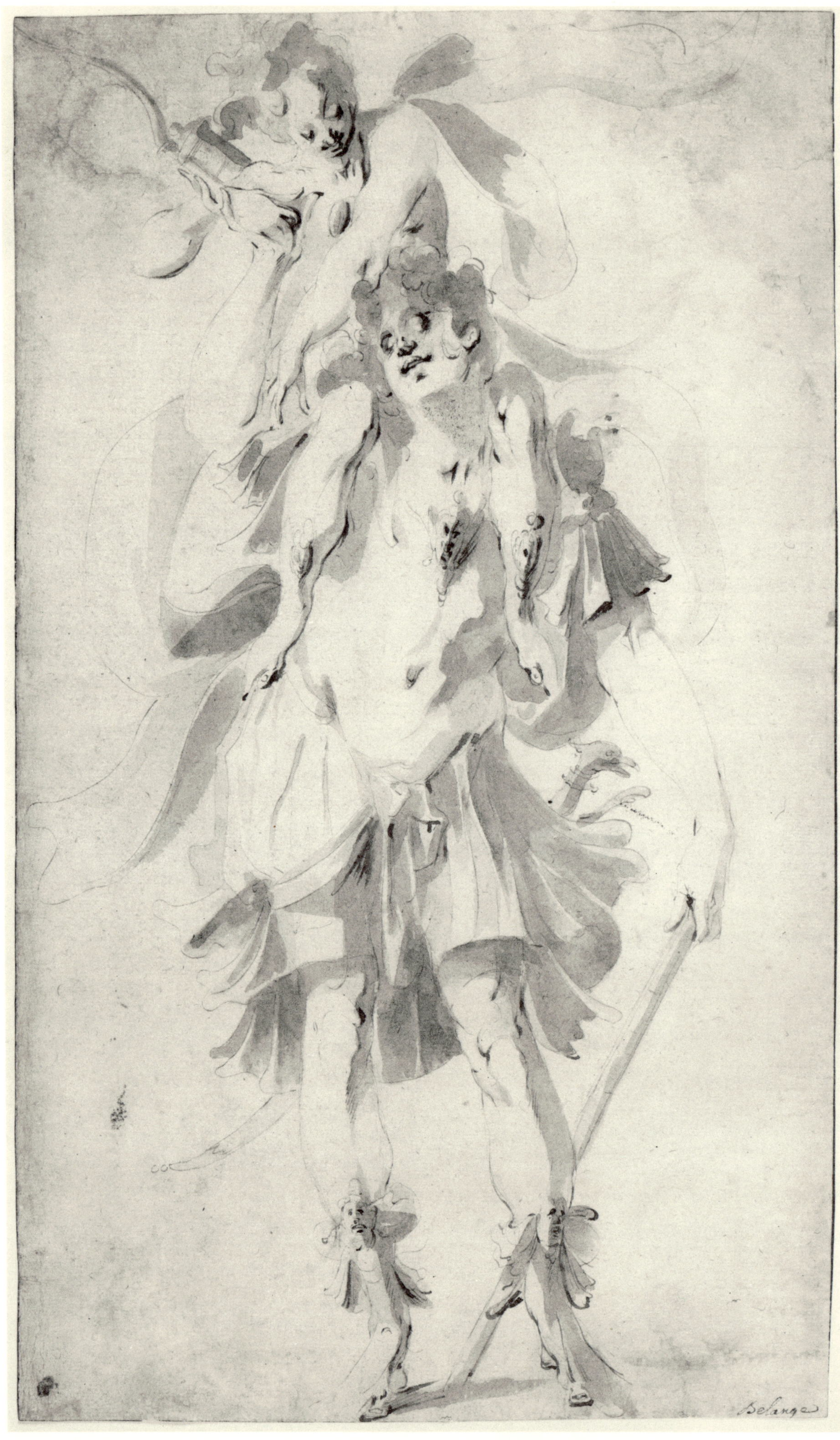

10

10
Diana and Orion
Pen and brown ink and brown wash; extraneous spots of red chalk and green paint
350 x 200 mm.
13¾ x 7⅞ in.
Coll.: John S. Thacher
Pierpont Morgan Library, New York

11-12
Diana and Orion
Walch 10, R.-D. 36
472 x 204 mm. (Boston second state)
18⁵⁄₁₆ x 8¹⁄₁₆ in.

11
Unique first state
Etching, touched with black chalk and pen and brown ink
Bibliothèque Nationale, Paris

12
Second state
Etching, additional etching, burnishing, burin, and drypoint
Etched, lower right: *Bellange;* in margin: "Gaudet amans nympha si raptor Agenore nata / Dum sua tergoribus per freta furla vehit / Qua mihi nunc Impleut placidam solatia mentem / Dum mea sic humeras pulchra Diana gravat." (Just as the loving abductor rejoices in the nymph Europa while he carries her off on his back through the raging sea, so now solace fills my happy mind while beautiful Diana thus burdens my shoulders.)
Watermark: grapes (?)
Museum of Fine Arts, Boston. Otis Norcross Fund. 40.155

13
GIORGIO GHISI
Italian, 1520/1-1582
Diana and Orion
Engraving, 1556, after Luca Penni
Bartsch 43
362 x 251 mm.
14¼ x 9⅞ in.
Museum of Fine Arts, Boston. Katherine Eliot Bullard Fund. 62.947

The giant hunter Orion, blinded by Oenopion for having raped his daughter Merope, was loved by Diana, goddess of the moon and the hunt, who here sits on his shoulders to guide him. Bellange's image exhibits a connection with the School of Fontainebleau both in subject matter and in pictorial source. Diana was a favorite subject for decorations at the palace of Fontainebleau, because it was used as a royal hunting lodge, and also because the mistress of King Henri II was Diane de Poitiers. Giorgio Ghisi's engraving of 1556 records Luca Penni's designs for a series of tapestries on the theme of Diana made some three years earlier for the Chateau at Anet, west of Paris, on the Eure, built for Diane de Poitiers.

Whereas Bellange's print shows close compositional and technical relationships to that of Ghisi, his preliminary drawing is a much freer rendition. The drawing and Ghisi's print are similar in their ornamental elements, in the eagle-headed sword and the masks and ribbons on the sandal tops. They are different in that Bellange exaggerated the contrasts between the huge Orion and the diminutive Diana and has made the pose less stable. In the drawing Orion does not grasp Diana's leg (as in both prints), nor she his neck (as in the Ghisi). The drawing is permeated by a softly flickering light, created by the application of the wash, that emphasizes the immaterial and mythical aspects of the subject.

Bellange seems to have referred more closely to the Ghisi print when he came to execute his etching. In its composition he more nearly equates the sizes of the two figures. He adopts Penni's motif of Orion's arm encircling Diana's leg, and he changes the billowing band of drapery into a substantial hunting net. Bellange follows the engraving in altering Orion's stance and the length and angle of his spear, and he adds the large dog, all of which increase the stability of the print's composition in contrast to the quivering, sinuous balance of the drawing.

Moreover, in the finished print, Bellange's technique emulates that of Ghisi's engraving. Patterns of hatching, cross-hatching, dot and lozenge, and stippling, are to be found in the etching, although they are less systematic than in the engraving.

A working proof of the etching exists, rare in Bellange's oeuvre. In both proof and drawing, the eyes of Orion are blank and sightless; the iris is only indicated in the finished state. The proof is executed entirely in etching. The composition is outlined completely, and hatched lines shade and model much of the drapery, while arms and legs (but not faces) have been stippled. Chalk and pen lines indicate additions to Orion's net and to his cloak. An indented stylus line reduces the width of the dog's right foreleg. These additions and changes are made in the following state.

The second and completed state shows not only additional etching but also drypoint and burin work and even burnishing of some of the etched lines of the first state. The new etched work includes hatching to shade and further model the draperies fluttering below Diana's quiver and to the right of Orion's staff. Orion's net is lengthened, and drapery added below it, and that side of his tunic is darkened. Horizontal lines are added to part of the background behind the figures. Etched stipples model and add texture to the faces of both Diana and Orion.

There is, moreover, additional engraving, which is more apparent here than in any other print. The burin was used to add short, parallel, curving strokes to round the faces, arms, and legs, and in the draperies to darken receding folds and shade areas such as Orion's tunic behind the bow above his right knee. Much of the new parallel shading on the ground and on the plant at the left was executed with the burin. Whereas the inner contour of the dog's right foreleg was re-etched, the shading between the forelegs was engraved.

Several areas were burnished to erase or lighten etched work visible in the proof impression. The upper outline of Diana's left arm was considerably reduced in strength, and later the drypoint was used to draw additional curls. The shading on the skirt over her left leg as well as the tunic over Orion's chest appear to have been burnished. The strong outlines of Orion's curls were burnished, thus softening his hairline, and etched dots were added to bring face and hair together into one unit.

The new work, both additive and subtractive, brings together into broad areas of light and shade what had been smaller segments, uniting the two figures into a single shape with a shadowed side, as may be seen in preceding prints (cat. nos. 5-8). The whole is enlivened by a surface pattern of flickering lights and shadows, achieving much the same results as found in the original drawing.

S.W.R.

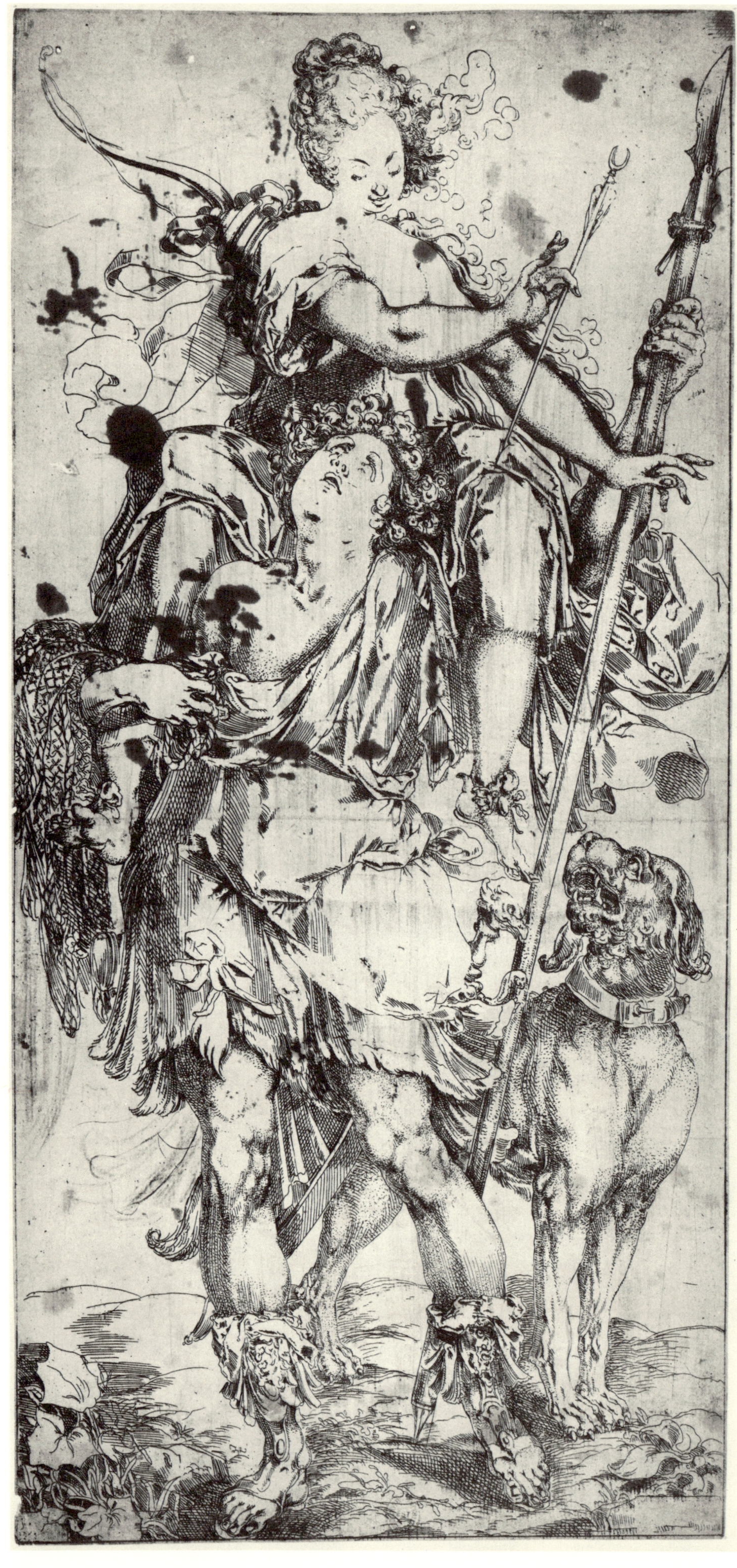

11

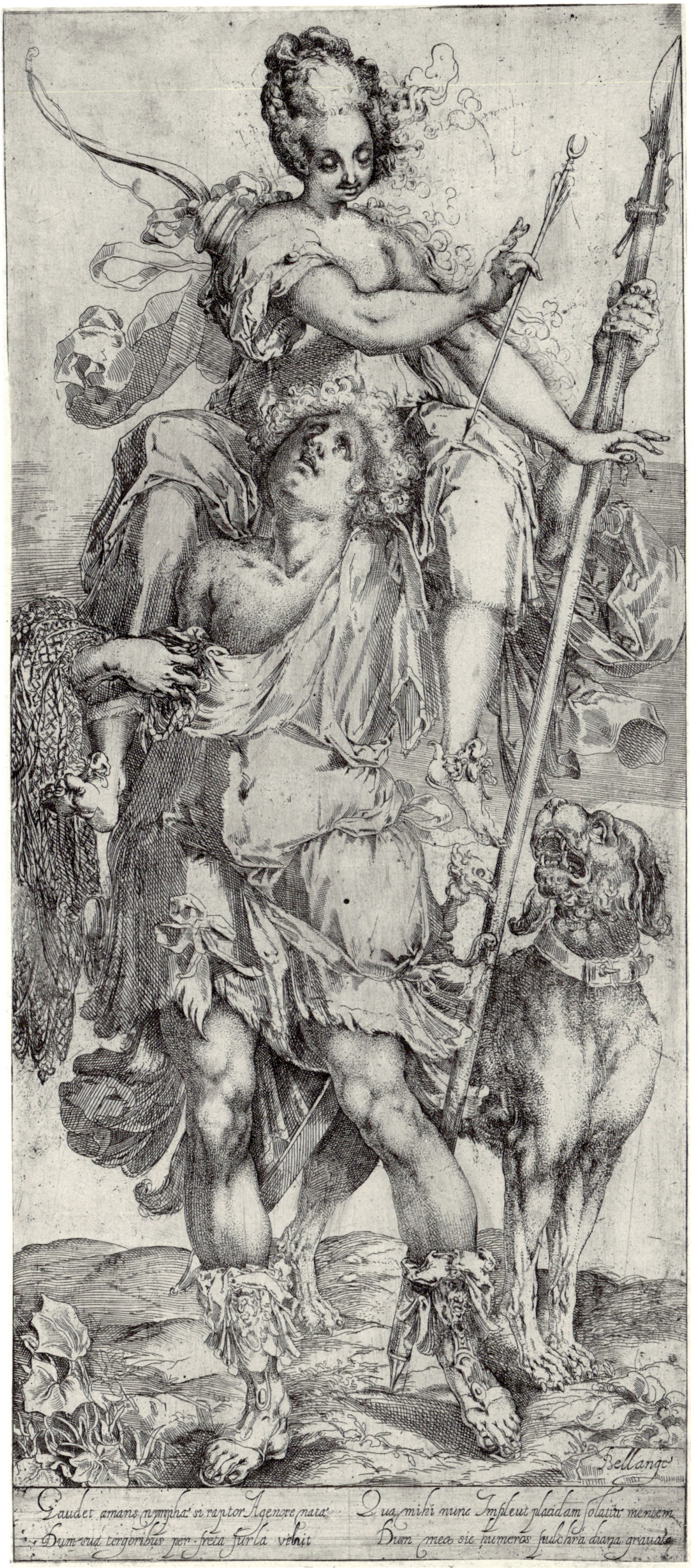

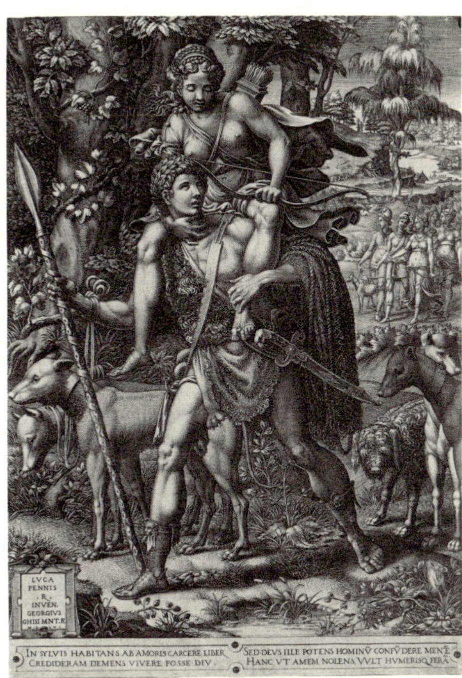

13

Bellange
Gaudet amans nympha si raptor Agenore nata
Dum sua tergoribus per freta furla vehit
Qua mihi nunc Impleut placidam solatiis mentem
Dum mea sic humeros pulchra diana grauata

12

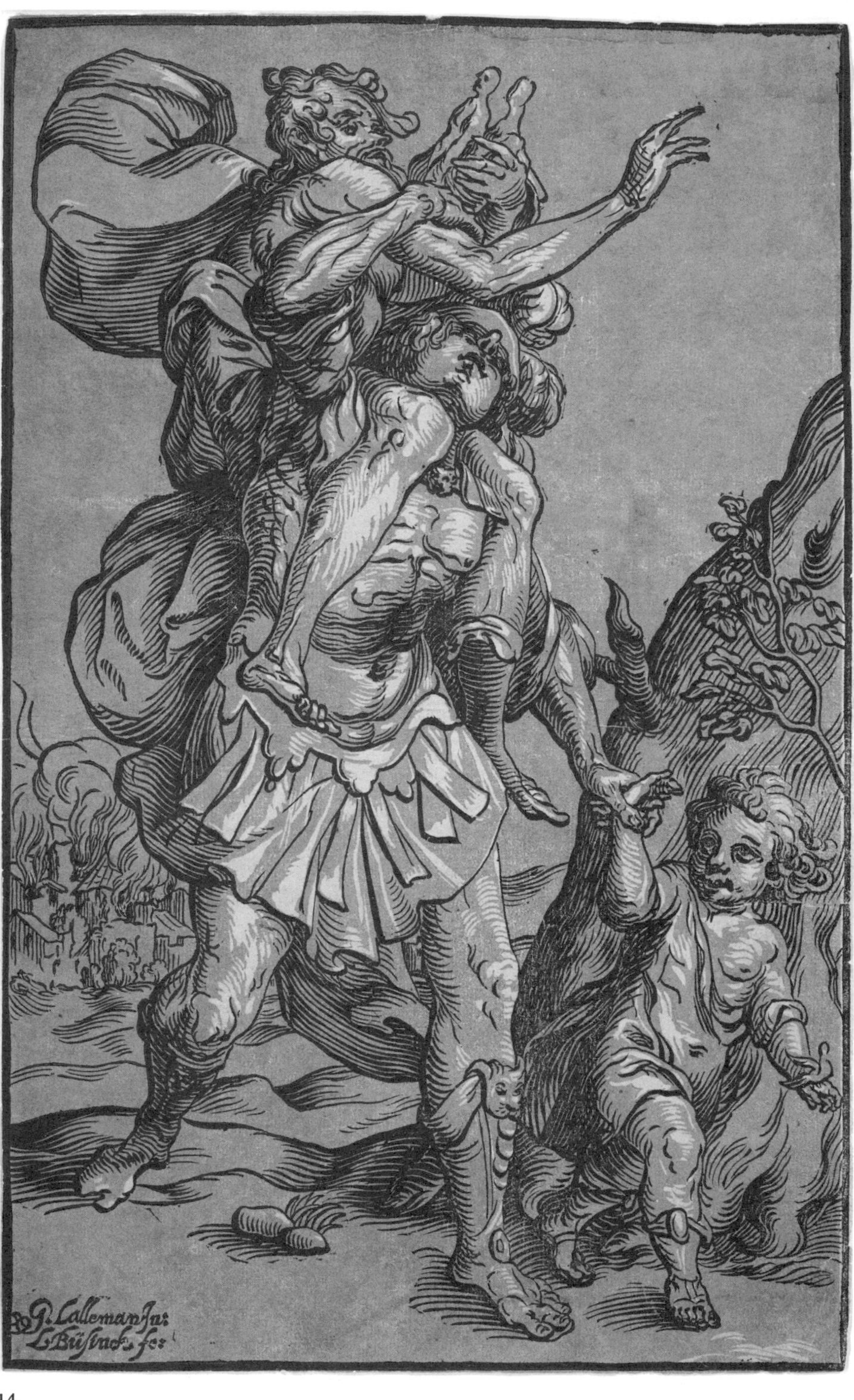

14

14
Ludolph Büsinck
Germany, 1599/1602-1669 (active France, ca. 1623-1630)
Aeneas and Anchises
After Georges Lallemand (1570- ca. 1635)
Chiaroscuro woodcut
2 blocks: black and brown
Hollstein 22
343 x 216 mm.
13½ x 8½ in.

Lower left: *G. Lalleman. In:/ L. Büsinck fe:*
Museum of Fine Arts, Boston. Bequest of W. G. Russell Allen. 1975.352

A native of Nancy, Georges Lallemand went to Paris around 1601, where he ran an atelier attended by such students as Pierre Brebiette, Nicolas Poussin, Michel Dorigny, and Philippe de Champaigne. Although Lallemand remained in Paris until his death around 1635, he is known to have maintained contact with Lorraine, particularly with the court, and may have been related to Jacques Lallemand (1560-1636), a cabinetmaker in the duke's employ. In 1617 François de Vaudémont, brother of Duke Henri II, attended the baptism of Lallemand's son Henri.

Lallemand's paintings show the influence of both the second School of Fontainebleau and the new Caravaggesque realism, but in his graphic work his style is more closely associated with Bellange. Lallemand was probably close in age to Bellange and was certainly aware of his work. A number of drawings previously attributed to Bellange have been reassigned to Lallemand, and Lallemand's etching *The Beheading of John the Baptist* was formerly given to Bellange.[1]

Lallemand's designs were reproduced as chiaroscuro woodcuts by Ludolph Büsinck in Paris between 1623 and 1630. Several derive directly from etchings by Bellange, while another seems to reflect what may be a lost composition.

Lallemand's design for *Aeneas and Anchises* is based on Bellange's *Diana and Orion*. The trail of relationships represented by these two prints says much about image-borrowing in the sixteenth and seventeenth centuries. Bellange's etching was based on Giorgio Ghisi's engraving after Luca Penni's design. Penni's figures in turn derive ultimately from those in Raphael's fresco *The Fire in the Borgo,* many times repeated in engravings. The Büsinck woodcut returned to nearly the same subject matter originally painted by Raphael.

Georges Lallemand was responsible in large part for the popularity of Bellange in Paris, and his studio there accounts for such artists as Brebiette, Vouet, and Dorigny coming under the sway of Bellange's style and subject matter, at least for a time (see also cat. nos. 21 and 68).

A.N.W.

1. Catalogued by Robert-Dumesnil as a print by Bellange after Lallemand, vol. 5 (Bellange), no. 14.

15-18
The Gardeners

15
Gardener with an Urn and Reticule
Etching
W.11, R.-D. 44 (first state)
343-350 x 185-198 mm. (plate)
13¾ x 7¹³⁄₁₆ in.
Lower right, autograph: *Bellange*
Museum of Fine Arts, Boston. Otis Norcross Fund. 40.163

16
Gardener with a Basket on Her Arm
Etching
W.12, R.-D. 42 (first state)
278-283 x 160-164 mm. (plate)
11⅛ x 6⁷⁄₁₆ in.
Lower right, autograph: *Bel.f*
Coll.: Robert-Dumesnil (Lugt 2200)
Museum of Fine Arts, Boston. Otis Norcross Fund. 40.161

17
Gardener with an Ornate Basin
Etching
W.13, R.-D. 42 (first state)
309-316 x 166-173 mm. (plate)
12⁷⁄₁₆ x 6¹³⁄₁₆ in.
Lower left autograph: *Bellange f*
Watermark: grapes
Museum of Fine Arts, Boston. Otis Norcross Fund. 40.162

18
Hortulana
Etching
W.14, R.-D. 41 (first state)
300-306 x 166-171 mm. (plate)
12¹⁄₁₆ x 6¾ in.
Lower right autograph: *Bellange*
Lower left: *Hortulana*
Museum of Fine Arts, Boston. Otis Norcross Fund. 40.160

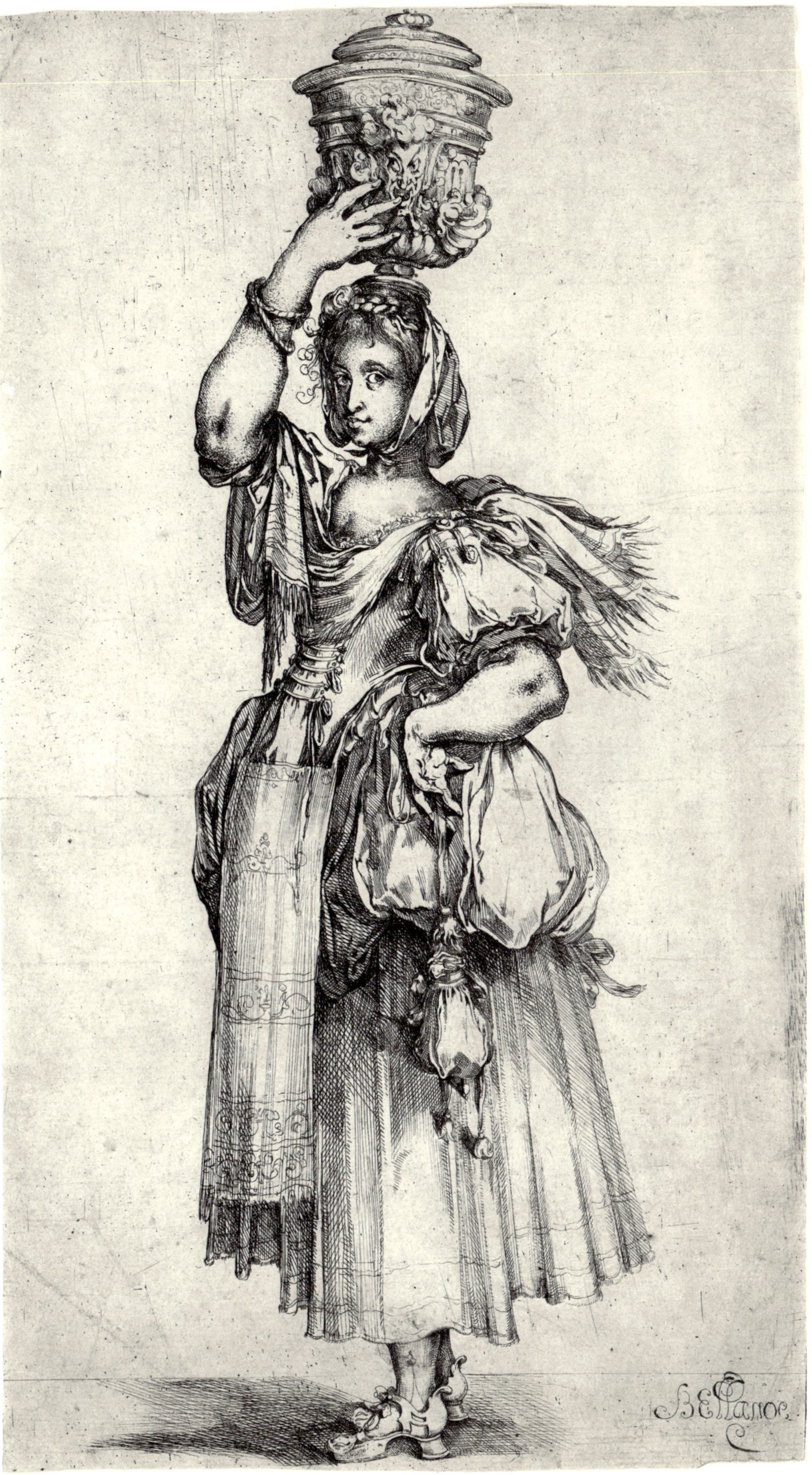

15

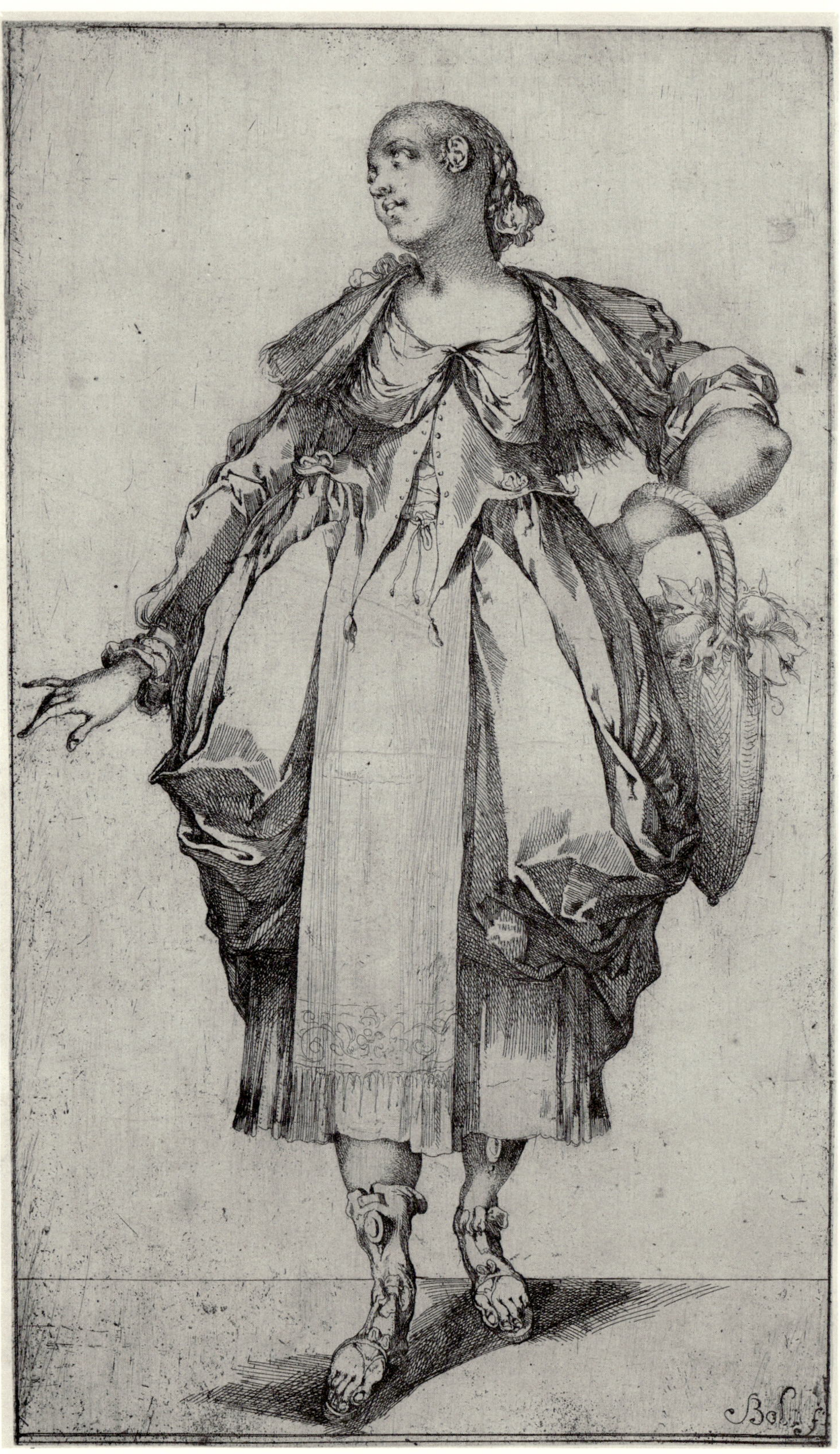

16

These four etchings are known as the Hortulana series, after the title given by Bellange to one of them (cat. no. 18). The word *hortulana* means gardener, and is not known in classical Latin. Although none of the prints have quite the same dimensions—indeed, the plate measurements vary considerably—it is reasonable to assume that they were conceived and executed together, for the actual height of the figures in all four is roughly the same.

Gardener with an Urn and Reticule (cat. no. 15) is the largest and the figure is slightly slimmer and less cramped in the space allotted her. Her pose varies only slightly from that of no. 17, which in turn is a mirror image of the pose in no. 18. Three of the gardeners wear costumes that lace up the bodice, a peasant fashion of that time, and all four gardeners wear aprons. One gardener (cat. no. 17) wears an armor-like corselet similar to that of Saint Catherine (cat. no. 20). The peasant image is reinforced by the fact that all four women are shown carrying something. In the many single-figure costume prints issued in the sixteenth century, such as those by Jost Amman, only women of the lower classes were represented carrying anything heavier than a purse or fan. The large receptacles that Bellange's gardeners carry, a figured urn, an ornate basin, and a watering can, are more fantastic than useful despite the fact that mannerist goldsmiths actually produced work of this type.[1] The ornate sandals the gardeners wear are also not practical for work. Bellange uses similar "classical" footgear on figures in the *Martyrdom of Saint Lucy* (cat. no. 24).

A pen and wash study for the *Gardener with an Urn and Reticule* (cat. no. 15) is in Stockholm. This and other related drawings in the Louvre, the British Museum, and at Stockholm are included in collections of theatrical costume designs. It has been suggested that Bellange created these courtly gardener images in connection with a ballet celebrating the completion of Henri II's Italian garden in 1611. However, no documentation for such an event has been found. While a ballet-related origin for these etchings is possible, Hortulana figures are in fact part of a previously undescribed iconographic type. An engraving by Ambrogio Brambilla, active in Rome from 1579-90, to be used as a game called *Pela il chiù*,[2] represents such a figure, labeled "Ortolana," along with many other small pictures of people illustrating the different trades and occupations. These figures certainly are part of a late sixteenth century popular imagery that has not yet been thoroughly studied.

Matthaeus Merian's copies of Bellange's *Hortulana* series are dated, as are his other copies of Bellange's etchings, to 1615-16, Strasbourg (fig. 3). These copies are much reduced in size, and three of them are reversed. Merian has set Bellange's figures in country landscapes that are peopled with additional figures and has added Latin verses of an amatory nature. As far as we know, they are not classical quotations but contemporary verses, perhaps created for the occasion. Interestingly, the title of the series, *Hortulana,* appears on Merian's copy of *Gardener with a Basket on Her Arm* (cat. no. 16), whereas in Bellange's original it appears on another (cat. no. 18).

The Hortulana prints were popular with Bellange's contemporaries, as attested by the fact that Abraham Bosse copied Merian's copies in Paris in 1622.

A.N.W.

1. Many imaginative patterns for elaborate vessels appear in prints of the sixteenth century, such as those by Paul Flindt.
2. Reproduced in Paolo Toschi, *Stampe popolari italiani,* Milan, 1964, pl. 146.

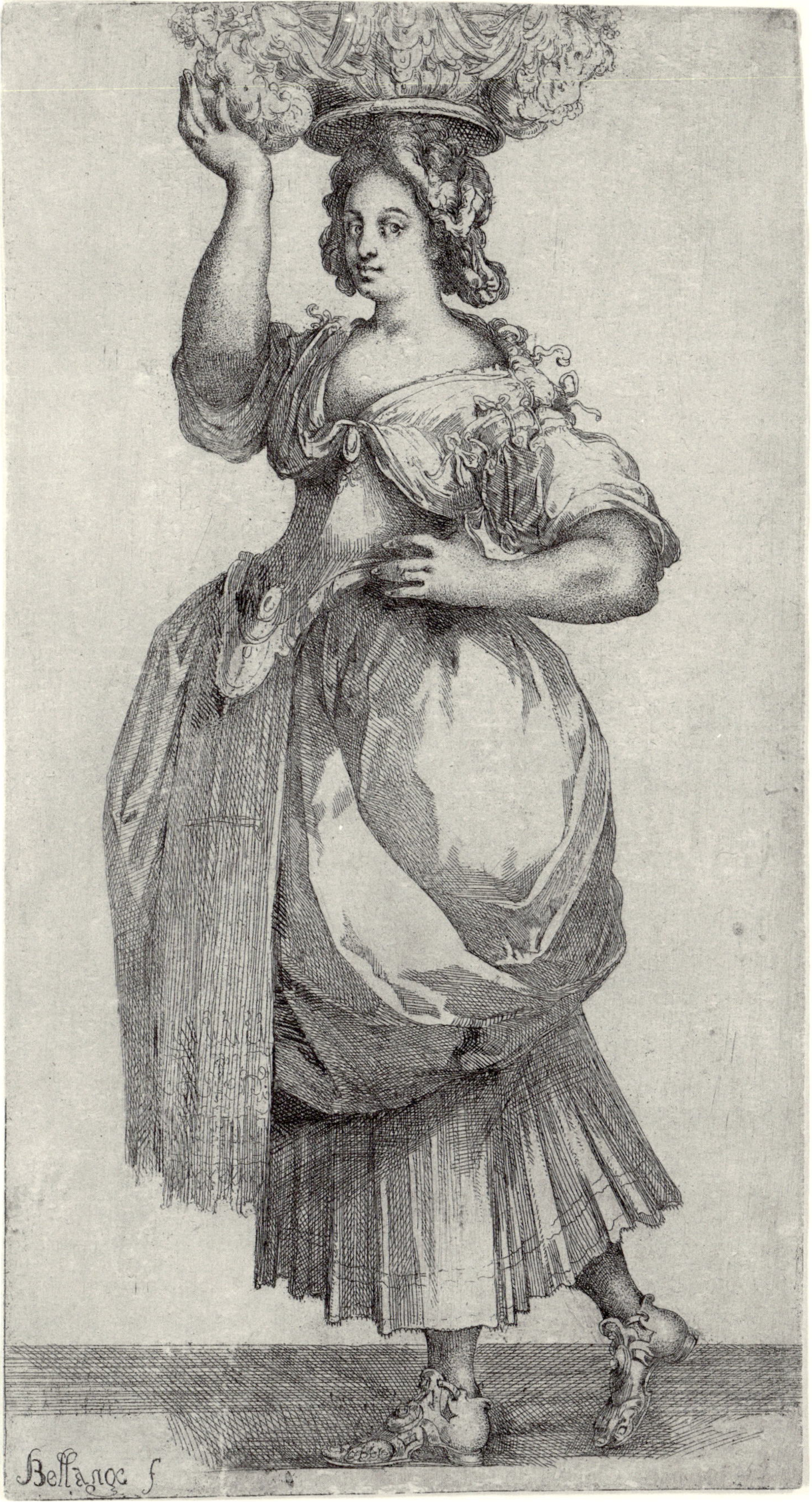

17

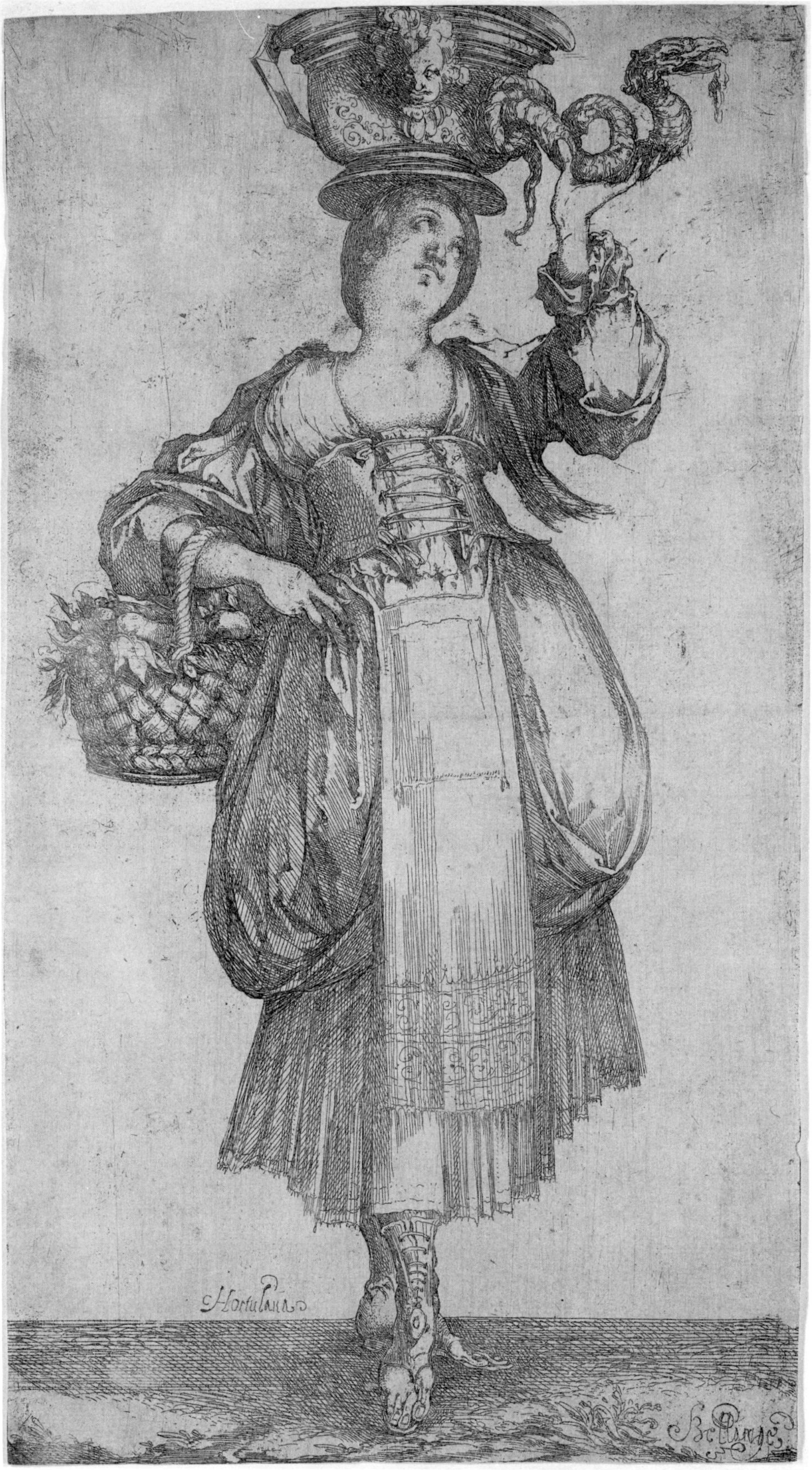

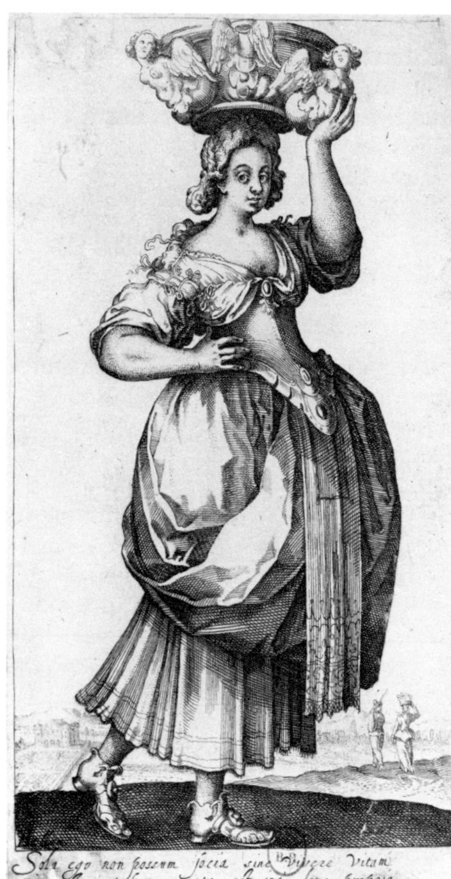

Fig. 3. MERIAN, *Gardener*, etching after BELLANGE (cat. no. 17). Bibliothèque Nationale, Paris

18

19

LUDOLPH BÜSINCK

Germany, 1599/1602-1669 (active France, ca. 1623-1630)

Girl with Fruit Baskets

Woodcut, 1629

Hollstein 25

318 x 218 mm.

12½ x 8⅝ in.

Lower left: *1629/L. Büsinck. inv. et scu:/ Cum privileg: Mariette ex*

Metropolitan Museum of Art, New York. Elisha Whittelsey Fund, 1955

Ludolph Büsinck executed a number of chiaroscuro woodcuts in Paris after Lallemand's designs (see cat. no. 14).[1] *Girl with Fruit Baskets,* a black line woodcut of his own design, based on Bellange's *Hortulana,* and dated 1629, was issued by Mariette in Paris. Rather than reproducing a specific gardener, Büsinck selected pose, costume, and attributes from several of Bellange's designs, and recombined them to form a new image.

A.N.W.

1. An essay and a catalogue of Büsinck woodcuts by Wolfgang Stechow appear in the *Print Collector's Quarterly,* 25 (1938), 392-419 (essay); and 26 (1939), 348-359 (catalogue).

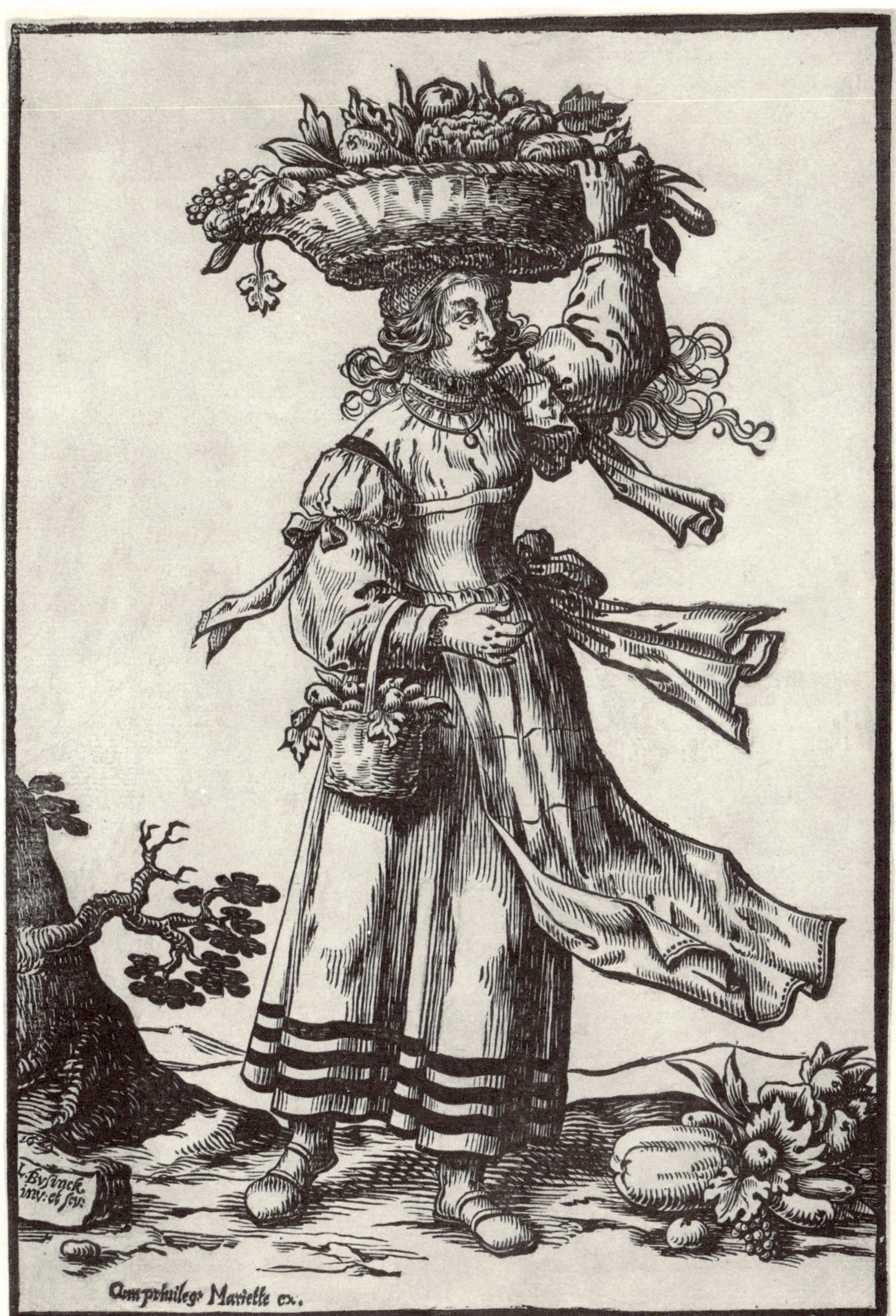

19

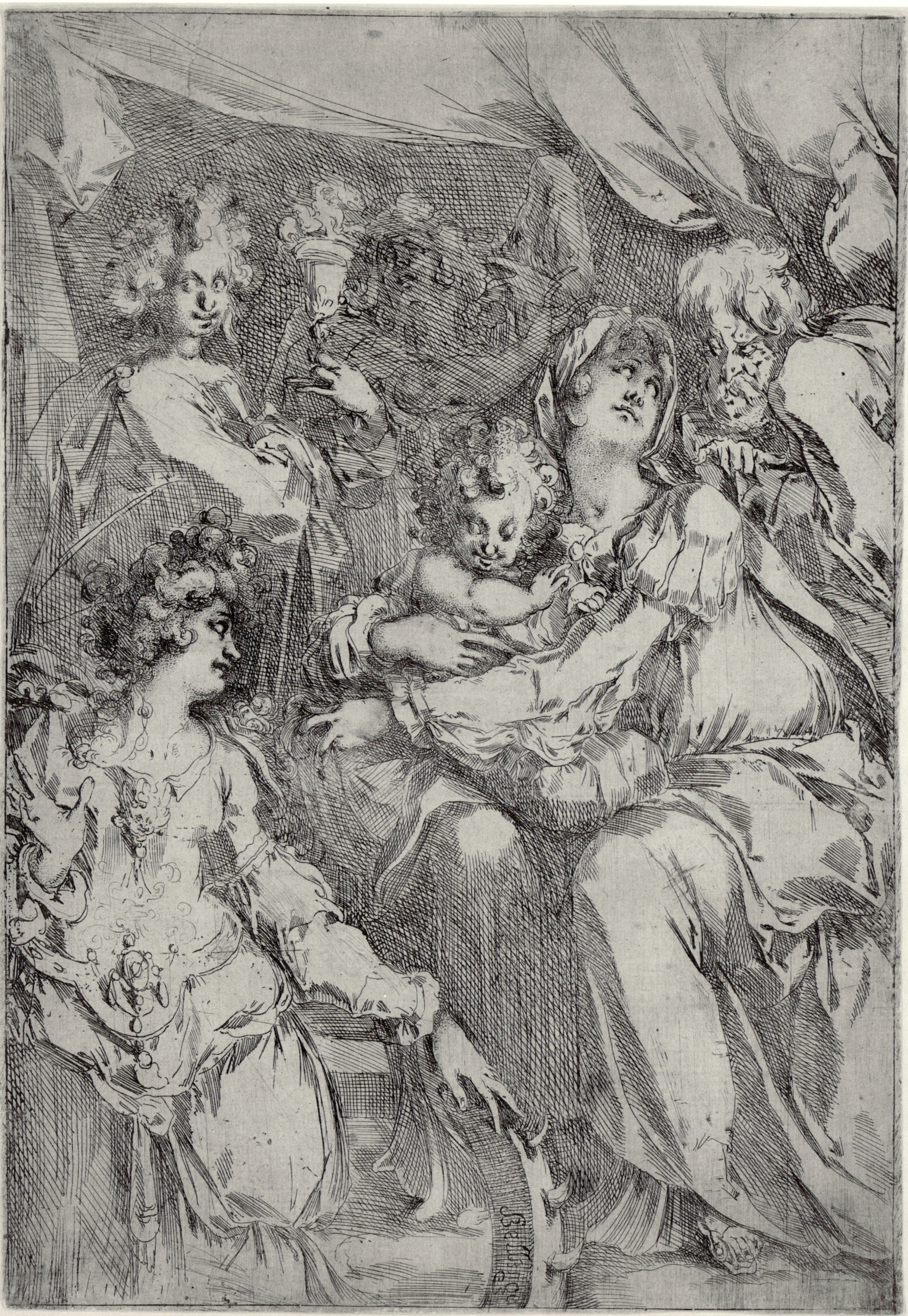

20

The Holy Family with Saint Catherine, Saint John, and an Angel

Etching
W.15, R. -D. 11 (first state)
263-267 x 182-187 mm. (plate)
10½ x 7⅜ in.
Metropolitan Museum of Art, New York. Elisha Whittelsey Fund, 1956

This plate, less densely worked than others, is one of the most harmonious and painterly of Bellange's prints. Its ultimate source is to be found in compositions by Parmigianino, very probably known to Bellange through etchings of the School of Fontainebleau, such as that by Master L. D. (Zerner 57).[1] The technique is also similar to Fontainebleau etchings, for it is lightly and freely etched, with the flesh only sparsely stippled. The design is composed of broad areas of light and transparent shadows, with relatively little insistence on strong contour lines. Elongated forms are selectively lighted and seen as flat planes with little or no interior modeling, arranged in a strong and rhythmic pattern against the shadows. The result is close in its effect to the drawing of the *Holy Family* (cat. no. 22), with the pale, cross-hatched shadows of the etching finding their equivalent in the delicate washes of the drawing.

S.W.R.

1. Henri Zerner, *Ecole de Fontainebleau, Gravures* Paris, 1969, illus.

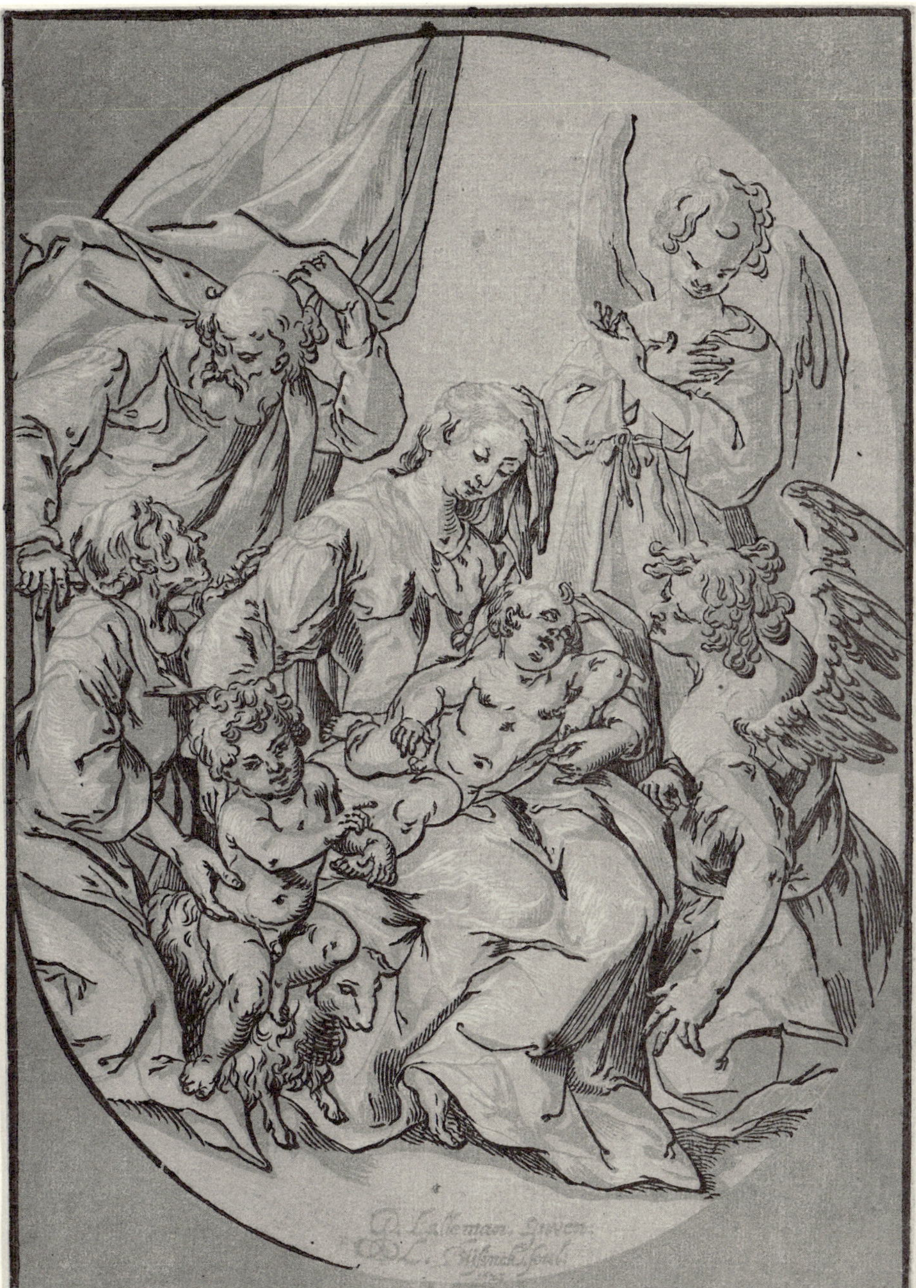

21

21

Ludolph Büsinck
Germany, 1599/1602-1699 (active France, ca. 1623-1630)
Holy Family in an Oval Frame
After Georges Lallemand (1570-ca. 1635)
Chiaroscuro woodcut
3 blocks: black, gray, light gray
Hollstein 3
305 x 210 mm.
12 x 8¼ in.
Lower center: *G. Lalleman. Inven:/ L. Büsinck. Scul:/ 1623*
Museum of Fine Arts, Boston. Harvey D. Parker Collection. P1718

Büsinck's chiaroscuro woodcut of 1623 after Lallemand (see cat. no. 14) seems to recall Bellange's *Holy Family with Saint Catherine* (cat. no. 20). The poses and expressions of saints Catherine and John of the etching are repeated in the woodcut in the figures of the two angels. Another Holy Family composition (cat. nos. 22 and 23) is brought to mind by Joseph's gesture of holding back the curtain. It is also possible that the woodcut refers to a lost composition by Bellange.

A.N.W.

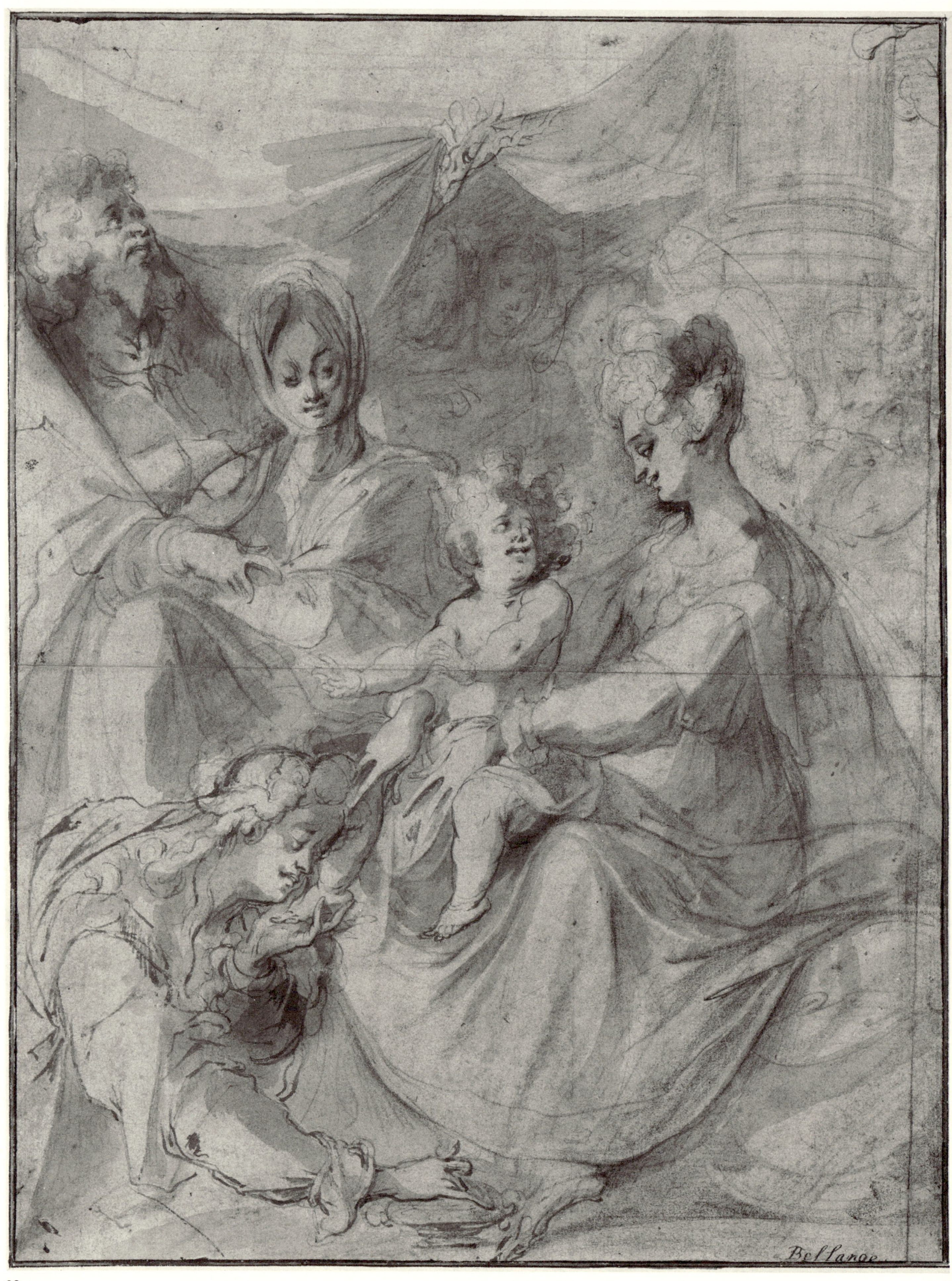

22

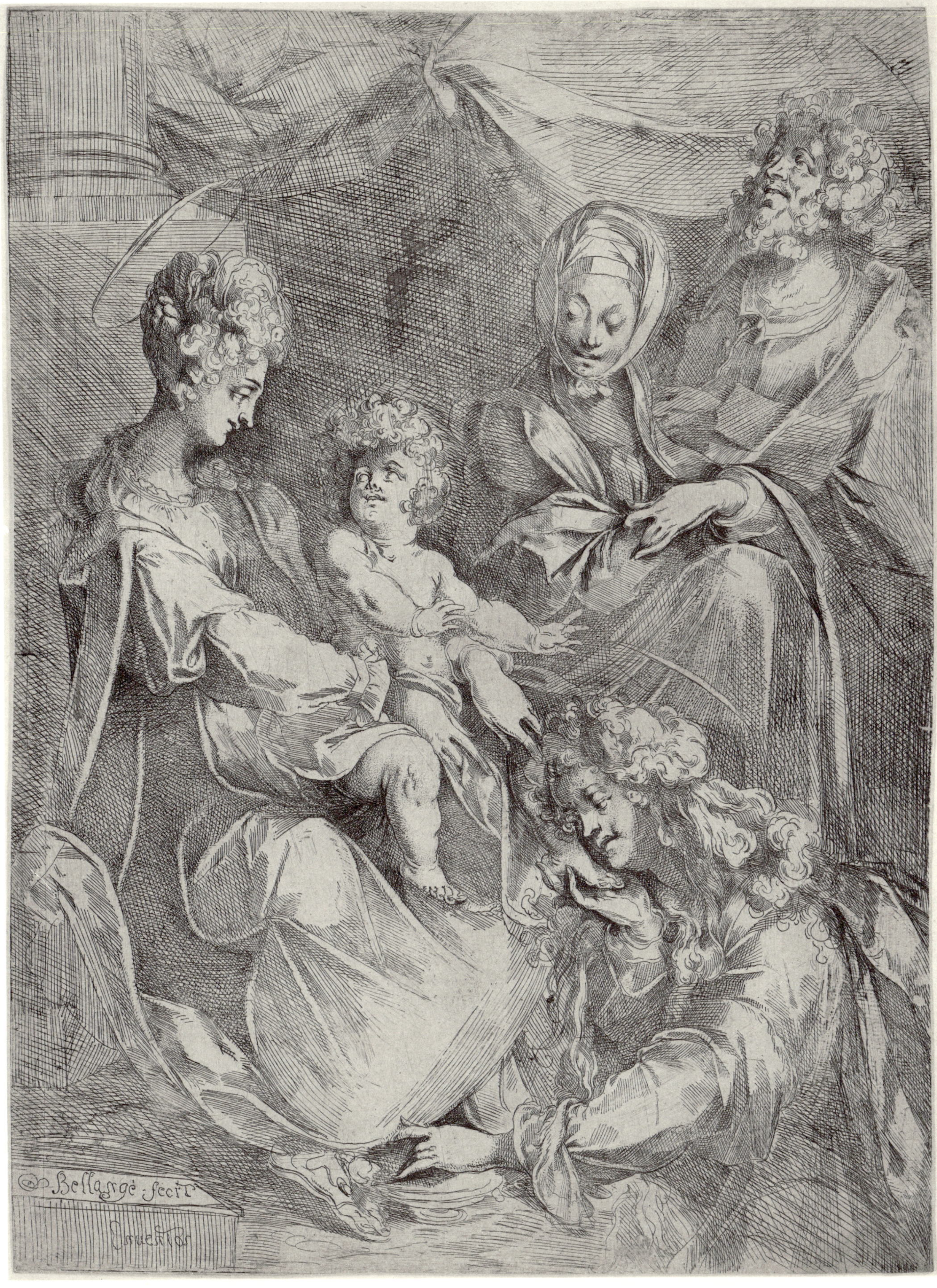

23

22
The Holy Family with the Magdalen, Saint Anne, and Three Angels
Pen, brown ink, and wash over black chalk on paper toned with ocher chalk. The use of a stylus is evident.
339 x 253 mm.
13 3/8 x 10 in.
Watermark: shield with 4, S, M (Wiener Pl. 15, no. 3; cf. Briquet 9838, Lorraine, 1587)
Coll.: Egmont
Yale University Art Gallery, Library Transfer, 1961

23
The Virgin and Child with the Magdalen and Saint Anne
Etching, burin, and burnishing
R.-D. 10 (first state); rejected by Walch
329-333 x 236-240 mm. (plate)
13 1/8 x 9 7/16 in.
Lower left, etched: *Bellange fecit / Inuentor*
Watermark: grapes
Coll.: Soliman Lieutaud (Lugt 1682)
Museum of Fine Arts, Boston. Otis Norcross Fund. 40.121

This drawing, with its overlays in several media, is one of the handsomest of Bellange's finished compositional studies. Colin Eisler has commented on the unusually stable and contained composition.[1] It has a more psychologically unified scheme than is common in Bellange's work, for the participants focus their attention on one point, the Child. Only Joseph gazes upward. A soft glow illuminates the harmoniously arranged group, emphasizing their long, gracefully curving forms.

The drawing bears clear signs of tracing with a stylus.[2] With some exceptions the incised lines follow the major contours of draperies, the column base, the heads of the five main figures and their hands, the child's body, and the Magdalen's hair. The Virgin's skirt was traced along its hemline but not on its interior folds. Her halo was moved closer to her head. The Magdalen's right hand was redrawn with the stylus to elongate the thumb, and a halo added above her head. The angels were not traced, nor do they appear in the print made after this drawing.

The etched outlines of the print echo the slight alterations made with the stylus on the drawing sheet. The image is reversed, implying that the drawing was indeed traced in order to transfer the design to the plate. (No remnants of etching ground or of chalk adhere to the verso of the drawing sheet, however.) The plate was approximately one centimeter narrower than the drawing, and the composition was reduced by this amount at the side with the column, eliminating the cradle beside the Virgin.

Both Eisler and Walch see a hand other than Bellange's in this print. Walch accepts Bellange's initial etching of the plate but feels that so much of the completed work is alien to Bellange's technique and style that she rejects the print. She also suggests that the plate may have been completed without his knowledge.[3]

Indeed there is poor draughtsmanship in certain areas, notably the awkward folds of the Virgin's cloak and skirt, the Magdalen's unresolved torso, the overcomplex folds covering Saint Anne's right arm, and the flat definition of Saint Joseph's left arm and sleeve. If one can see beyond this to the initial line etching, it is possible to accept much of the drawing as by Bellange himself. The autograph qualities of hair, hands, and toes find comparison in the first state of *Diana and Orion* (cat. no. 11). The Virgin, before her profile was altered by added hatching, finds a counterpart in the *Virgin with the Child Standing on His Cradle* (cat. no. 6) and to the central saint in *Three Holy Women* (cat. no. 38). Saint Anne's features are drawn similarly to Diana's as well as to the statue of Diana in *The Martyrdom of Saint Lucy* (cat. no. 29), and to the Virgin in *The Adoration of the Magi* (cat. no. 31).

It is possible to believe that the disquieting elements of the etching are due to its having been completed by someone other than Bellange. That this unknown artist did not have the drawing before him seems likely when one remembers that the stylus lines traced only the hemline of the Virgin's skirt. The strange, star-like folds of its interior would have been someone else's invention. Most importantly, it is the lack of a strong formal pattern of light and shade, so evident in the drawing and in other prints by Bellange, that leads one to conclude that he himself did not complete the print.

S.W.R.

1. "A New Drawing by Jacques de Bellange at Yale," *Master Drawings*, vol. 1, no. 4 (1963), 32 ff.

2. The sheet has not been squared, but the effect of squaring is achieved by old folds or cuts.

3. Walch, p. 215.

24
Pietà
Etching (and burin?)
W. 17, R.-D. 8 (first state)
313-320 x 193-200 mm. (plate)
12 5/8 x 7 7/8 in.
At the right vertically: *Bellange Eques In Incidebat*
Watermark: numeral 4 with letters
Des Moines Art Center. Dr. and Mrs. Peder T. Madsen Fund

Bellange's extraordinary print of Mary mourning the dead Christ is an enduring image of despair. These adult counterparts of Bellange's favorite image, the Madonna and Child, are placed in a blackened, burned-out world which they alone seem to light. The living agony of Mary is expressed by her violently upturned head which radiates a vivid halo. The Christ, whose expired human form rests heavily upon the knees of his mother, has only the weak glimmer of a dying halo, as if his vitality no longer fueled the glow. The contorted gesture of Mary's right hand raised to her heart recalls her gesture of questioning amazement at the time of the Annunciation (cat. no. 42), while the nail-wounded hand of Christ parallels her left hand. The massive folds of the drapery of Mary's dress display the nude, tortured body of Christ. A basket, once filled with yarn, now holds the instruments of the Passion.

Though an image of great and immediate impact, the plate must have caused Bellange a good deal of labor. The position of Christ's left arm is awkward and seems to have been corrected.[1] Technical problems plagued the etcher: many of the lines are too widely bitten to hold the ink properly, as along the contour of Christ. Tones are laboriously built up with hatching and flicks. Stippling is largely confined to the flesh areas: the effect is like slowly polished, radiant marble. Apparently the original series of parallel lines in the sky did not provide enough black to make the heavily worked figures emerge from the darkness. Bellange added additional vertical lines on the right and hatching on the left to thicken and deepen the darkness, increase the contrast, and thus strengthen the image. It would be fascinating to have the working proofs of this print. Bellange realized the necessity of simplification to achieve a dramatic and powerful effect, and in the *Pietà*, contrary to his inclination, suppressed details of costume. He emphasized movement with lines which describe contours and creases. With light, he picks out strands of Christ's hair and folds along Mary's knees and neckline to provide a web of white lines which weave together the dark forms.

Many writers have seen this print as proof of Bellange's great interest in the art of Italy. Reed (1962) suggested that the composition has a strong relationship with the lost drawing of the *Pietà* by Michelangelo for Vittoria Colonna, known from many engravings. On the other hand, Schab[2] prefers to see the Christ as coming from Michelangelo's sanguine drawing in the Albertina,[3] and, with Blunt and Walch, feels that Bellange may have made a visit to Italy. We would agree with Schab's idea that Bellange's print "reflects a pathos and breadth of Michelangelo's late style which could not have been derived from the harsh, mechanical contemporary engravings . . ."[4] We do not agree, however, with Schab's conclusion that Bellange had to have seen Michelangelo's drawings in Italy, for this implies that he was so dependent on his sources that he could not express these emotions on his own. The way in which he consistently used the work of others was to extract certain formal components—compositions, figure types—and invest them with his own personal sense of drama, to give the borrowed images a new life.

A recitation of the many engraved and etched descendants of Michelangelo's *Pietà* drawing is unnecessary here, for De Tolnay[5] provides ample illustration. We would, however, call attention to some remarks by Dimitri Tselos[6] on the meaning of the *Pietà* image for the late sixteenth century. Tselos emphasizes that Italy did not import this iconographical theme from medieval Germany, but both countries derived it from the Byzantine mystical tradition dating from the tenth century. Nowhere does the Bible narrate this event of the Virgin holding her dead son. A *Pietà* image, therefore, is the non-narrational, ceremonial last presentation of the body of Christ to the faithful.

Many of the Pietà images which appeared toward the end of the sixteenth century surely owed their popularity to Saint Filippo Neri's Cult of Pity (Pietà), which he associated with the veneration of the mysteries of Mary at his church of Santa Maria in Valicella, built in Rome in 1575.[7] One does not need to establish a particular link between Saint Filippo Neri and Lorraine in order to explain Bellange's print,[8] for there were so many Pietà images available for Bellange to see. Many of these images depended upon the Michelangelo drawing. However, Bellange's print, like Goltzius' engraving (B. 273) after Spranger, and El Greco's *Pietà* (New York, Hispanic Society), all share a pictorial impact and a spiritual quality that make them more than mere repetitions of a famous picture.

A.N.W.

1. Bellange needed to make several adjustments to obtain the precise relationship of the figures that he wanted. A pen drawing in the Feilchenfeld Collection, Zurich, may be a preliminary study for the etching. While the general relationships of the bodies and the expression of emotion are the same, considerable rearrangements have been made in the print. In the drawing, Christ's head is turned downward, his right arm is unsupported, and his legs are stretched out. His halo is larger. Mary's arms are both raised to her breast. In the print a more striking image is achieved. Christ's body is drawn up higher, hiding Mary's midsection, with its transparent, clinging clothing. Her left arm reaches down to touch her son, creating a closer relationship between the figures. Before, Mary was isolated, even from the object of her grief. Bellange focuses attention on this psychological touch by highlighting the white sleeve of Mary's arm, now the largest area of light in the print.

2. "Master Drawings and Prints from European and Private Collections," William H. Schab Gallery, New York, cat. no. 55, p. 66.

3. Reproduced: Vienna, Albertina catalogue, 1972, no. 27.

4. Schab, "Master Drawings."

5. Charles De Tolnay, *Michelangelo*, Princeton, N.J., Princeton University Press, 1971, vol. 5, pls. 340-364.

6. Dimitri Tselos, "The Pietà; the enigma of its origins and meanings," paper read at the College Art Association, Washington, D.C., 1975.

7. This church had twelve chapels dedicated to the mysteries of the Virgin, one of which, the Cappella della Pietà, had as its altarpiece Caravaggio's *Deposition*.

8. The one instance of Saint Filippo Neri's involvement in politics came when he intervened on behalf of King Henri IV of France with Clement VIII. Henri IV was the brother of Catherine de Bourbon, wife of Henri II of Lorraine.

25

Matthaeus Merian
Germany, 1593-1650
Reverse copy of Bellange *Pietà*
Etching, ca. 1615
Wüthrich 89
304 x 196 mm.
12 x 7¾ in.
Lower right: *Bellange*
Museum of Fine Arts, Boston. Gift of William H. Schab. 40.227

Merian's first dated etching is from 1609. The next year he studied in Zurich with Dietrich Meyer and with Christoph Murer. In 1611, at the age of about 17, Merian went to Nancy to work with Frederick Brentel on the *Pompe funèbre de Charles III*. Merian's name appears on the title page of the first section, as well as on the first sheet of section 3, *The Entry of Henri II*. Wüthrich[1] has interpreted this to mean that Merian was a full-fledged collaborator and not the mere "garçon" mentioned in the contract for the project (see Introduction). It was during the work on the *Pompe funèbre* that Merian must have become acquainted with Jacques Bellange, since Bellange etched a small portion of *The Entry of Henri II* on which Merian worked (see cat. no. 1). Whether or not Merian or Brentel actually taught Bellange to etch at this time cannot be known, however.

Though Bellange's independent etchings date from after Merian's sojourn in Nancy, Merian was aware of them, for he etched eleven copies which were published in Strasbourg by Jacob van der Heyden and are dated 1615-16 by Wüthrich.[2] Merian's contact with Van der Heyden probably came about through his connection in Nancy with Frederick Brentel and Hermann de Loye, both of Strasbourg. Merian's copies reproduce Bellange's original etchings, but make them neat, tidy, and more comprehensible through the addition of landscapes, titles, and verses. Ten of the eleven are reversed. (See cat. nos. 15-18, 25, 36, 37, and 39.) Abraham Bosse[3] praised Merian, along with Callot and Frisius, for having perfected etching by making it consistent and reliable. Merian's technique and his aesthetic seem to have been well suited to each other.

One looks in vain through the remainder of Merian's prints, which number over 700, for some hint of a lasting influence from Bellange, for there is none. Merian

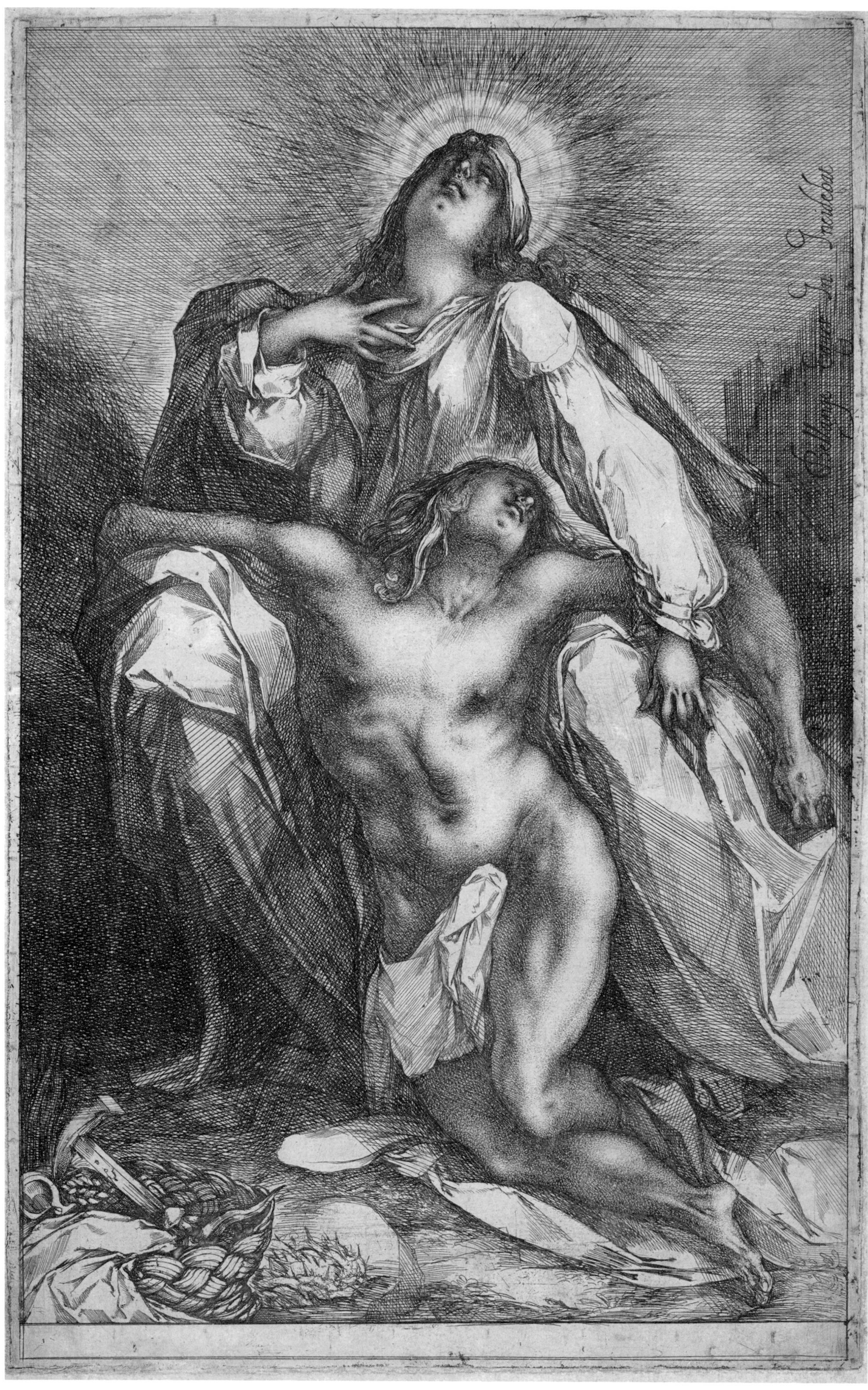

spent the rest of his life etching formularized landscapes, topographic views, title pages, and book illustrations. His youthful flirtation with Jacques Bellange's images is intriguing.

A.N.W.

1. L. H. Wüthrich, *Das druckgraphische Werk von Matthäus Merian d. Ae.*, vol. 1, p. 18.

2. Merian's copies of Bellange's etchings are all listed and reproduced in Wüthrich, who dates them to Basel, 1615-16. These prints, with their Wüthrich numbers, are:
Melchior, W. 85 (cat. no. 36) after Bellange *Caspar* (cat. no. 34)
Caspar, W. 86 after Bellange *Balthasar* (cat. no. 33)
Balthasar, W. 87 (cat. no. 37) after Bellange *Adoration of the Magi* (cat. no. 31)
The Three Women on Their Way to the Tomb, W. 88 (cat. no. 39) after Bellange *Three Holy Women* (cat. no. 38)
Pietà, W. 89 (cat. no. 25) after Bellange *Pietà* (cat. no. 24)
Hortulana, W. 90 after Bellange *Gardener with a Basket* (cat. no. 16)
—." W. 91 after Bellange *Hortulana* (cat. no. 18)
—." W. 92 after Bellange *Gardener with an Ornate Basin* (cat. no. 17)
—." W. 93 after Bellange *Gardener with an Urn and Reticule* (cat. no. 15)
Blind Hurdy-Gurdy Players, W. 94 after Bellange *Blind Hurdy-Gurdy Player* (cat. no. 27)
Fighting Beggars, W. 95 after Bellange *Two Tramps Fighting* (cat. no. 26)

3. Abraham Bosse, *Traité des manieres de graver en taille douce . . .*, Paris, 1645.

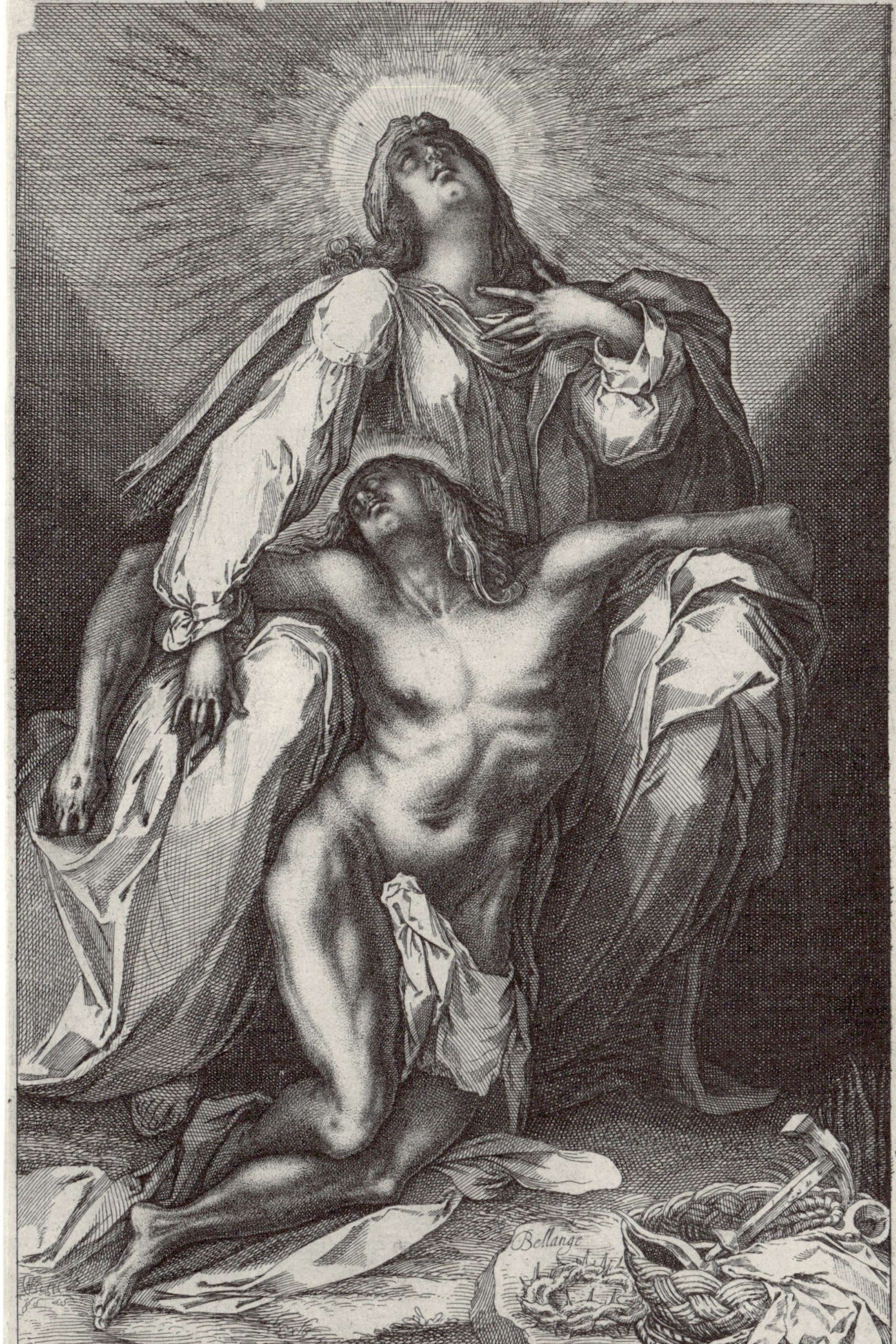

25

26
Two Tramps Fighting
Etching, drypoint, and burin
W.18, R.-D. 46 (first state)
314 x 214 mm. (Yale impression)
12⅜ x 8 7/16 in.
Lower right: *Bellange fecit* (*t* on the borderline)
Watermark: grapes
Yale University Art Gallery. Everett V. Meeks, B.A. 1901, Fund

27
The Blind Hurdy-Gurdy Player*
Etching and burin
W.21, R.-D. 45 (second state)
295-301 x 175-180 mm. (plate)
11 13/16 x 7 1/16 in.
Lower left, etched: *Bellange.fecit.;* lower right, engraved: *Le Blond excud*
Squared in pencil
Museum of Fine Arts, Boston. Otis Norcross Fund. 40.164

*Another impression, in better condition, is in the collection of the Minneapolis Institute of Arts; however, its existence was discovered too late for inclusion in the exhibition.

Two blind men are gripped in a vicious struggle. One, a hurdy-gurdy player, digs his fingers into the throat of the other, who flails a staff in the air and clenches his right hand, as if in pain. This other man wears a hat with a shell, the sign of a pilgrim from the shrine of Saint James at Compostella in Spain. Bellange's *Saint James* (cat. no. 52) wears the same clothing as this pilgrim. Their struggle takes place in a landscape which is only briefly indicated. An extremely low horizon places the viewer's eye level with the dog, while the horizontal lines of the "sky" negate the space, creating an effect which is monumental and oppressive. This spatial treatment was also used by Bellange in several other prints, including the *Pietà* (cat. no. 24) and in most of the *Apostles.*

The *Blind Hurdy-Gurdy Player* sounds his instrument. His face is gaunt; he has empty eyes and his gap-toothed mouth is opened in song. The dark "sky" and low ground focus all attention on the pathetic figure, whom Bellange has spotlighted as if on an empty stage. There is no sympathy on the part of the artist, only a detached fascination with this creature's ugliness in contrast to his beautiful instrument. Bellange has suppressed distracting details of clothing such as we see in the *Two Tramps Fighting,* in order to emphasize the depiction of ugliness. Bellange's etching technique is splendidly used to create broad areas of shadow needed for dramatic light effects. Stippling and hatching techniques are now perfectly integrated to form rich darks. The outline of the figure is simpler and more compact, in contrast with Bellange's earlier figures. He has now learned to etch with the freedom, ease, and power of his wash drawings.

Iconographically, one other print by Bellange deals with the subject of blindness—the *Diana and Orion* (cat. nos. 10-12), but this is most likely coincidental. It is interesting to compare Bellange's treatment of the blindness of Orion with that of the tramps. In the *Diana and Orion* the cruelty of Orion's situation is merely implied—one must know the story to realize that Orion is blind. To most viewers, this would appear to be a light and appealing scene. By contrast, the horrible image of the hurdy-gurdy player on the attack, or the *Blind Hurdy-Gurdy Player's* more abstract yet terrifying grandeur, are sordid. Bellange seems to be expressing his disgust for the ravaged human beings who sound the beautiful instruments that they cannot see.

Though Walch has placed the two tramp etchings somewhat apart in her chronology, it is appropriate to treat them together. Numerous writers have tried to explain the apparent "popular realism" of these two etchings in contrast to the artistocratic worldiness of Bellange's other works. Blunt[1] has suggested that the extremes of beauty and ugliness found in Bellange's prints are really two aspects of the same aesthetic. A. Hyatt Mayor[2] found that the *Pietà* and the *Two Tramps Fighting* exhibit the same "Baroque luxury of pain." Walch has placed Bellange's beggar prints in the category of popular realism. This concept should be more closely examined, for the theatrical lighting, unreal space, and the clothing of the tramps deny a "realistic" reading of the prints. The fighting beggars wear the same open-toed footgear as the Hortulana maidens (cat. nos. 16, 18), while their clothing is metamorphosed into flesh just as the Apostles' is. The hurdy-gurdies, so lovingly described and ornamented, are typical Bellange touches. Rather than etching genre scenes taken from life, once more he has turned to his sources to create works rich in reference, if ambiguous in meaning.

The sources of Bellange's beggar images have been traced by Walch, who with Sudeck,[3] sees Annibale Carracci's and Villamena's large single-figure beggar prints as the immediate prototypes. Many writers have shown that there is a long northern tradition of the representation of blind beggars, often associated with a moralizing or satirical message such as the parable of the blind leading the blind.

The hurdy-gurdy[4] was invented in the late middle ages and was considered to employ advanced principles of harmony. Originally found in the courts, by the fifteenth century it was associated exclusively with tramps and beggars, and in France, had a specific connection with blind men.[5] Among sixteenth century representations of blind hurdy-gurdy players in art, Brueghel's painting, *The Blind Leading the Blind,* illustrating the parable, is perhaps the best known example. Hurdy-gurdy players appeared in numerous sixteenth century prints, including works by Hans Sebald Beham, and Goltzius.[6]

A second tradition, that of fighting beggars, can be traced in the works of Bosch and Pieter Aertsen, though the meaning of the theme is unclear.[7] Bellange was probably familiar with both blind hurdy-gurdy players and fighting beggars as subject matter for art. He may have reinterpreted the theme of the blind leading the blind in an image such as Goltzius', which represents two blind Compostella pilgrims, one carrying a hurdy-gurdy, stumbling about and grasping at each other in a woodland.[8]

Whatever thematic overtones Bellange's prints convey, they remain ambiguous, for his lack of sympathy renders them so. Of all the prints dealing with the theme of the blind beggar, Bellange's evoke the most disgust and horror. Merian's reverse copies of 1615-16 were issued, it would seem, immediately after the appearance of Bellange's originals. Merian attempted to clarify the meaning of the *Two Tramps Fighting* by adding the inscription: *Mendicus mendico invidet* (Beggar envies beggar).

Bellange's contribution to the blind beggar theme in art was the emphasis on ugliness, which added a new emotional impact to the traditional subject matter and stimulated its popularity in seventeenth century France. Weigert's estimate that over thirty prints[9] made in the seventeenth century in France have

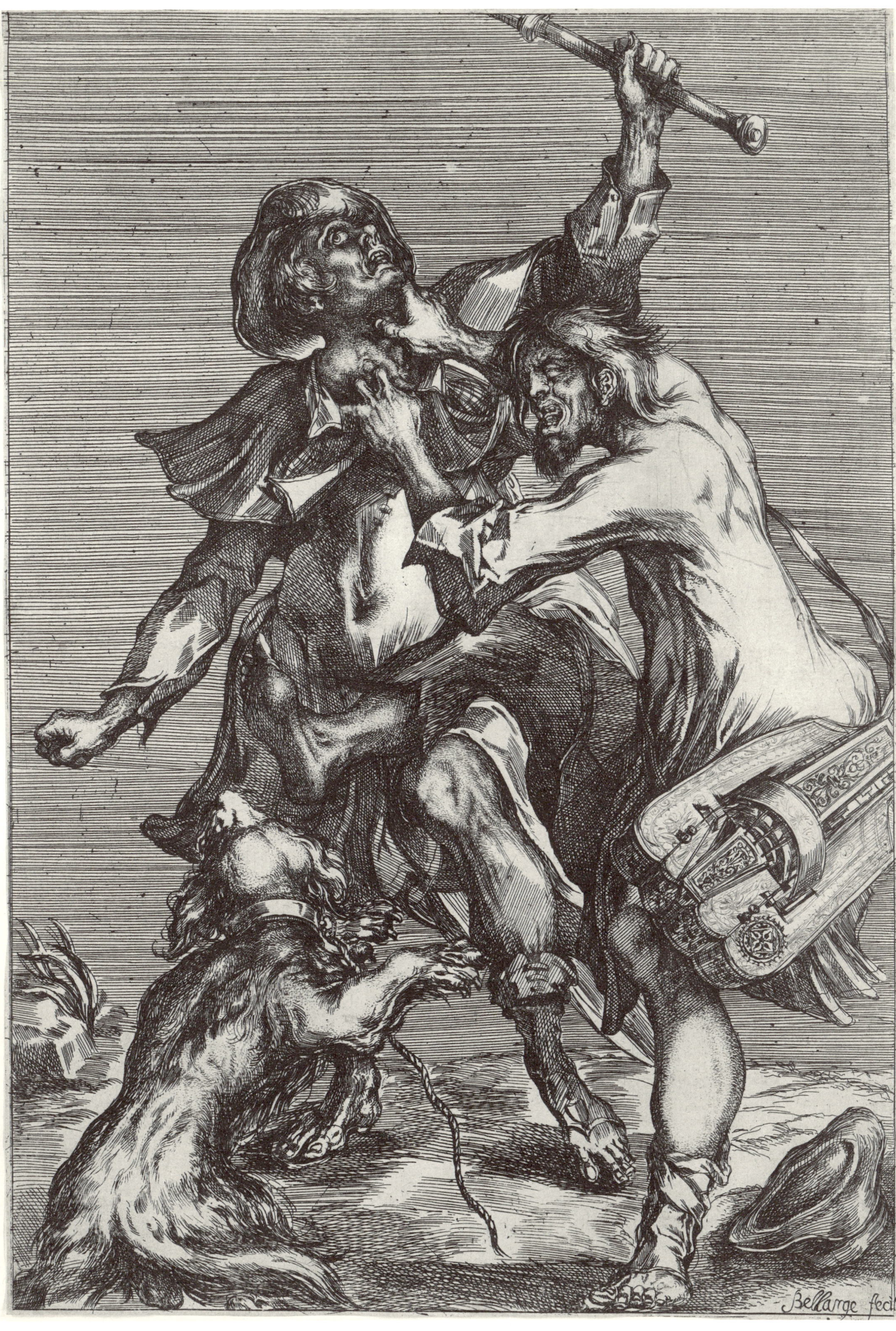
Bellange fecit

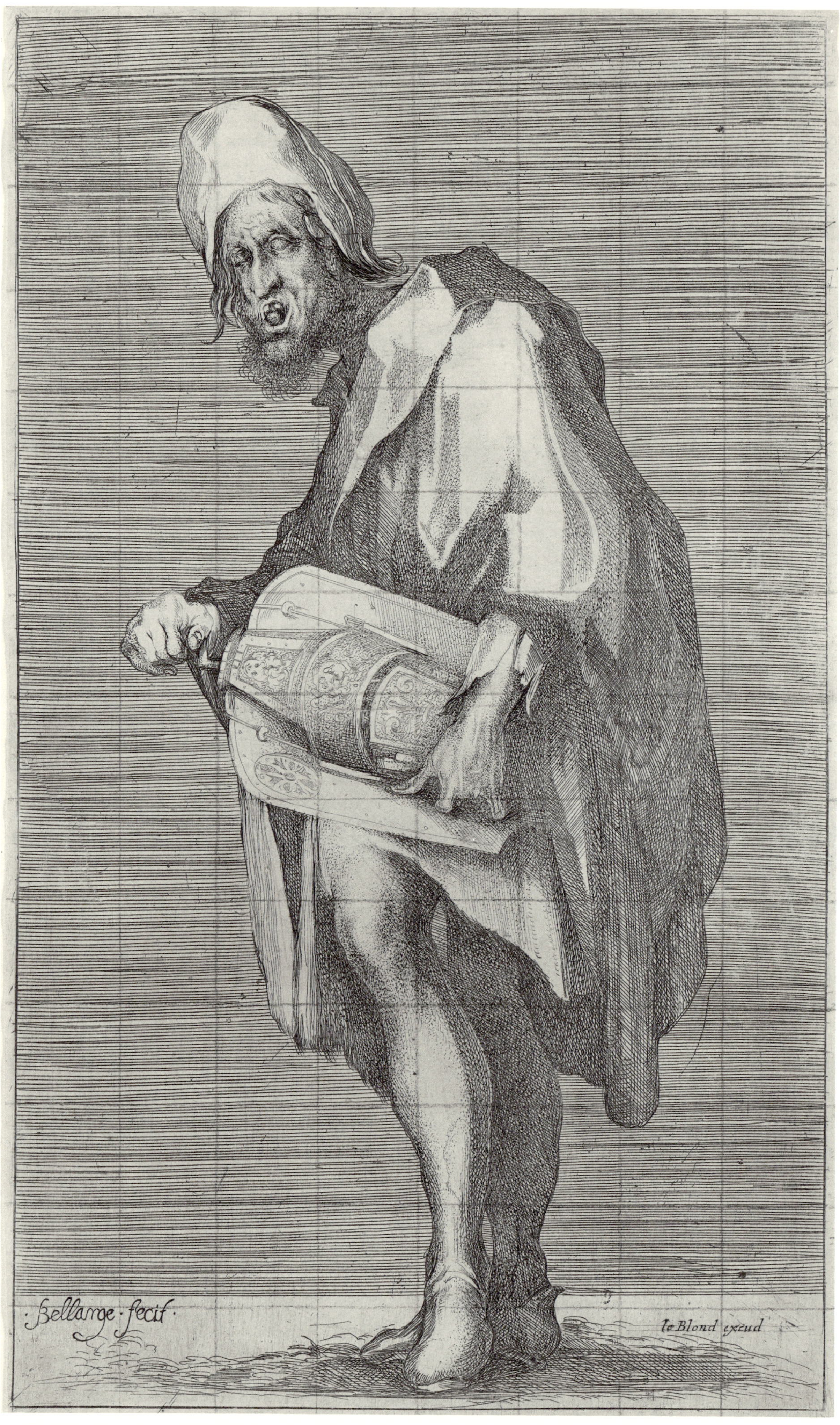

Bellange fecit
le Blond excud

a direct link with Bellange's two prints suggests the impact of these images. In Lorraine, George de La Tour's paintings *Le Joueur de vielle* and *Rixe de musiciens* depended heavily on Bellange's prints. Also in Lorraine, Jean Appier, called Hanzelet, and Jacques Callot etched blind hurdy-gurdy players. The Bellange plates were among those reissued by Le Blond in Paris.

A.N.W.

1. Anthony Blunt, *Art and Architecture in France, 1500 to 1700*, Pelican History of Art, 24, London, 2nd ed., 1957.
2. A. Hyatt Mayor, *Prints and People*, New York, Metropolitan Museum of Art, 1971, 454.
3. Elisabeth Sudeck, *Bettlerdarstellungen vom Ende des XV. Jahrhunderts bis zu Rembrandt*, Studien zur deutschen Kunstgeschichte, vol. 279, Strasbourg, 1931.
4. Anthony Blunt, "The Joueur de vielle of Georges de La Tour," *Burlington Magazine*, 86 (1945), 108 ff.
5. The Blunt article (1945) mentions a fifteenth century poem "in which a King of Portugal displays to a French knight with great pride an instrument called a *Chifonie*, which is a kind of Vielle. The French knight says scornfully that in France they are never seen "fors aveugle portant" and goes on: *"Ainsi vont li aveugles et ly Povres Truant,*
De si fais instrumens li Bourgeois esbattant
En l'apella depuis un instrument truant
Cars ils vont d'huis en huis leur instrument portant,
Et demandant leur pain" (Chronique manuscrit de Bertrand du Guesclin).
This fragment quoted from Terrasson's *Dissertation historique sur l'instrument nommé la Vielle*, in *Mélanges d'histoire et de litterature*, 1768.
6. Beham, Hollstein 239; Monogrammist COR. MET., Bartsch 53; Bosch, Riggs 12, 19 (Timothy Riggs, *Hieronymus Cock*, unpublished Ph.D. thesis, 1971, Yale University); Goltzius, Hollstein 111.
7. Bosch, Riggs 10; Pieter Aertsen, Sudeck (1931), pl. 7.
8. Reproduced in Hollstein, 111.
9. These include works by or after Büsinck, della Bella, Daniel Rabel, Ferdinand Elle, Sebastien Vouillement, Ragot, van de Venne, G. Isaac, Matthieu le Nain, Sebastien le Clerc, and H. Bonnart.

28
Military Scene
Etching and burin
W.19, R.-D. 37
275-279 x 216-220 mm. (plate)
11 x 8 11/16 in.
Below on the shield: *Bellange Eques in incide.*
Watermark: arms of Dachsbourg (Dabo); a shield with eight batons (Wiener Pl. 13, no. 7)
Wesleyan University, Davison Art Center

According to the descriptions of Basan,[1] Huber-Rost,[2] Gandinelli,[3] and Robert-Dumesnil, this print represents a warrior standing, a woman seated, leaning against a drum, and additional figures, with a city in the distance. Nineteenth and twentieth century attempts to identify the subject of the print as Judith and her servant in the camp of Holofernes or as an allegory of Bellona have been based upon these traditional descriptions. Tietze-Conrat[4] and Nicole Walch have pointed out that the seated figure could not possibly be a woman, were one to compare it with other, unquestionably female, figures in Bellange's prints. In particular, Walch shows that the treatment of the hair and the prominent musculature are more characteristic of Bellange's masculine figures. We would add that Bellange decorously never allows the skirts on his women to reveal leg as high as the knee. The fact that the seated figure is apparently male has led us to a renewed investigation of the iconography of Bellange's print.

Torquato Tasso's epic, *Gerusalemme liberata*, was completed in 1574 and published in 1581. It was very popular, and eleven illustrated editions appeared within the first forty years.[5] Countless painters drew from the celebrated romantic episodes of Tancred and Clorinda, Rinaldo and Armida, and Erminia among the shepherds. In about 1605 Ambroise Dubois executed the first painted *Gerusalemme* cycle for the Cabinet de la Reine at Fontainebleau. The eight paintings illustrate the story of Clorinda in Cantos I-III and XII. When Bellange visited Fontainebleau in 1608 he would surely have seen the Cabinet de la Reine with its newly completed cycle. Given the fashionable nature of Tasso's epic, and the fact that Margherita Gonzaga, wife of the Duc de Bar, was from Mantua, where Tasso worked, Bellange would have had ample reason to see Dubois' paintings. Relationships can be found between three of the paintings in the Cabinet de la Reine and two of Bellange's etchings.[6]

A figure in Dubois' *Tancred Baptizing Clorinda*[7] bears comparison with the reclining figure in Bellange's print. The mortally wounded Clorinda lies in the foreground, leaning against a draped rock; nearby are her helmet and sword, and her figured shield, which serves as a *repoussoir*. In the background are the round towers and walls of Jerusalem. The figure in Bellange's print is by no means identical, yet the hand raised in a gesture of weariness, the face staring vacantly upward, the feet crossed at the ankles are suggestively close. If indeed this beautiful and memorable painting is the prototype for Bellange's reclining figure, the sexual ambiguity that has been the source of past confusion may now be explained. Though Bellange's own figure is male, its source was female, dressed as a man.

A figure that appears in another Dubois painting, *Crusader's Camp before Jerusalem*,[8] may have been the inspiration for Bellange's standing warrior. Although this figure type is a very common motif of sixteenth and seventeenth century painting, it is possible that Dubois' painting was the specific source of Bellange's warrior in this, and subsequently, several other of Bellange's prints. In addition to similarities of pose and costume, both the Dubois and Bellange warriors serve the same compositional function and close the composition at the right. Both images show the walls and towers of Jerusalem in the distance.

The depiction in prints of soldier groups clothed in diverse costumes goes back to the fifteenth century, for example, Dürer's *Five Soldiers with a Turkish Rider* (B.88).[9] The large number of antique-costume military prints made around the year 1600 provides the type for the Bellange etching. If one compares Bellange's print with engraved or etched illustrations for any of the twenty cantos of *Gerusalemme liberata* it becomes clear that Bellange's etching does not depict a specific narrative incident from the epic. Instead, Bellange made a "capriccio" whose imagery may have been derived from Tasso. He transformed and updated the traditional military-costume fantasy print by using elements associated with a fashionable

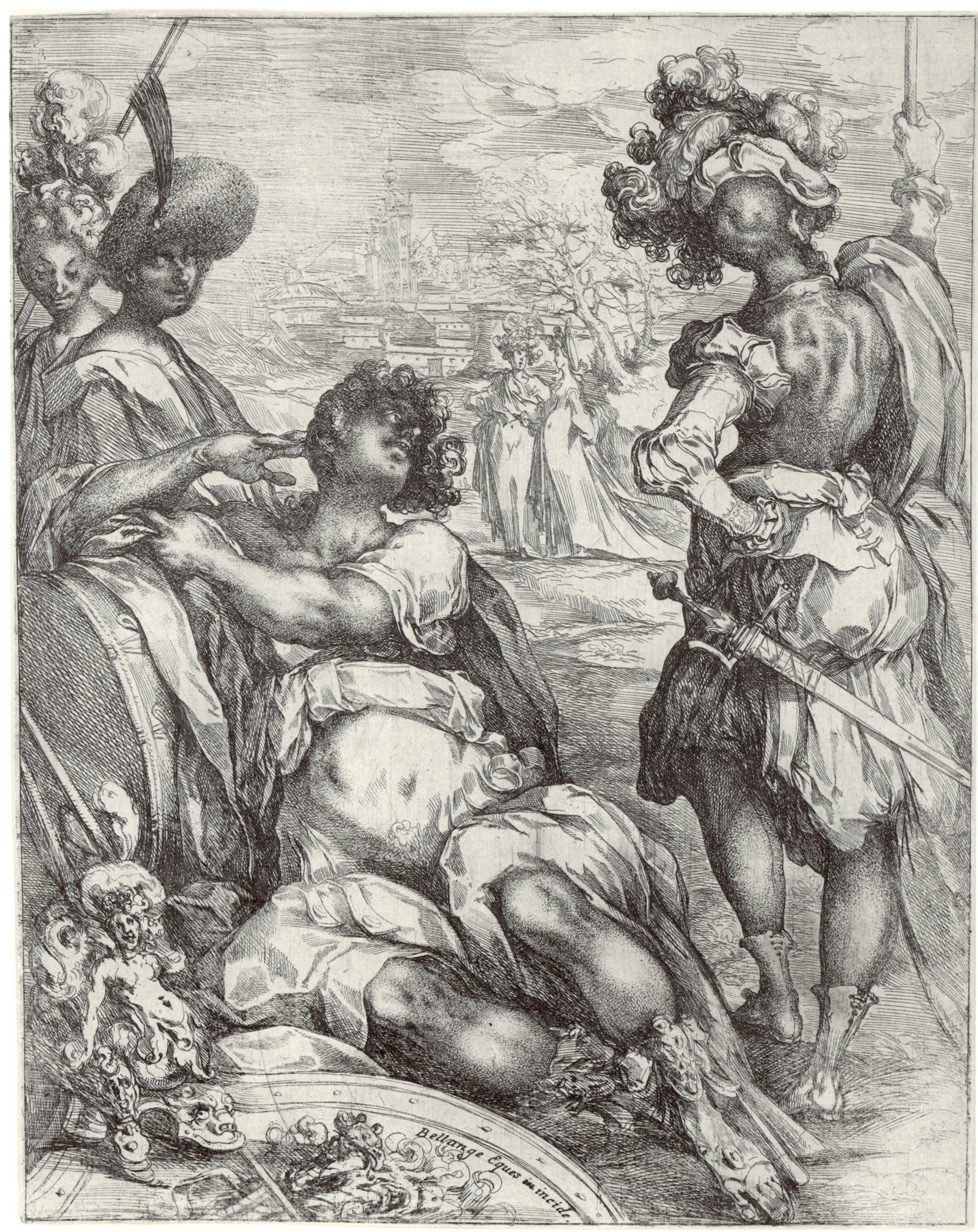

28

epic. Thus, the seemingly vague title of *Military Scene*, suggested by Walch, is appropriate.

A.N.W.

1. F. Basan, *Dictionnaire des graveurs anciens et modernes depuis l'origine de la gravure*, Paris, 1767.
2. M. Huber and C. C. H. Rost, *Manuel des curieux et des amateurs d'art*, vol. 7, Zurich, 1804.
3. Giovanni Gori Gandinelli, *Notizie degli intagliatori*, vol. 1, Siena, 1808.
4. E. Tietze-Conrat, "Zum Oeuvre des Jacques Bellange," *Mitteilungen der Gesellschaft für vervielfältigende Künst, Beilage der graphischen Künste*, 1930, p. 15.
5. Among the better-known illustrations were those by Bernardo Castello (1604) and Antonio Tempesta (1607). The usual format was one illustration per canto, for a total of twenty.
6. Two of the paintings are discussed in this entry. For the third painting, see cat. no. 24.
7. Reproduced in *Fontainebleau*, vol. 1, National Gallery of Canada, Ottawa, 1973, p. 214, pl. 205.
8. Reproduced in Anthony Blunt, *Nicolas Poussin*, London, Phaidon, 1967, p. 22, fig. 16.
9. See Walch, p. 111.

29
The Martyrdom of Saint Lucy
Etching and burin
W. 16, R.-D. 15
461-465 x 348-352 mm. (plate)
18³⁄₁₆ x 13⅞ in.
Lower left: *Bellange* (autograph)
Watermark: hunting horn in shield (see Briquet 7862)
Museum of Fine Arts, Boston. Otis Norcross Fund. 40.129

30
ANTON EISENHOIT
Germany, 1553-1603
Ecce Homo
After Taddeo Zuccaro
Engraving, 1590
Hollstein 1
375 x 450 mm.
14¾ x 17¾ in.
Metropolitan Museum of Art, New York. Elisha Whittelsey Fund, 1951

Lucy of Syracuse enraged her fiancé by giving away her wealth in gratitude for her mother's cure and was betrayed as a Christian. An attempt was made to burn her alive, and then she was stabbed in the throat.[1] The statue of Diana at the upper left corner of the print probably represents the pagan cult figure that Lucy refused to worship. The statue holds a flaming lamp that is an attribute of Diana as the moon goddess, as well as of Saint Lucy, whose name means light.

This was probably Bellange's first large plate. The print is crowded with figures in diverse attire, posture, and gesture. In the center is Saint Lucy, with halo, surrounded by a crowd whose expressions reveal varying degrees of awareness of the violent event. The crowd here distracts, stares out, competes for attention. One can wander through the crowd, admire the clothing, ponder the many curious faces, as was likely intended. One can marvel at an obelisk constructed upon an arch. Even Bellange's frivolous signature is a delight.

The composition and several of the individual figures were borrowed from a number of outside sources. Oberhuber[2] has suggested that Bellange knew Agostino Carracci's engraving[3] of Veronese's *Martyrdom of Saint Justina* (fig. 4). There are indeed strong similarities between the two prints, although Bellange was apparently interested only in the lower two-thirds of the engraving. The main architectural features of Carracci's print, including the steps with the central figure group, the high column base upon which a soldier stands, and the distant landscape with domes and towers, can be found in Bellange's *Martyrdom of Saint Lucy*. Saint Justina, on her knees on a stepped platform, is held by her captors, including a muscular, bare-armed man who reappears in Bellange's print. The curved plinth on which the soldier stands was the source of the Diana statue's vase-like base.

The extravagantly suited soldiers[4] at the lower edge of Bellange's print have been identified by Walch as another significant borrowing from Anton Eisenhoit's *Ecce Homo*, an engraving of 1590, after Taddeo Zuccaro. Bellange also obtained from Eisenhoit's print the spirited pointing and reaching gestures, and additional bits of architecture. The series of shaded, columniated arches in the Eisenhoit engraving are abbreviated in the Bellange etching to form a strong vertical accent in the background.

A third source of figures in the *Martyrdom of Saint Lucy* was Bellange's own print, *Military Scene* (cat. no. 28), which itself probably relied on figures in Ambroise Dubois' paintings at Fontainebleau. Saint Lucy is a slightly modified version of the reclining youth in the military print.[5] The standing full-length soldier seen from the rear in the *Saint Lucy* is really the soldier in the *Military Scene* who has changed his armor to match his companions from the Eisenhoit engraving.

The robed figure at the far right of the *Martyrdom of Saint Lucy*, whose head is bent over so far that his chin touches his shoulder, may have been inspired by a figure in a third Dubois painting at Fontainebleau, *Clorinda and Argante Leaving Saladin to Fight the Crusaders*.[6] In addition to having similar poses, the figures in both painting and etching fulfill the identical function of terminating the composition at its edge. As previously discussed (see cat. no. 28) Bellange had most certainly seen Dubois' paintings at Fontainebleau in 1608.

A.N.W.

1. The Roman heroine Virginia died from a stab wound in the throat, which explains why certain eighteenth century writers identified this print as the *Death of Virginia*.
2. Konrad Oberhuber, *Zwischen Renaissance und Barock. Das Zeitalter von Brueghel und Bellange*. Exhibition catalogue, Graphische Sammlung Albertina, Vienna, Nov. 1967-Feb. 1968, p. 253.
3. Bartsch 78.
4. Bellange used this compositional device, which allows the viewer to enter into the space of a picture, only rarely. In general he seems to have preferred a simpler, more enclosed format, keeping his composition restricted by the plate itself.
5. This implies a slight shift in the chronology proposed by Walch, who places the *Martyrdom of Saint Lucy* earlier than the *Military Scene*.
6. Reproduced in Blunt, *Poussin* (1967), vol. 1, p. 23, fig. 17.

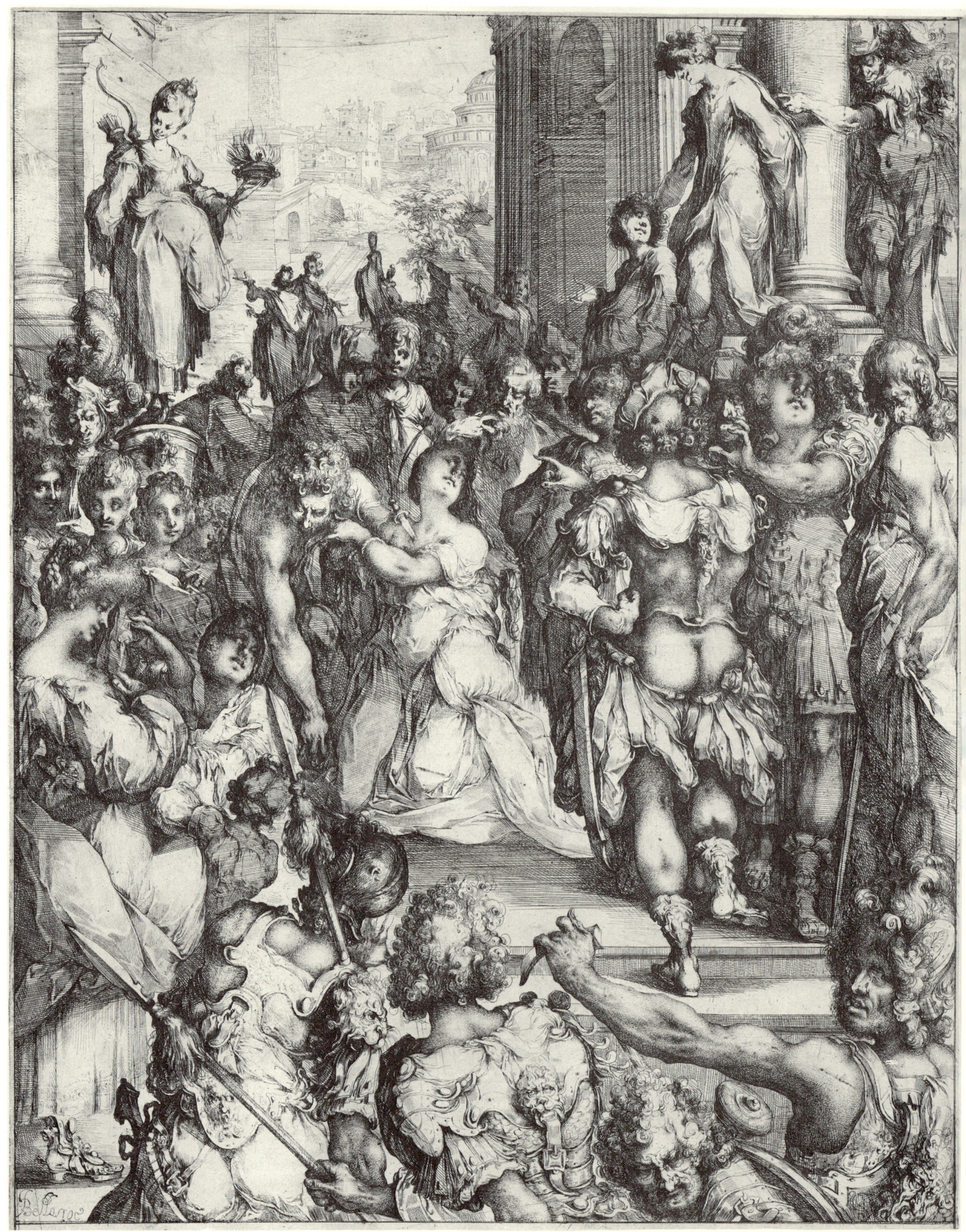

29

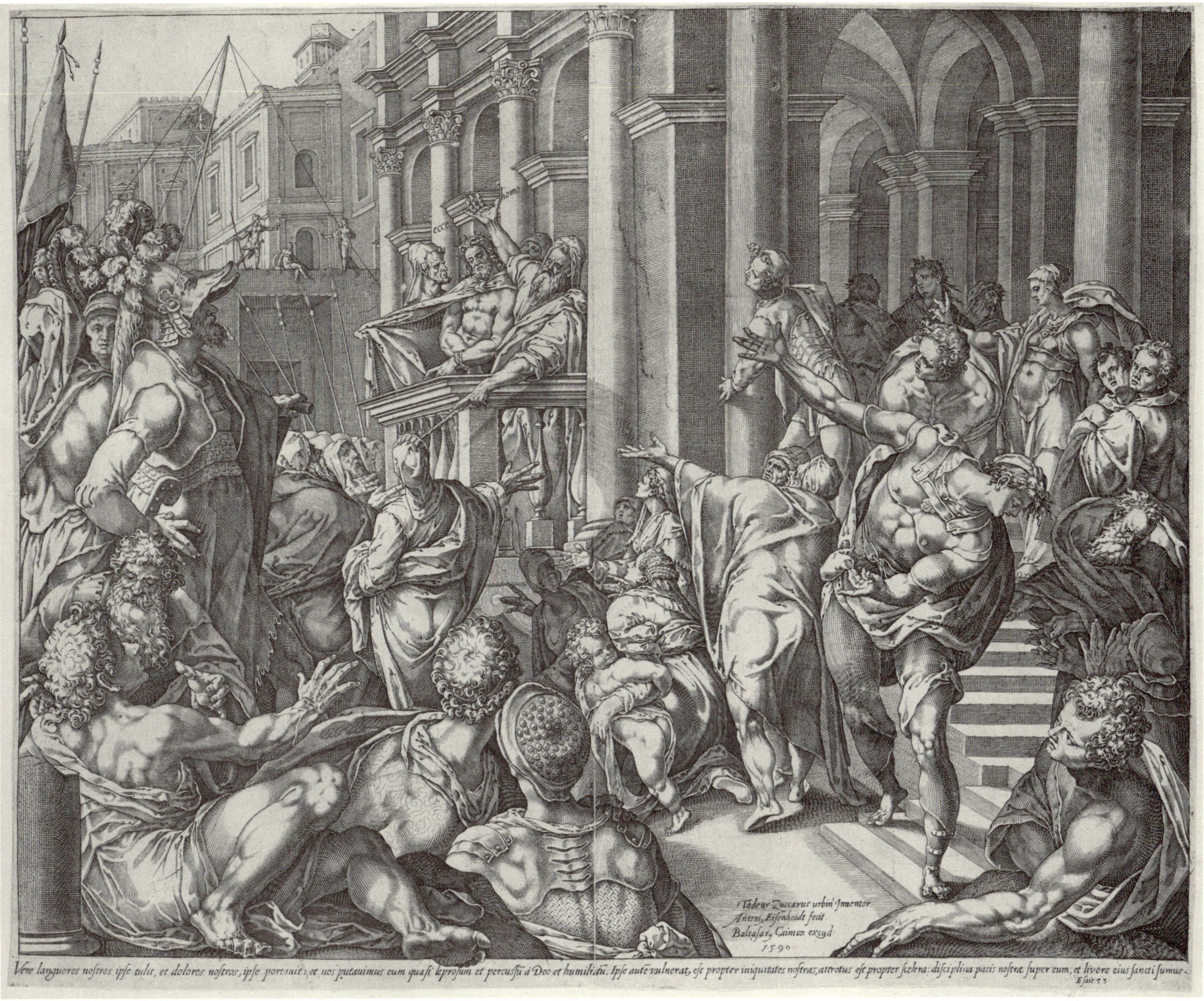

30

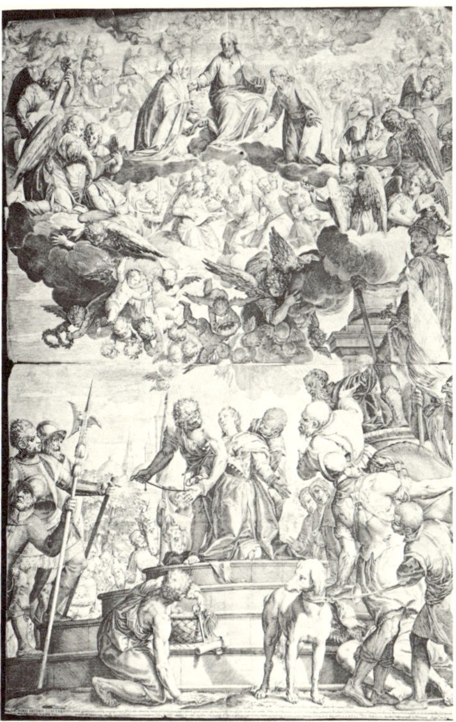

Fig. 4. CARRACCI, *The Martyrdom of Saint Justina*, etching after VERONESE.

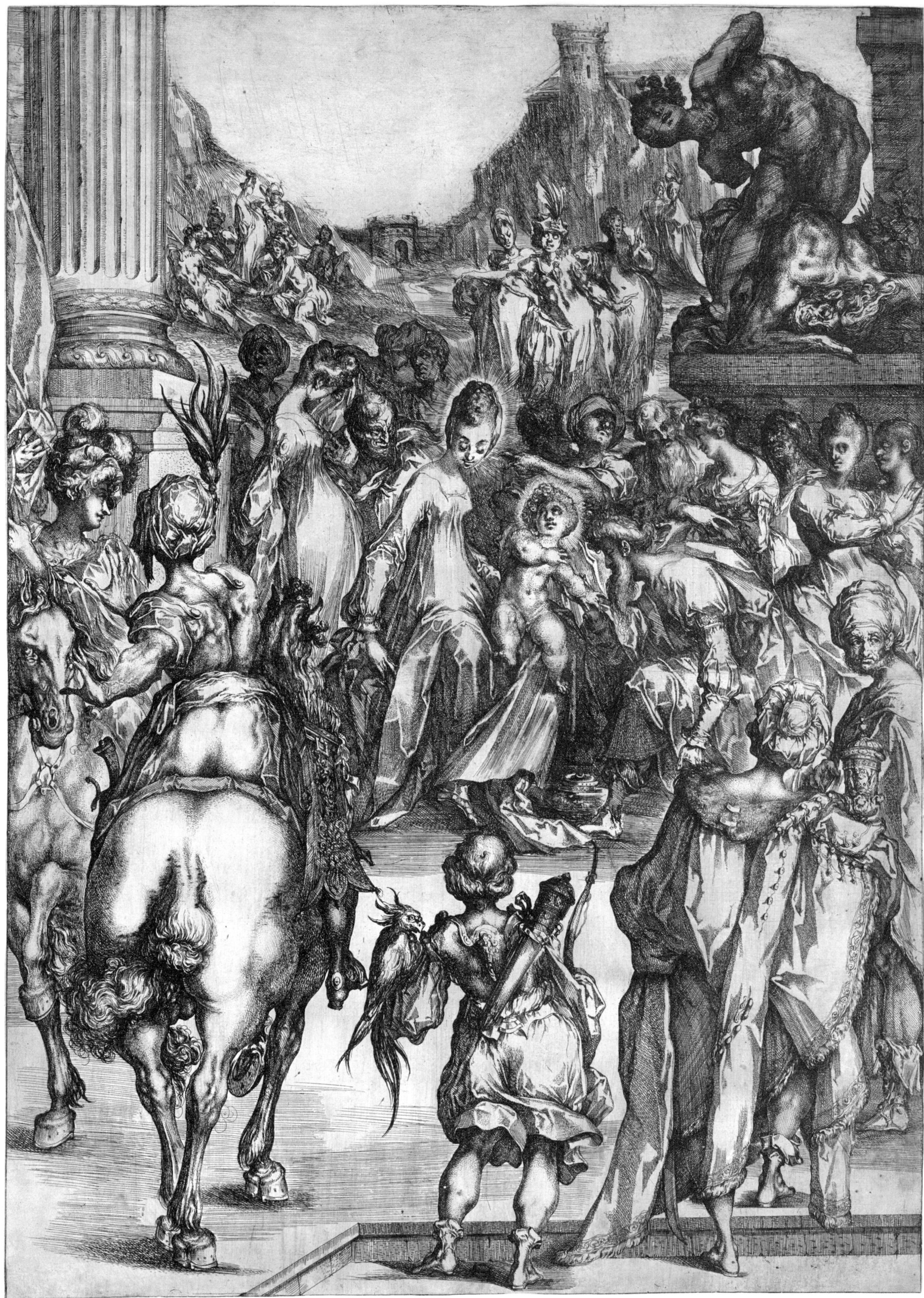

31

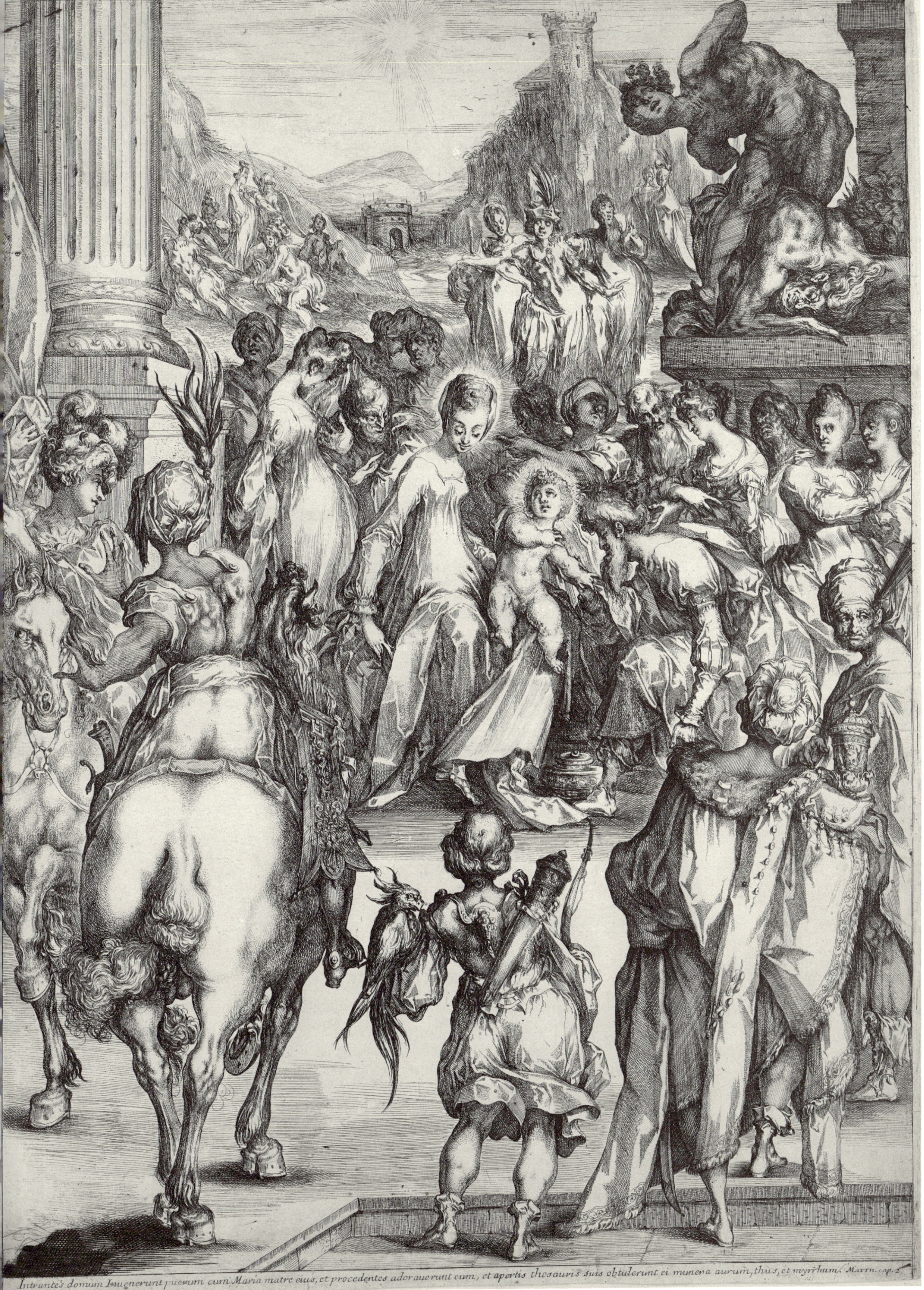
Intrantes domum Inuenerunt puerum cum Maria matre eius, et procedentes adorauerunt eum, et apertis thesauris suis obtulerunt ei munera aurum, thus, et myrrham. Matth. cap. 2.

31-32
The Adoration of the Magi
Etching and burin
W.20, R.-D.2
601-608 x 423-438 mm. (plate)
23¹³⁄₁₆ x 17¼ in.

31
First state
Printed on two sheets of paper, joined
Watermark (on lower sheet): crossed arrows (Briquet 6283, an Italian watermark but found at Troyes, 1578)
National Gallery of Canada, Ottawa

32
Fifth state
In lower margin, engraved: *Intrantes domum . . . thus et myrrham. Matth. Cap.2.*
Watermark: double-headed eagle; countermark: *LEBLOYS*
Museum of Fine Arts, Boston. Otis Norcross Fund. 40.106

Ambitious in both its size and its composition, which contains over thirty figures, the *Adoration of the Magi* has an overall design that is balanced and rhythmic. It presents the Virgin with the Child sitting unsupported on her knee surrounded by a swaying circle of admirers. There is a strong emphasis on the decorative silhouettes of the prominent foreground figures, and there is no rational occupation of space in this mannerist tableau. It is punctuated by characters with strange faces and extravagant gestures, ornamented with exotic attire and accessories. Walch notes the similarity between elements of Bellange's print and Agostino Carracci's *Adoration of the Magi* etched after Baldassare Peruzzi.[1] The placement of the column with a rider below, and the boy with a parrot, are alike in both prints.

This exceptionally fresh and bright impression can be characterized as a proof, for, although the image is complete, the plate has yet to receive Bellange's name, and in order to print it, two sheets of paper were joined horizontally across the center. The unusually large size of the plate, nearly two feet high, would have required especially large sheets to print. Impressions of subsequent states seem to have been printed on one sheet, both in Nancy and in Paris. Since prints of this size were usually folded in order to place them in albums, it is not unusual to find a horizontal crease.

Even in this earliest known state considerable corrections have been made in the plate. Originally, as Walch points out, a towered city similar to that in the *Military Scene* formed the distant view, surmounted by the great star. Faint traces remain visible after scraping and burnishing. The hands of the woman at the far right edge have been burnished and redrawn with the burin. Considerably more work was executed with the burin, most noticeably the curved strokes that model the horse's rump and the right legs of both the boy and the king in the foreground.

The fifth and last state of the print contains engraved additions that do not appear to have been made by Bellange. A brief summary of the intervening states will help reconstruct the history of the plate. Bellange's name is added to the plate in the second state. The third state bears in addition an inscription from Matthew and the name of the Parisian publisher Van Merle. This is the only one of Bellange's plates to bear his name, although seventeen others were published in Paris by Le Blond. The fourth state still bears the artist's and publisher's names, but changes have been made to the image. The heads of both the Virgin and the Child were altered by burnishing and engraving; the shapes appear as they do in the fifth state, the Virgin's head shorter, and the Child's narrower. A hilly background and the star in a different shape were engraved sketchily. The new work appears to cater to a change in taste. As Walch says, it was not done by Bellange. Besides stylistic considerations, other evidence suggests a posthumous date for the reworking. Van Merle was presumably active until his death in 1682, and Walch proposes that this reworking, visible in the fourth state, may not have been done until the mid-century.

In the fifth state both the artist's and the publisher's names have been removed, suggesting a date after 1682. Numerous engraved additions have been made to the plate; only the most significant are mentioned here. The heads of Virgin and Child were more strongly defined in the proportions they took on in the fourth state, and the landscape was completed and strengthened. Two foreground figures, the rider and the king seen from the rear, bear additional parallel shading that darkens their flesh; the king's robe was further shaded as well. The face and arm of the man gesturing behind the child were also darkened.

The effect of the new work is to suggest a more volumetric placement of the figures in space. The foreground king and rider no longer read as planar barriers, but instead the new shading has made them more plastic and they now provide a more gradual spatial transition toward the central group. In combination with the revised facial proportions of the Virgin and Child, the reworking suggests an alteration to Bellange's design—insofar as it was possible—in order to appeal to a later taste for optical reality and naturalism.

The impression is well printed and the plate in reasonably good condition. It is interesting to speculate how many impressions of this stylistically old-fashioned print were sold long after the demise of Bellange and of mannerism. The watermark of this impression of the "renovated" fifth state has not been identified, but its large size and regularity have more in common with eighteenth century marks than with those of the early seventeenth century.

S.W.R.

1. Walch, p. 114.

33-35
The Three Magi

33
Balthasar
Etching
W.26, R.-D. 34 (identified as Casper) (second state)
284-287 x 162-166 mm. (plate)
11⁵⁄₁₆ x 6½ in.
Lower left, etched: *Bellange* (autograph); lower left, engraved: *Le Blond excud*
Watermark: grapes
Coll: Camberlyn (Lugt 514)
Museum of Fine Arts, Boston. Otis Norcross Fund. 40.152

34
Caspar
Etching
W. 27, R.-D. 33 (identified as Melchior) (second state)
278-283 x 161-166 mm.
11⅛ x 6½ in.
Lower left, etched: *Bellange* (autograph); lower right, engraved: *Le Blond excud.*
Traces of letters, etched and scraped away at left: *REX*
Metropolitan Museum of Art, New York. Elisha Whittelsey Fund

35
Melchior
Etching
W. 28, R.-D. 35 (identified as Balthasar) (second state)
279-284 x 160-167 mm.
11³⁄₁₆ x 6⁹⁄₁₆ in.
Lower right, etched: *Bellan* (autograph); lower left, engraved: *Le Blond excud*
Watermark: grapes
Coll: AA (Lugt 62a, unidentified)
Museum of Fine Arts, Boston. Otis Norcross Fund. 40.154

36
MATTHAEUS MERIAN
German, 1593-1650
Melchior (reverse copy of Caspar, W. 27)
Etching, ca. 1615
Wüthrich 85
11 x 7⅛ in. (approx.)
Inscribed: *Tres Magi / Melchior Rex Nubia Bellange invent: Jac: ab Heydé excu./Argentina.*
Watermark: serpent (similar to Heawood 3770)
Metropolitan Museum of Art, New York. Gift of Harry G. Friedman, 1962

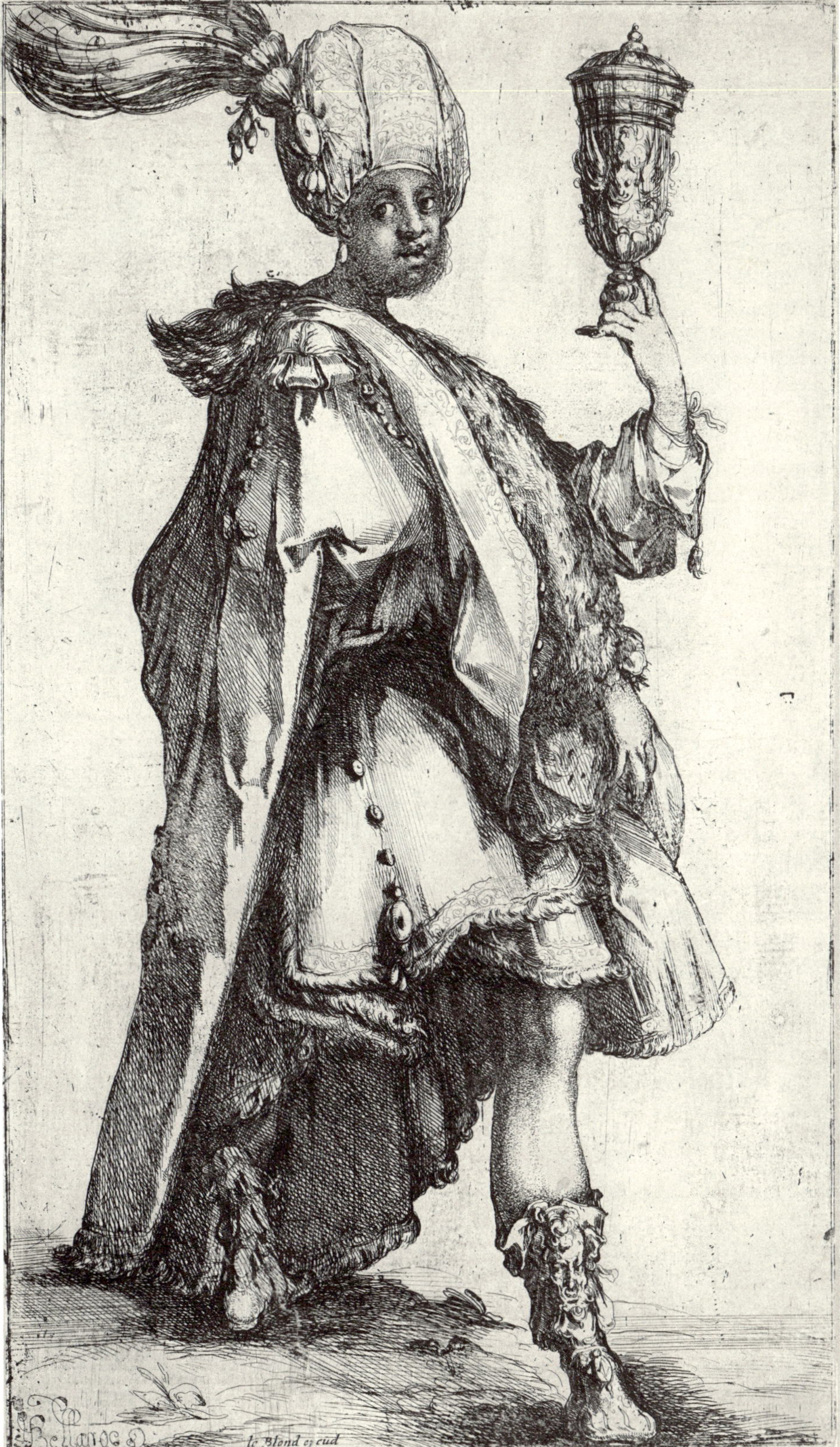

33

37
Matthaeus Merian
German, 1593-1650
Balthasar (reverse copy of king in *Adoration of the Magi*, W. 20)
Etching, ca. 1615
Wüthrich 87
11 x 7⅛ in. (approx.)
Inscribed: *Baltasar Rex Saba/Bellange inventor*
Watermark: serpent (similar to Heawood 3770)
Metropolitan Museum of Art, New York. Gift of Harry G. Friedman, 1962

The Three Magi are etched with a versatility and sureness of technique that proclaim Bellange's full grasp of the medium. He employs a variety of strokes and a full range from pale and fine to dark, heavy lines. There are no retouches with the burin.

It is unusual to find the Magi represented independently of the Holy Family and executed on separate plates. Like the *Hortulana* (cat. nos. 15-18) the kings may be costume studies, as if for a court masque or entertainment. The prototypes for Bellange's trio are to be found in prints depicting Turks or other orientals in exotic dress, such as those of Schongauer and Dürer. That there still was a Germanic taste for this kind of print is supported by the fact that, when Matthaeus Merian copied them, he substituted a more elaborately costumed king from the large plate of the *Adoration of the Magi* (cat. no. 31) for the more simply robed *Melchior.* Merian titled his copies, and Robert-Dumesnil follows these identifications. Walch prefers another system, naming Balthasar as the Moorish king, Caspar as the old king, and Melchior as the young one.[1]

In Merian's reverse copies the linear patterns of etched hatching are more regular and systematic. He added a profile to the head of one (cat. no. 37). The figures have space surrounding them; plumes are no longer cut off at the borderline as in Bellange's original versions. The vitality and tension have diminished.

S.W.R.

1. Although Walch has "corrected" Merian and Robert-Dumesnil's titles for the *Three Magi*, it should be noted that throughout history there has been no standardization of the iconographic system of these personages. Some writers call Caspar the youngest, others Melchior. Balthasar is generally the Moorish king.

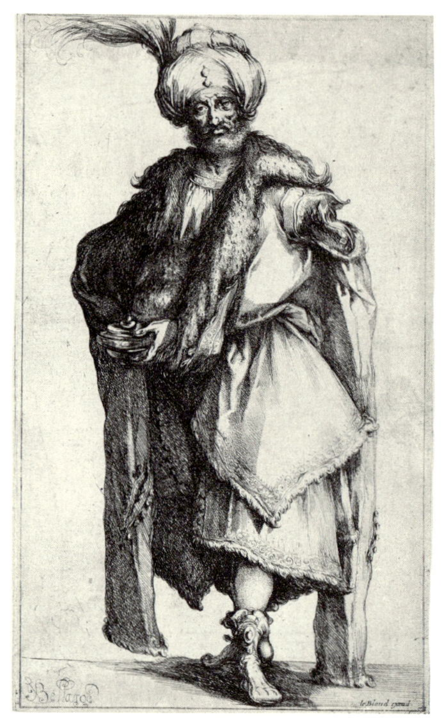

34

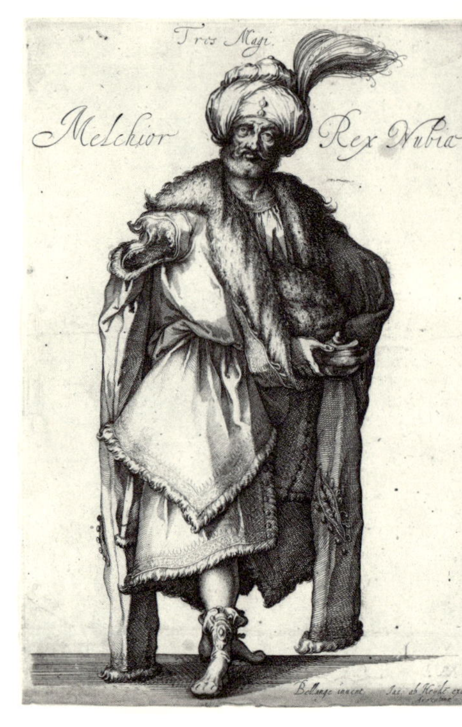

36

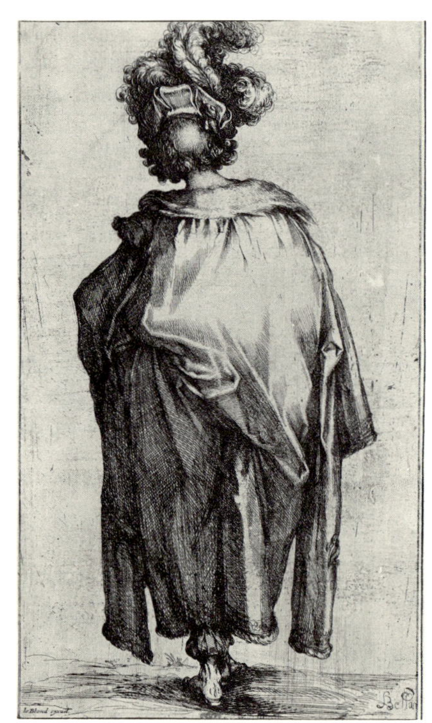

35

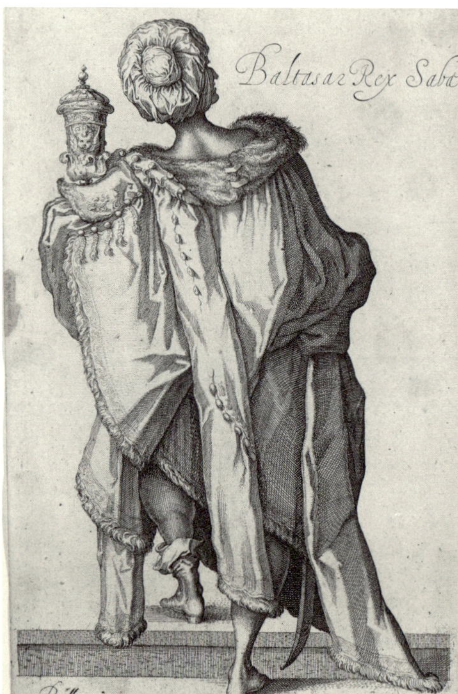

37

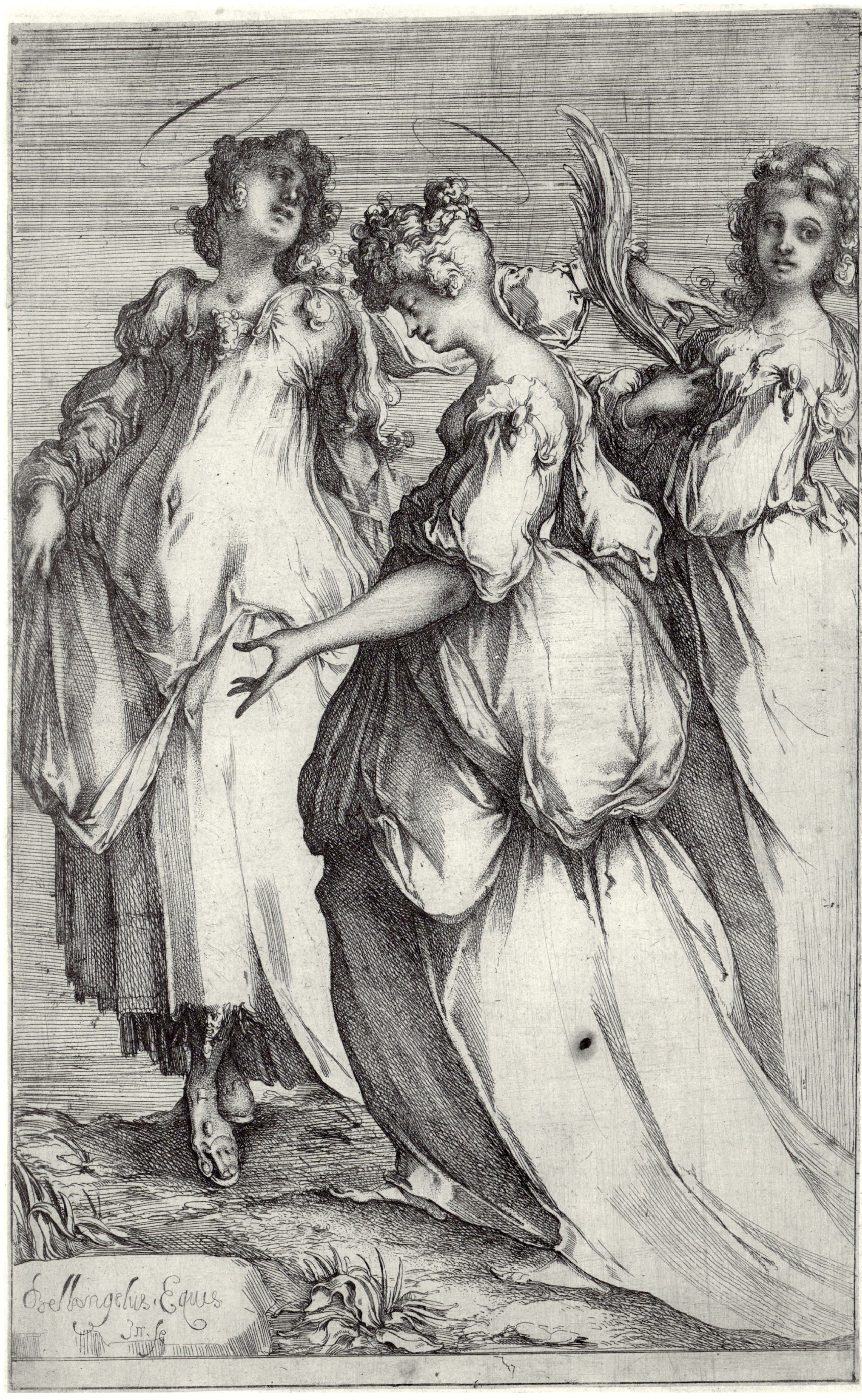
Bellangelus. Eques
In. fe

38
Three Holy Women
Etching
W.22, R.-D. 13 (only state)
316-322 x 196-202 mm. (plate)
12 11/16 x 7 15/16 in.
Lower left, etched: *Bellangelus.Eques/ In.fe* (autograph)
Museum of Fine Arts, Boston. Otis Norcross Fund. 40.125

39
Matthaeus Merian
German, 1593-1650
Reverse copy of *Three Holy Women* (W.22)
Etching, ca. 1615
Wüthrich 88
306 x 192 mm.
12 1/16 x 7 9/16 in.
Lower left: *Bellangelus Eques/Inv:*; lower margin: *Et cum preterisset Sabbatum, Maria Magdalene, et Maria Jacobi, et Salome emerunt aromata, ut venirent et ungerent eum. Mar. XVI.*; lower right: *J. ab / Heyden / excu.*
Watermark: serpent (similar to Heawood 3770)
Impression trimmed at top
Museum of Fine Arts, Boston. Harvey D. Parker Collection. P. 4294

Although the three women are based on Sadeler's engraving after Spranger, *The Three Holy Women Going to the Tomb*,[1] Bellange's etching contains no attribute pertinent to these particular women. Two have halos and the third carries the palm of martyrdom. Bellange did treat the subject of the three women at the tomb at least twice (cat. nos. 62 and 65).

As with the *Three Magi* (cat. nos. 33-37), Merian's reverse copy is more specific. He changed the palm frond to an ointment jar and added an inscription that identifies the subject as the *Three Women Going to the Tomb*.

Bellange's figures echo his own works. The head of the center saint repeats that of the Virgin (cat. no. 6), while her companion at the left relates to one of the gardeners (cat. no. 18). All three find parallels among the women in the crowd at the left of the *Carrying of the Cross* (cat. no. 40).

In this print there are numerous ornaments, on sleeve, bodice, and antique sandals. A comparison with Bellange's later *Three Women at the Tomb* (cat. no. 62) reveals the elimination of incidental detail in that print and a dependence on the forms themselves for expressive purposes.

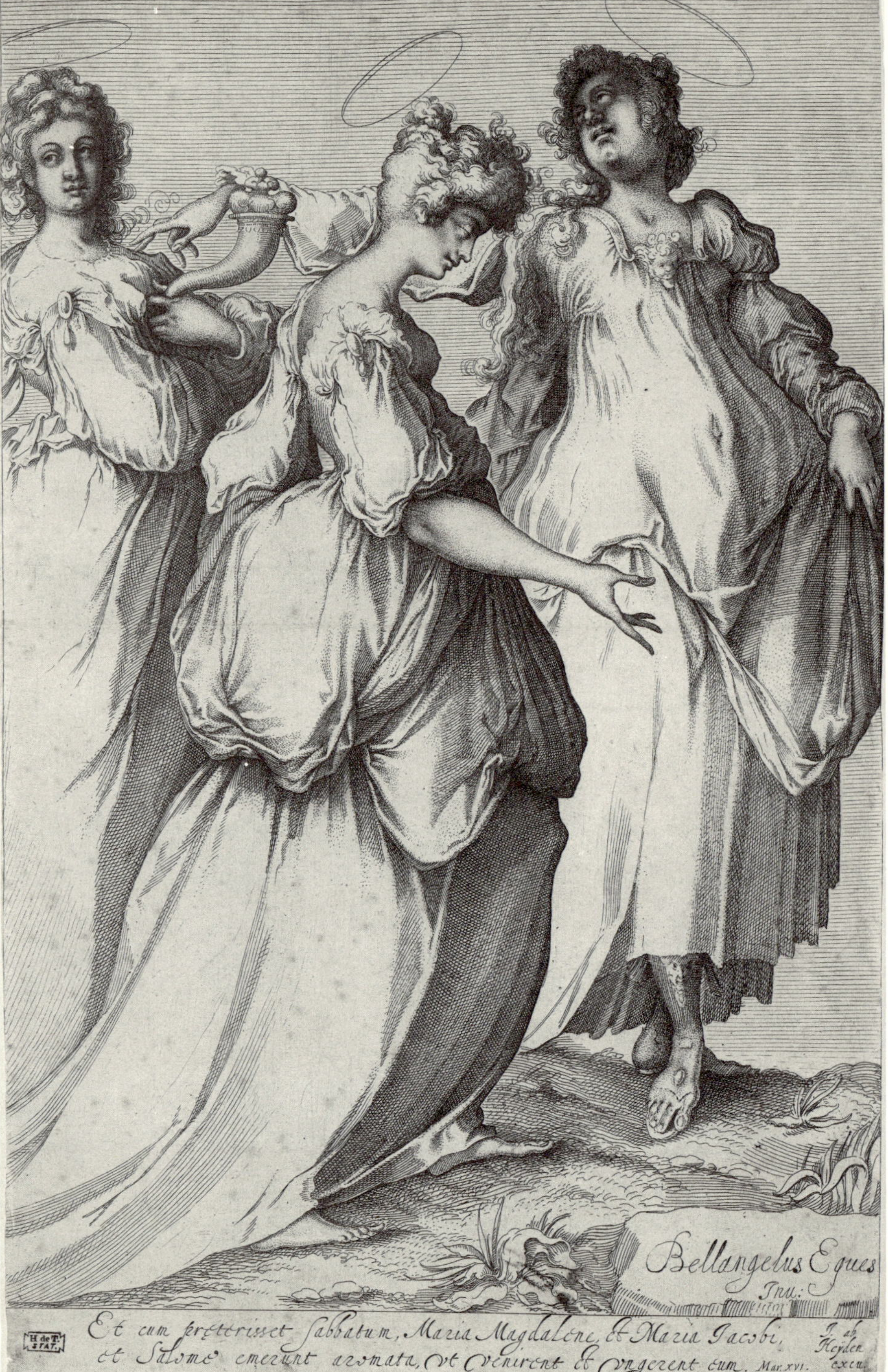

39

S.W.R.

1. Walch, p. 117, note 199. Repr. F.-G. Pariset, "Bellange and Lagneau," in *Studies in Western Art III*, Princeton, N.J., Princeton University Press, 1963, pp. 118 ff. fig. 7.

40
The Carrying of the Cross
Etching and drypoint
W. 23, R.-D. 7
411-414 x 581-588 mm (plate)
16⁵⁄₁₆ x 23³⁄₁₆ in.
Lower left on stone: *Bellange Eques in: incide.*; in margin: *Vere languores . . . sancti sumus* [Isaiah 53, 4]
Undeciphered watermark
Metropolitan Museum of Art, New York. Elisha Whittelsey Fund, 1949

41
MARTIN SCHONGAUER
German, ca. 1450-1491
The Road to Calvary
Engraving
Lehrs 9
11⁵⁄₁₆ x 16¹⁵⁄₁₆ in.
Metropolitan Museum of Art, New York. By exchange, 1935

Bellange's print depicts Christ, fallen under the burden of the cross, on the way from Jerusalem to Calvary. He is surrounded by a large crowd of soldiers and spectators, and is preceded by the two thieves. A man near him who reaches out to take up the cross is Simon of Cyrene. Although Simon is mentioned in Matthew 27:32 and Mark 15:21, only Luke 23:26-34 gives an account of the procession and the crowd as well. Luke states: *"Great numbers of people followed, many women among them, who mourned and lamented over him. Jesus turned to them and said, 'Daughters of Jerusalem, do not weep for me; no, weep for yourselves and your children . . .' "* This passage, which has been interpreted as an appeal to the pity of the reader, accounts for the presence of the weeping woman and the mother and child in Bellange's print.

Among the group of women is one who holds out a cloth toward Christ. This is Saint Veronica, who is not mentioned at all in the Bible but comes from legendary sources. Bellange's print, therefore, is not a literal Biblical illustration but one that compresses various narrative and traditional events into a single image. In addition, fanciful elements have been incorporated into the scene, such as the view of Jerusalem with a Trajanic column, and a statue designed by J. Bellange, sculptor.

For pictorial analysis, Bellange's *Carrying of the Cross* may be broken down into the following components: the figures borrowed from Martin Schongauer's *Road to Calvary* (cat. no. 41); the group of women and children with Saint Veronica; and the cut-off *repoussoir* figure of a woman.

The *Road to Calvary* was the largest plate engraved by Schongauer, and it was one of the largest of all early Northern engravings. Despite the problems involved in preserving such a large sheet, many impressions have survived to our day, testifying to the great admiration it must have inspired. Like a few great seminal images in the history of art, Schongauer's *Road to Calvary* inspired a great many copies and adaptations. Ivins once wrote: *"It would be a boring and thankless task to attempt to trace out all the occasions on which other men mined in the quarry of its richness."*[1]

Among the specific borrowings most often made by artists from the Schongauer engraving are the hooded riders and the guard whipping Christ, seen from the rear. The Schongauer inventions adapted by Bellange include the position of Christ, the two thieves seen from the rear (although their place in the composition is changed), the hooded riders, the horse and rider seen from the rear, the group of women seated in the distant rocky landscape, and the architecture of Jerusalem. Schongauer's small boy and the dogs have been replaced by Bellange's mourning women, and Veronica. We do not know whether Bellange worked from an original impression of the Schongauer engraving, or from a copy.

Throughout the sixteenth century it was common for artists to use elements of the Schongauer engraving in combination with other pictorial and iconographic themes. Both Dürer's *Carrying of the Cross* (B.37) from the small woodcut Passion and Raphael's *Spasimo di Sicilia* are hybrids based on the Schongauer. Among works produced in France, Leonard Thiry's wash drawing made at Fontainebleau[2] quoted the Schongauer while adding mourning women and Saint Veronica. Jean Mignon's *Carrying of the Cross* (Zerner 29) recalls the Schongauer, and features mourning women, small figures on a distant hill, and a cut-off figure at the bottom of the composition.

Bellange's group of mourning women is derived from a compositional device quite common in the sixteenth century. Basically, it has a space-filling function. For instance, groups of similar figures appear in Giulio Romano's *Triumph of Scipio—VII*, a cartoon for tapestries made for François I (Hartt 266). An etching by Jean Mignon of *John the Baptist Preaching* (Zerner 55) contains a group of figures with a striking similarity to Bellange's group, as well as an enframement of nude children in which one is tempted to see a prototype for Bellange's child.

The *Carrying of the Cross* was Bellange's most ambitious etching. Although slightly smaller than the *Adoration of the Magi* (cat. no. 31, 32), it contains many more figures, over fifty in comparison with the entourage of thirty in the *Adoration*. Since it is possible for an artist to give the illusion of a crowd without actually depicting every member, it is indicative that Bellange chose to pack his crowds with figures. The enumeration accomplished certain goals, among which was allowing free rein for his powers of decorative invention. In Bellange's elaborately costumed crowds, a sense of unreality results from the juxtaposition of many styles from different lands and eras. In the *Carrying of the Cross*, he used the crowd to express a particular relationship between Christ and the viewer. Although Christ is surrounded by this throng, few of them seem to pay any attention to him, and he, oblivious to the circus swirling about him, gazes squarely outward. Bellange contrasted the paleness and simplicity of Christ with the darker complexity of the crowd. The etched lines forming Christ are lightly bitten, and fine, drypoint lines shade the cross. Unembellished by ornamental detail, Christ's simple, open, centrally placed figure becomes an area of rest for the viewer, whose eye continually returns to him, whose calm expression momentarily holds it fast.

The contrast between Christ and the crowd, which seems to be a microcosm of mankind, produces an effect quite different from that of the Schongauer engraving. The Schongauer is more strictly narrative: Christ is shown at the moment when he falls from exhaustion, helplessly suffering the outrages inflicted by his captors. Bellange's Christ halts in order to give the viewer a chance to contemplate him. The inscription at the bottom of the plate supports the notion that Bellange intended this interpretation. The verse, not from Luke, but from Isaiah 53:4, reads:

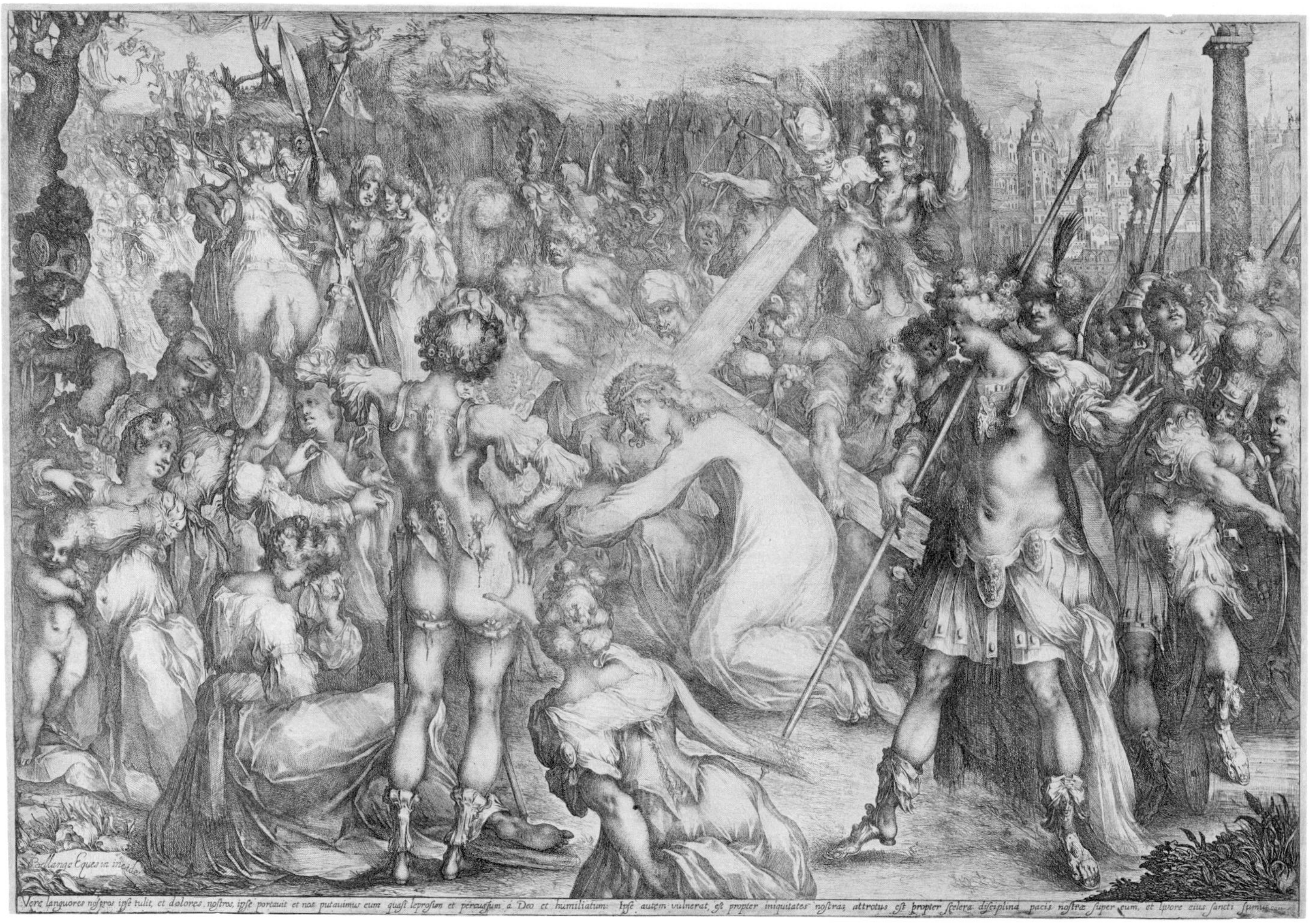

40 and detail

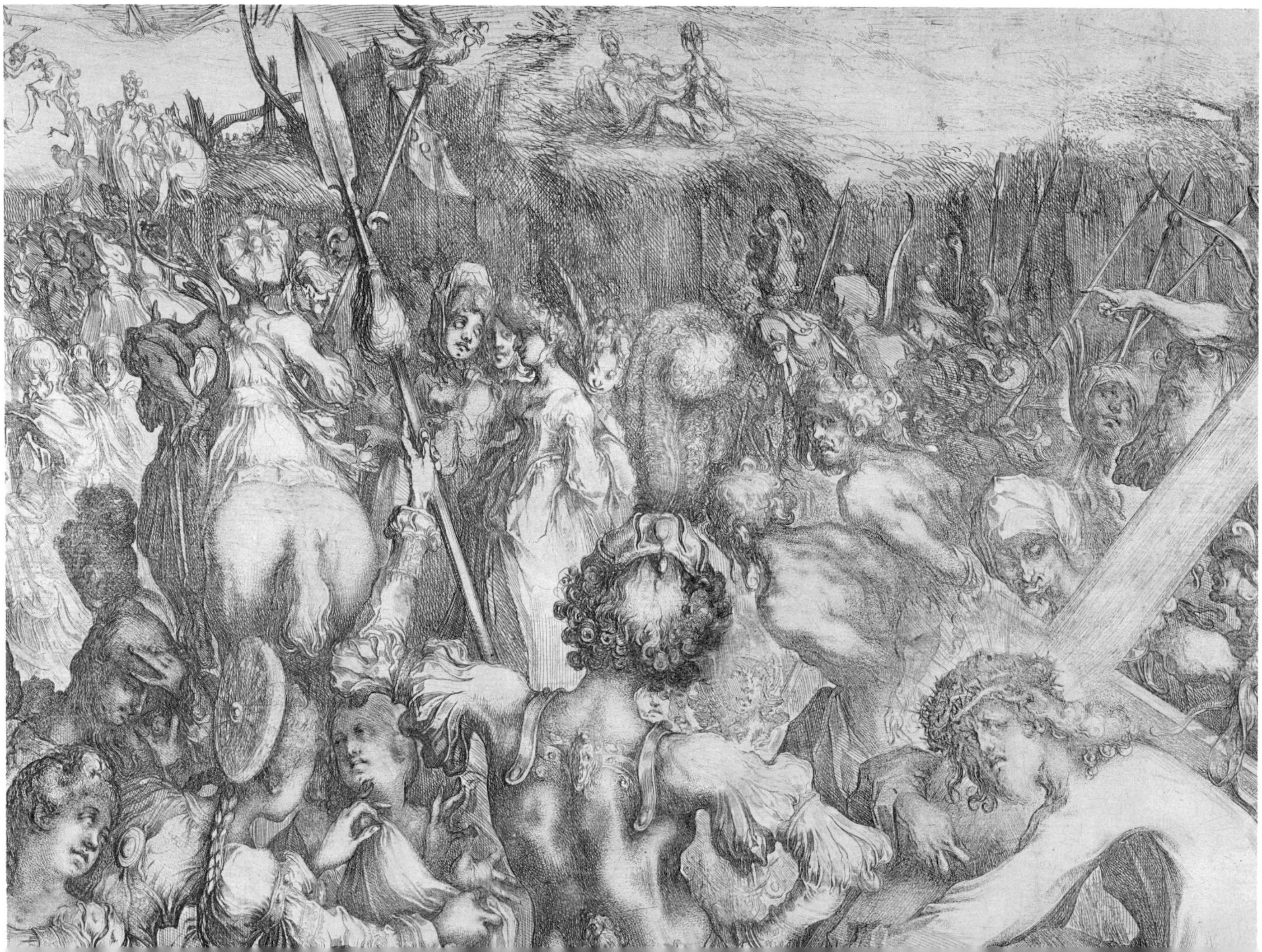

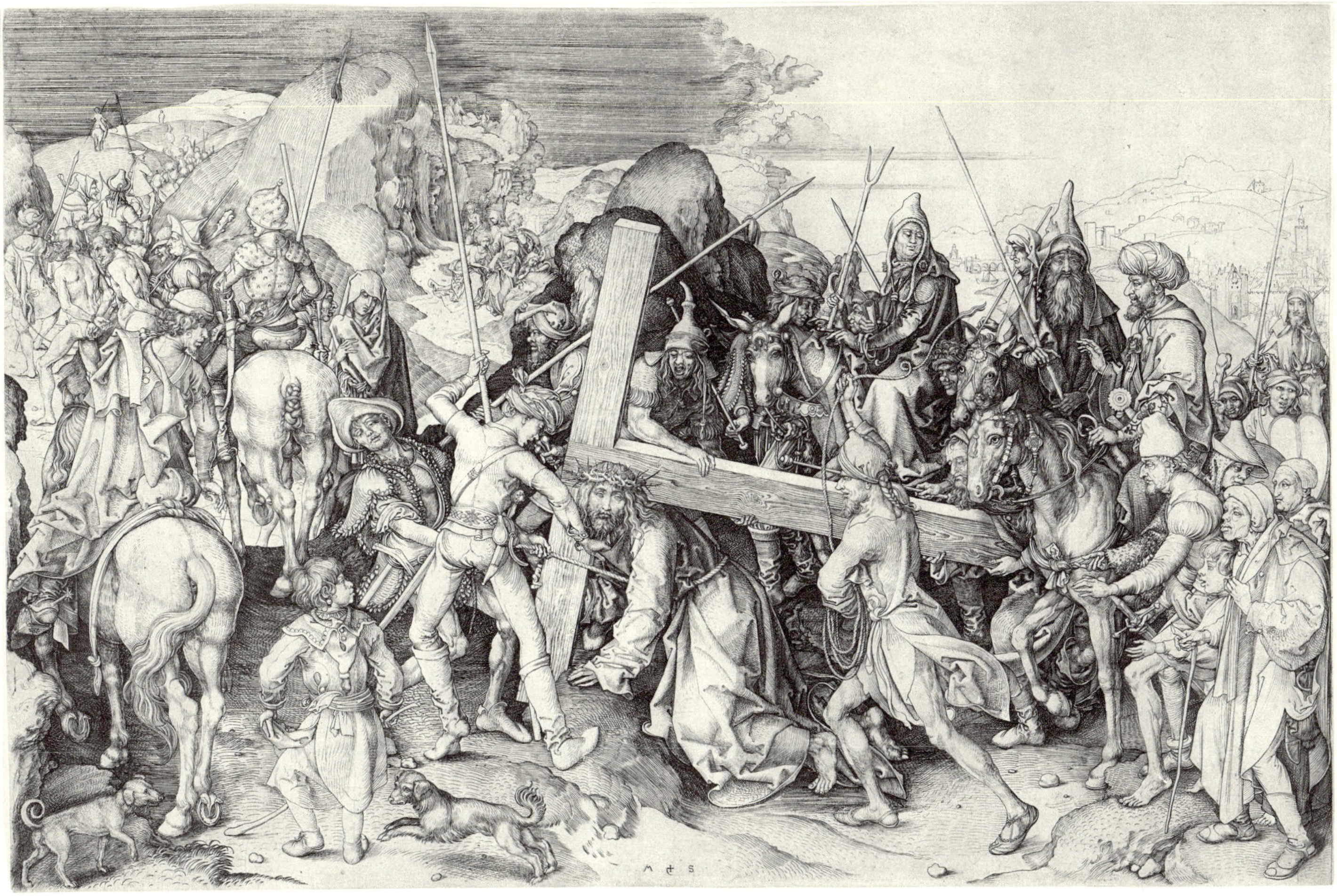

41

"Yet on himself he bore our sufferings
our torments he endured
While we counted him smitten by God
struck down by disease and misery;
but he was pierced for our transgressions,
tortured for our iniquities;
the chastisement he bore is health for us
and by his scourging we are healed."[3]

The viewer now knows that he is meant to be a part of the crowd. To reinforce this pictorially, Bellange added the figure of a woman, cut off at knee level, at the bottom edge of the center of the print. This standard Renaissance pictorial device causes the viewer to enter the illusionary space of the picture. If one then takes into account the depiction of Christ, the inscription, and the use of this *repoussoir* figure, the print can be interpreted as a moralizing image in which the artist intended the viewer to feel he is part of the tormenting crowd—mankind—for which Christ died. We do not know why this major print was made, but it is worth mentioning that the Benedictines established an order dedicated to the Holy Cross at Nancy in 1616, a year consistent with the possible dating of this etching.

A.N.W.

1. William M. Ivins, Jr., as quoted in *Prints by Martin Schongauer*, exhibition catalogue, Metropolitan Museum of Art, New York, 1971, p. 3.

2. Reproduced in *Fontainebleau* exhibition catalogue, National Gallery of Canada, Ottawa, 1973, cat. no. 224, plate 62.

3. The identical inscription is found on Eisenhoit's *Ecce Homo* (cat. no. 30).

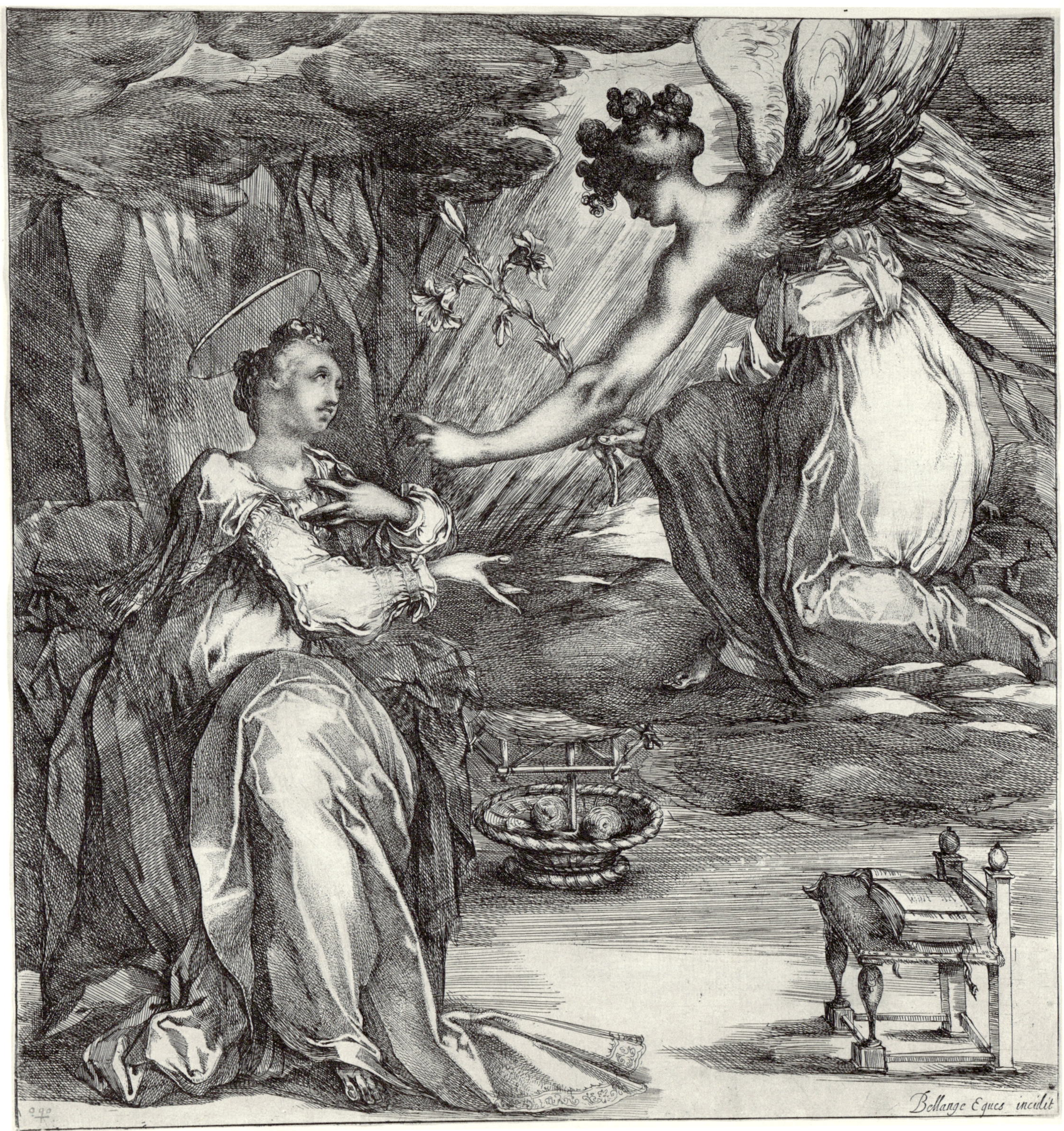

42

42

The Annunciation

Etching, touched with burin
W. 24, R.-D. 1 (second state)
340-343 x 315-321 mm. (plate)
13½ x 12⅝ in.
Lower right, engraved: *Bellange Eques incidit*
Art Institute of Chicago. The Print and Drawing Club Fund

The *Annunciation* heralds a change in style in Bellange's etchings. If one compares it with the early *Virgin with a Spindle* (cat. no. 8) one sees increased plasticity and movement in the figures. Light falls selectively on the twisting figures of Virgin and angel so as to suggest greater volume, a sense that is increased by the closer relationship of the draperies to the underlying limbs. The indeterminate, cloud-filled background is treated with greater subtlety and complexity than in the earlier print, and the atmosphere of the *Annunciation* is appropriately more expressive and mysterious.

The change in style is one of degree, not an abrupt change in kind, for these new elements are strongly tempered by Bellange's essential mannerist tendencies. Ornamental silhouettes, particularly the sharply defined angel's head, remain important, and tension remains between the implied plasticity of forms and their planar arrangement. Figure proportions continue to be exaggerated for formal purposes. Yet, although the angel's elongated arm fills a design need, it also serves a meaningful and expressive function.

In the later prints (The *Annunciation,* some of the *Apostles,* the *Raising of Lazarus),* one no longer finds the languid nonchalance that dominated the *Death of Portia,* the *Martyrdom of Saint Lucy,* or the *Virgin with a Spindle.* Instead there is a considerable increase of focussed energy and emotional intensity. It is in these late prints, such as the *Annunciation,* that Bellange employs a technique close to that of Barocci to define faceted drapery planes, executed in varied and subtle combinations of hatching and stippling, to bring a greater sense of relief modeling to surfaces.

It is not only to Barocci that Bellange looks at this time of change, but to Caravaggio or Caravaggesque ideals. A large painting of the *Annunciation* attributed to Caravaggio and dated 1609/10[2] would appear to be the altarpiece "by the hand of the famous painter Michelangelo" (i.e., da Caravaggio) presented by Duke Henri II in about 1616 to the primatial church in Nancy which was dedicated to the cult of the Annunciation.[3] (One may speculate on the Mantuan court's influence on Henri's choice, for on Ruben's advice in 1607 the Duke of Mantua purchased for his collection Caravaggio's *Death of the Virgin* [Louvre], rejected for its realism by the church that had commissioned it.) Bellange would seem to have known the Nancy painting, for his etched *Annunciation* echoes the composition, and quite specifically quotes the figure of the angel, by far the painting's most beautiful and striking feature.

As if to bear out this interest in a naturalistic style, Bellange's red chalk drawing of a kneeling figure, possibly a study for the angel in the *Annunciation,* may conceivably be a study from life.[4] The directness of concept and the simplicity of execution set it apart from the more numerous fanciful inventions in Bellange's oeuvre.

S.W.R.

1. It should be added to Walch's description that in the signed second state engraved flicks have been applied to the Virgin's face, which in the first state was modeled with etched stippling alone.

2. Musée de Beaux-Arts, Nancy. Valerio Mariani, *Caravaggio,* Rome, 1973, pp. 136 f., pl. 61.

3. A primatial chapter was authorized by the papacy for Nancy in 1602, and the provisional structure of the church was constructed in the heart of the *ville neuve* from 1608 to 1614 and dedicated to Notre Dame de l'Annonciation. The first primate was Cardinal Charles of Lorraine, brother of the reigning duke Henri II. The Dukes of Lorraine had had a special veneration for the Annunciate since the Battle of Nancy in 1477 when Duke René carried a banner depicting the Annunciation as his battle standard. The provisional primatial church (later Saint Sebastian) was endowed by Henri II with a painting of the *Annunciation* about 1616; according to a document of 1645 this altarpiece was by "the famous painter Michelangelo."

4. Ecole des Beaux-Arts, Paris, repr. J. Vallery-Radot, *Le Dessin française au XVIIe siècle,* Lausanne, 1953, pl. 9.

43

The Madonna with the Rose

Etching and burin
W. 25, R.-D. 4 (first state)
214-221 x 140-145 mm. (plate)
8⁵⁄₁₆ x 5¹¹⁄₁₆ in.
Lower left: *Bellange fecit*
Art Institute of Chicago. The Kate S. Buckingham Fund

The Madonna with the Rose is one of the smallest and most intimate of Bellange's late etchings. In this print he has returned to the subject matter he frequently depicted in his earlier works. *The Madonna with the Rose* so resembles Bellange's earlier *Virgin and Child* (cat. no. 7), allowing for minute differences in pose and in plate size, that one is tempted to think that both prints were based on the same drawing, or that the later print was based on the earlier one.

A comparison of the two prints shows much about the development of Bellange's etching technique. The ring-like halo in the *Virgin and Child* was worn by most of Bellange's saints, from Saint Augustine through the Apostles. Simultaneously, though less frequently, Bellange explored a more "naturalistic" depiction of the halo as radiant light. *The Madonna with the Rose* belongs to the latter group. The treatment of the halo corresponds to the general interest in light that Bellange's prints show in the late phase of his printmaking activity. In this print, rich darks are built up with parallel lines massed together to form overlays of tone. The tonal sections are contrasted with areas of light, produced by delicate biting, drypoint, or scraping. Stippling is largely confined to the flesh areas, but there is a small amount in the drapery. There are a few areas of burin work along the left sleeve and hand of the Madonna.

The plate was provided with a large lower margin, possibly for an inscription which was never added. A few flourish-like lines can be seen in the lower left corner below the signature where Bellange tested the etching ground. A scraped-out form can easily be discerned in most impressions of the print at the lower edge of the image, extending into the margin area. It appears to have been a coat of arms, possibly surmounted by a crozier. Bellange seems to have either used a previously worked plate which was imperfectly scraped down, or

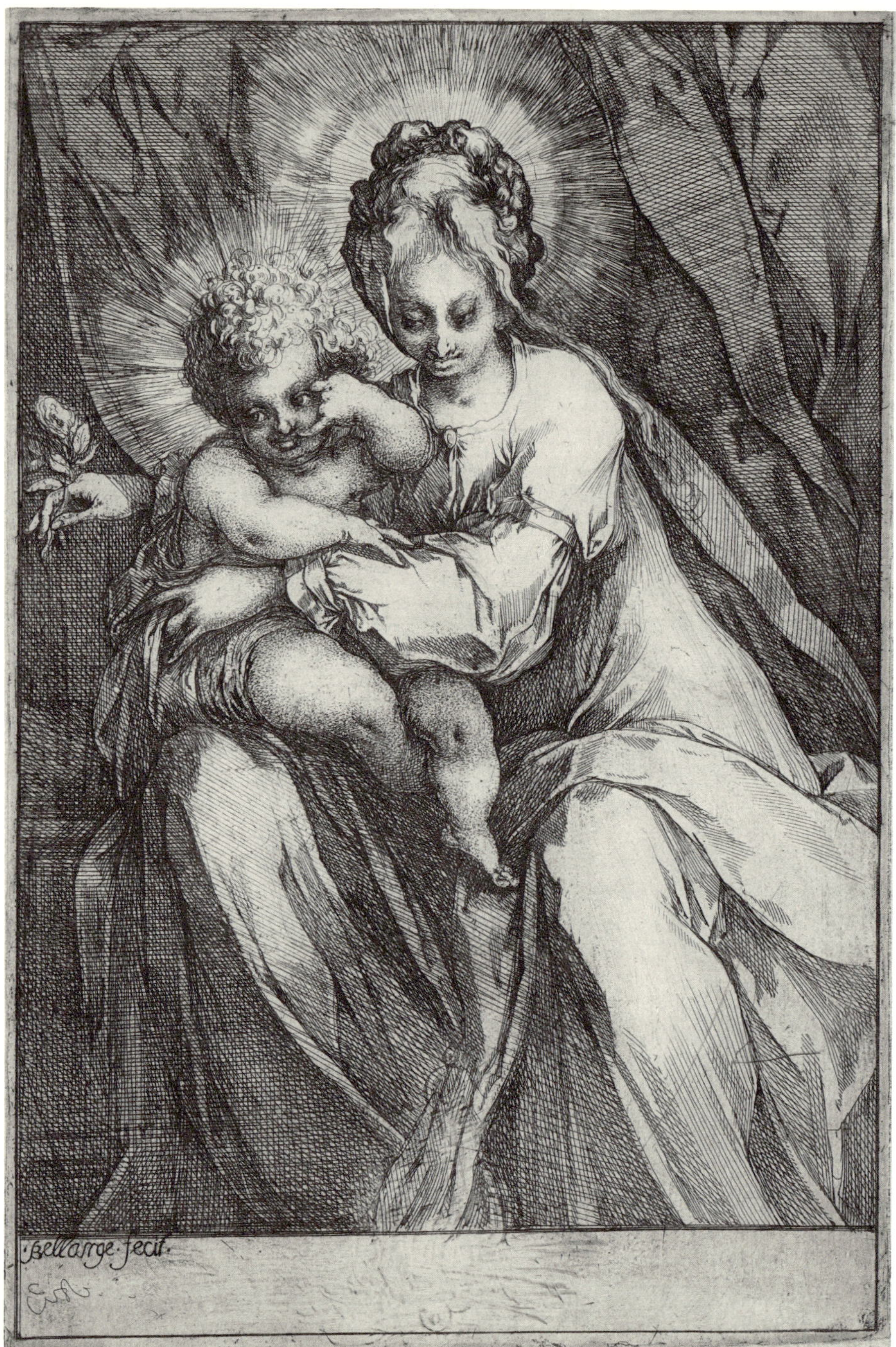

43

etched the coat of arms as part of his original design and then, for some reason, scraped it out.

A.N.W.

44

Rest on the Flight into Egypt

Pen and brown wash with touches of white over black chalk
240 x 200 mm.
9 7/16 x 7 7/8 in.
Lower right: *De Bellange* (probably autograph)
Watermark: crowned interlaced C's of Duke Charles III and Claude de France
Coll.: Berkeley Sheffield; Louis Deglatigny (Lugt 1768a); Maurice Gobin (Lugt 1124 a/b); Ludwig Burchard
Art Institute of Chicago. The Joseph and Helen Regenstein Collection

Although not a direct study for a print, this wash drawing[1] has characteristics in common with the late etchings. The washes that overlie a sensitive line drawing are handled in a deft and painterly manner. A flying putto, drawn in black chalk, appears at the upper left, recalling the fugitive angels in *The Holy Family with the Magdalen* (cat. no. 22).

Bellange's distinctly personal facial types appear in the pensive Madonna and the coy child. When one compares a late print such as the *Madonna with the Rose* to this drawing, it is apparent how far Bellange has advanced from the *Diana and Orion* (cat. nos. 10-12) in controlling the etching medium so as to suggest the graded tonalities and atmospheric possibilities of a wash drawing.

S.W.R.

1. See Harold Joachim, *The Helen Regenstein Collection of European Drawings*, Chicago, Art Institute of Chicago, 1974, p. 52f.

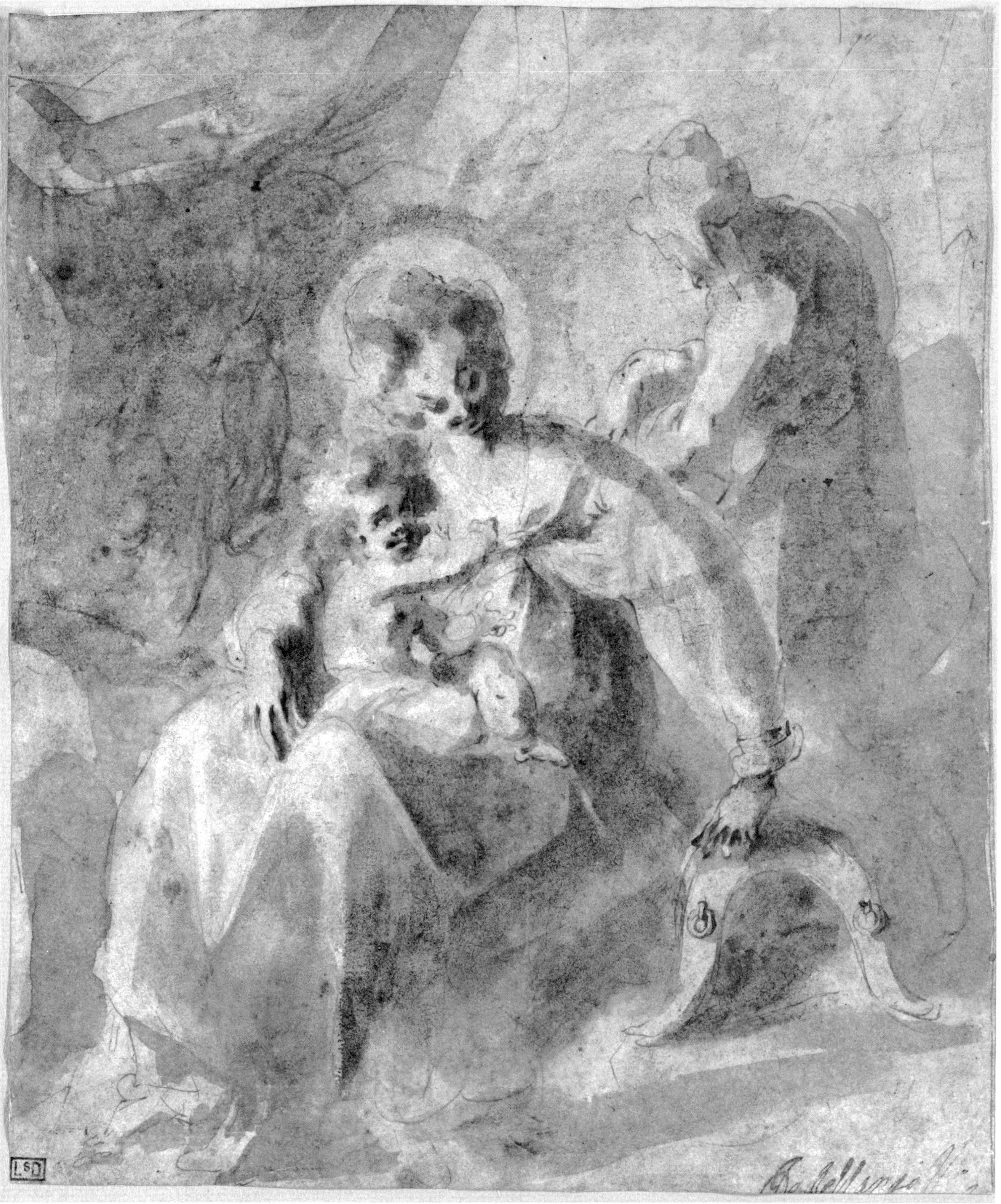

44

45, 47-61 The Apostles

45
Saint James the Greater
Etching
W. 29, R.-D. 31
280-289 x 160-168 mm. (plate)
$11\frac{3}{8}$ x $6\frac{5}{8}$ in.
Coll.: Robert-Dumesnil (Lugt 2200)
Museum of Fine Arts, Boston. Otis Norcross Fund. 40.147

46
FRANCESCO MAZZOLA (il Parmigianino)
Italian, 1503-1540
Saint James the Greater
Etching
Bartsch 8
122 x 70 mm.
$4\frac{13}{16}$ x $2\frac{3}{4}$ in.
Museum of Fine Arts, Boston. Bequest of W. G. Russell Allen. 1973.238

47
Saint Philip
Etching
W. 31, R.-D. 32
280 x 162 mm.
11 x $6\frac{3}{8}$ in.
Watermark: small grapes
Museum of Fine Arts, Boston. Otis Norcross Fund. 40.148

48
Saint Bartholomew
Etching
W. 32, R.-D. 23
283-290 x 163-168 mm. (plate)
$11\frac{3}{8}$ x $6\frac{5}{8}$ in.
Watermark: small grapes
Museum of Fine Arts, Boston. Otis Norcross Fund. 40.138

49
Saint Andrew
Etching and burin
W. 33, R.-D. 19
282-286 x 162-168 mm. (plate)
$11\frac{1}{4}$ x $6\frac{5}{8}$ in.
Museum of Fine Arts, Boston. Otis Norcross Fund. 40.134

50
Saint Thomas
Etching and burnishing
W. 34, R.-D. 25
284-290 x 164-169 mm. (plate)
$11\frac{3}{8}$ x $6\frac{5}{8}$ in.
Museum of Fine Arts, Boston. Otis Norcross Fund. 40.140

51
Saint Thomas
Etching
W. 35, R.-D. 30
282-290 x 162-170 mm. (plate)
$11\frac{3}{8}$ x $6\frac{11}{16}$ in.
Museum of Fine Arts, Boston. Otis Norcross Fund. 40.146

52
Saint James the Greater
Etching and burin
W. 36, R.-D. 20
288-293 x 163-172 mm. (plate)
$11\frac{1}{2}$ x $6\frac{3}{4}$ in.
Watermark: grapes
Museum of Fine Arts, Boston. Otis Norcross Fund. 40.135

53
Saint Simon
Etching and burin
W. 37, R.-D. 26
291-297 x 165-170 mm. (plate)
$11\frac{11}{16}$ x $6\frac{11}{16}$ in.
Watermark: small grapes
Museum of Fine Arts, Boston. Otis Norcross Fund. 40.141

54
Saint Matthias
Etching
W. 38, R.-D. 27
296-301 x 168-172 mm. (plate)
$11\frac{13}{16}$ x $6\frac{3}{4}$ in.
Coll.: Robert-Dumesnie (Lugt 2200)
Museum of Fine Arts, Boston. Otis Norcross Fund. 40.142

55
Saint James the Lesser
Etching and stop-out
W. 39, R.-D. 24
283-290 x 164-170 mm. (plate)
$11\frac{3}{8}$ x $6\frac{11}{16}$ in.
Metropolitan Museum of Art, New York. By exchange, 1959

56
Saint Peter
Etching
W. 40, R.-D. 18
292-297 x 163-168 mm. (plate)
$11\frac{11}{16}$ x $6\frac{5}{8}$ in.
Coll.: Robert-Dumesnil (Lugt 2200)
Museum of Fine Arts, Boston. Otis Norcross Fund. 40.132

57
Saint John
Etching, burin, and stop-out
W. 41, R.-D. 29
292-297 x 166-173 mm. (plate)
$11\frac{11}{16}$ x $6\frac{13}{16}$ in.
Museum of Fine Arts, Boston. Otis Norcross Fund. 40.145

58
Saint Philip
Etching and burin
W. 42, R.-D. 22
291-294 x 166-173 mm. (plate)
$11\frac{5}{16}$ x $6\frac{13}{16}$ in.
Watermark: small grapes
Museum of Fine Arts, Boston. Otis Norcross Fund. 40.137

59
Saint John
Etching
W. 43, R.-D. 21
279 x 158 mm.
11 x $6\frac{1}{4}$ in.
Watermark: small grapes
Museum of Fine Arts, Boston. Otis Norcross Fund. 40.136

60
Saint Paul
Etching
W. 44, R.-D. 28
285-290 x 163-168 mm. (plate)
$11\frac{3}{8}$ x $6\frac{5}{8}$ in.
Watermark: small grapes
Museum of Fine Arts, Boston. Otis Norcross Fund. 40.143

61
Christ
Etching
W. 45, R.-D. 17
296-299 x 170-176 mm. (plate)
$11\frac{3}{4}$ x $6\frac{15}{16}$ in.
Los Angeles County Museum of Art. Museum Purchase with Art Museum Council Fund

On the basis of stylistic considerations, Walch finds two groups among the series of apostles. The earlier group (cat. nos. 45, 47-53) presents the figure as an imaginatively arranged mass of drapery provided with a head, feet, and hands, but with no sense of underlying body.

Three apostles, one version of *James the Greater* and one of *Philip* (cat. nos. 45, 47) and the unique impression of *Mat-*

thew (fig. 5) were etched without any background shading. There are similarities in the inflated draperies (Matthew and Philip) and in the ground and shadows (James and Matthew) to the *Hortulana* series (especially cat. nos. 16 and 17). These three apostles probably antedate the shaded series where another version of James and Philip occur.

The probable prototype for *James the Greater* is Parmigianino's smaller and more lightly etched version of the same saint (cat. no. 46), where the pose and attribute are similar. As has often been noted, Bellange looked to Parmigianino not only as a designer but also as an etcher.

Thomas appears in two versions. In the first (cat. no. 50) the shape of his head has been altered and the burnishing necessitated by this move is clearly evident. The second version of Thomas (cat. no. 51) has the same ugly face as the *Blind Hurdy-Gurdy Player* (cat. no. 27).

The later group of apostles (cat. nos. 54-61) shows a deft handling of technique and greater emphasis on underlying structure. Although the decorative contours remain very important, these figures are illuminated so as to increase their plasticity. The resulting tangibility, especially in some of the more bizarre conceptions such as *John* or *Christ* (cat. nos. 57, 61) can be repugnant and at best is startling. To the ideals of the eighteenth and nineteenth centuries these holy figures would have indeed appeared "perverse and decadent."[1]

In her eloquent analysis of the *Christ,* Walch draws attention to the mandorla- (or flame-) shaped figure. Like some strange plant form, it rises from the ground. The body widens at the hips and has a swollen abdomen; it tapers again to a narrow chest and shoulders, and is topped by a bulbous head with heavy-lidded eyes, fleshy lips, and curling hair. The silhouette is decorative, accented by draperies drawn into triangular points and swelling extravagantly beside arm and hips. The lighting is strong and crosses the figure on a diagonal, accenting its serpentine pose and at the same time emphasizing the plasticity of some parts. These late apostles are voluminous but virtually weightless. In Bellange's saints, refined beyond human terms, we must see the embodiment of the ideals of courtly taste. Esthete and aristocrat, this is a Christ who never washed his disciples' feet.

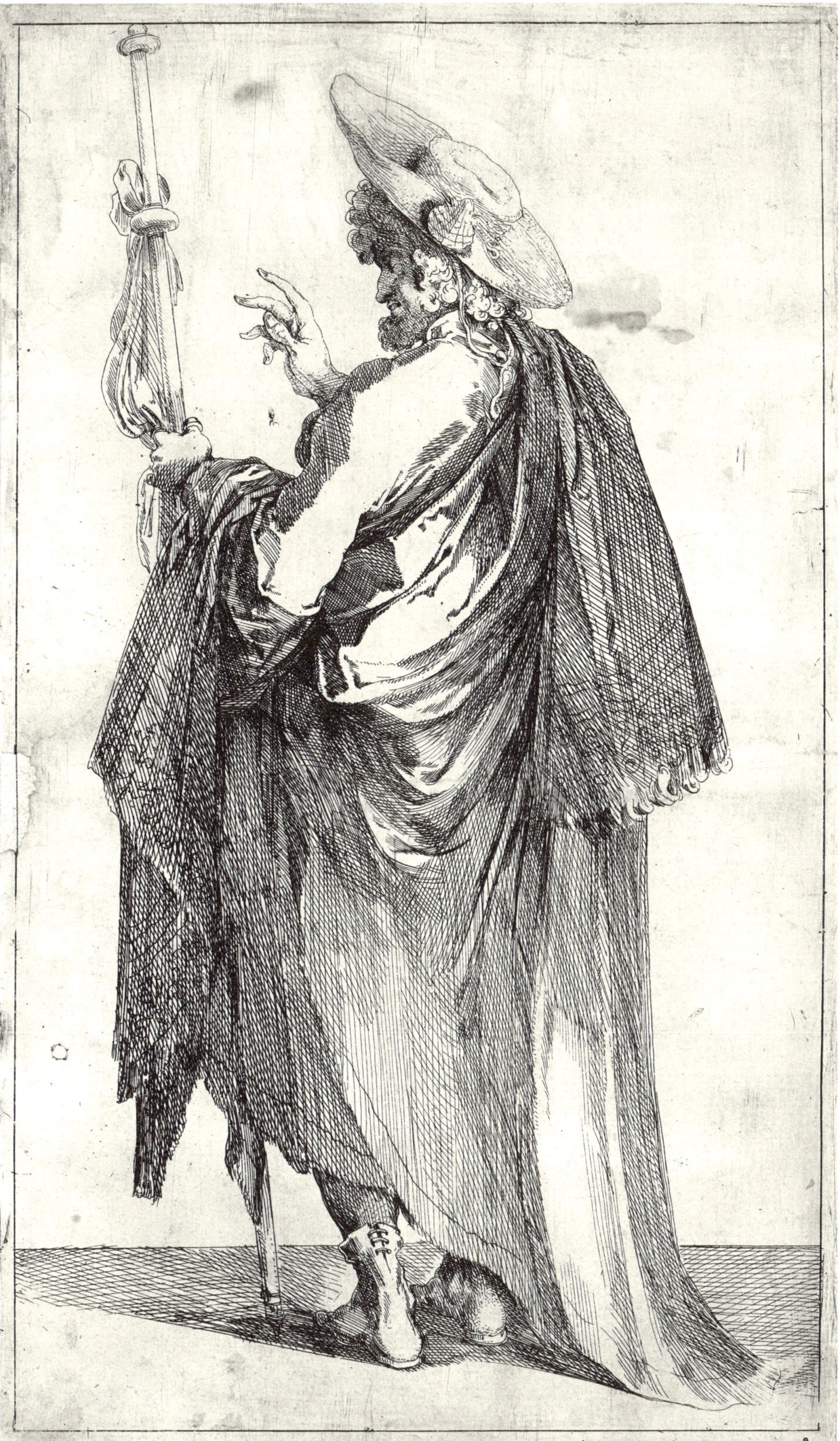

45

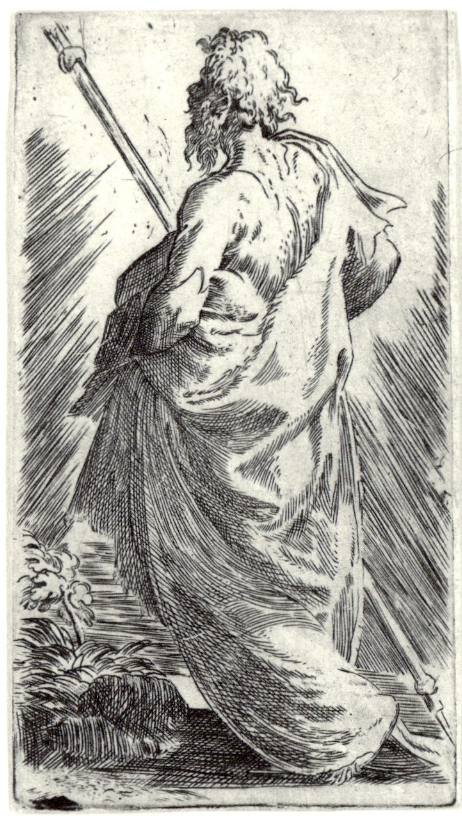

46

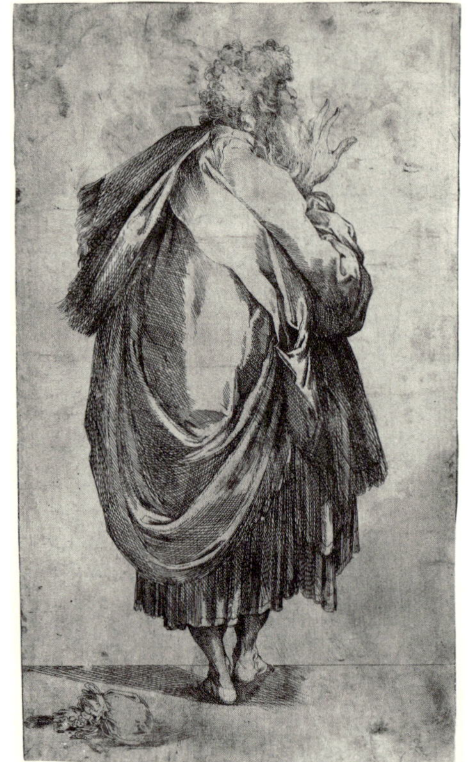

Fig. 5. BELLANGE, *Saint Matthew*, etching. Kupferstichkabinett, Staatliche Museen, Berlin

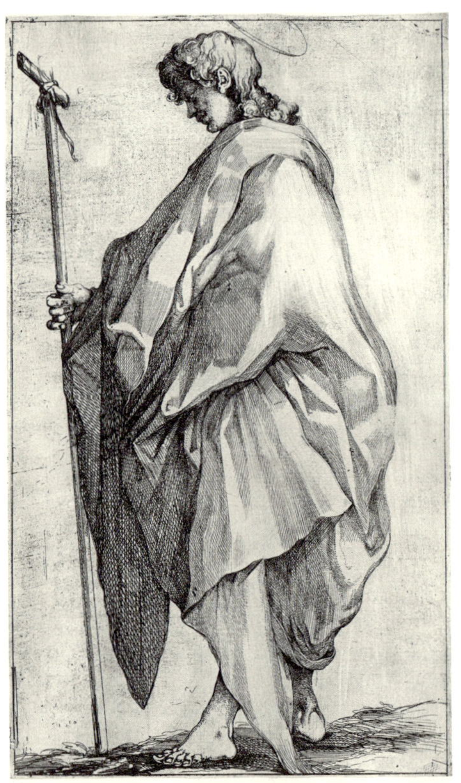

47

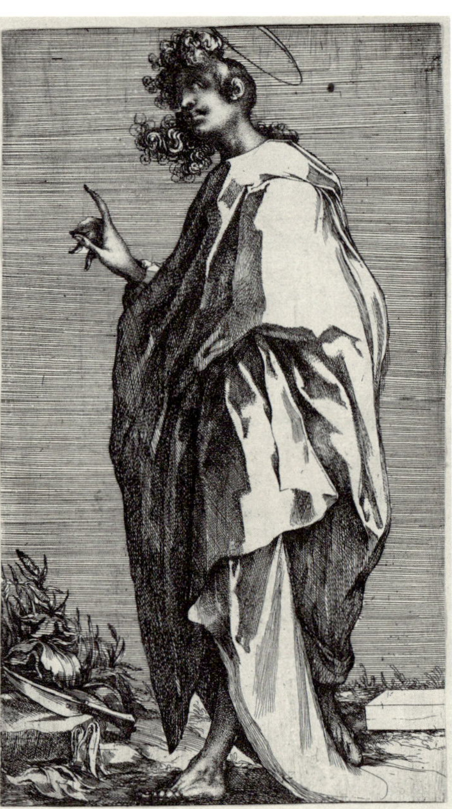

48

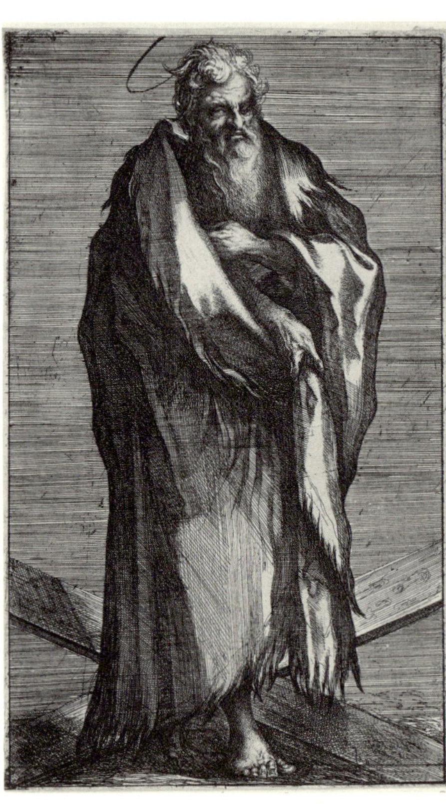

49

In contrast, *Peter* (cat. no. 56) is the most sober and monumental of the series. A sculptural prototype is suggested for him, and for *Paul* (cat. no. 60) as well. Ultimately it is Michelangelo's *Moses* for the tomb of Julius II, many times imitated, such as in the four fathers of the church, executed in marble by the workshop of Florent Drouin in Nancy for the tomb of Charles of Vaudémont, Bishop of Toul and Verdun. Commissioned in 1588, the tomb was located in the Church of the Cordeliers, adjacent to the ducal palace.[2]

In *James the Lesser* and one version of *John* (cat. nos. 55 and 57) one finds an application of stop-out varnish, lightening the background shading along the outer left contour of the figure. This seems to have been done in order to make a stronger contrast between the dark side of the figure and the background's intermediary tone. In *James* there is also burnishing to create a more subtle transition between the two tones of the background. Although the results are not totally satisfactory, Bellange's willingness to experiment is significant.

In his time Bellange was not alone in portraying religious subjects with affectation and as sensuous, super-elegant beings. At the Palace of Fontainebleau in 1608 Bellange could have seen the Chapel of the Trinity in process of being decorated by Martin Fréminet (1567–1619). Begun as early as 1606, the chapel was worked on continuously until Fréminet's death and completed thereafter. Bellange would have found much to admire there. Sylvie Béguin remarks on Fréminet's "entirely profane charm" in the vault figures,[3] and, indeed, some of these kings of the Old Testament are brothers to Bellange's apostles in their very shapes, as well as in their serpentine poses, elegant draperies, and suave deportment.

S.W.R.

1. John Shearman, *Mannerism,* New York, Penguin Books, 1967, p. 16.
2. Pierre Marot, *Le Vieux Nancy,* Nancy, 1970, p. 85, illus.
3. "Two Projects by Martin Fréminet for the Chapel of the Trinity at Fontainebleau," *Master Drawings,* vol. 1, no. 3 (1963), 32.

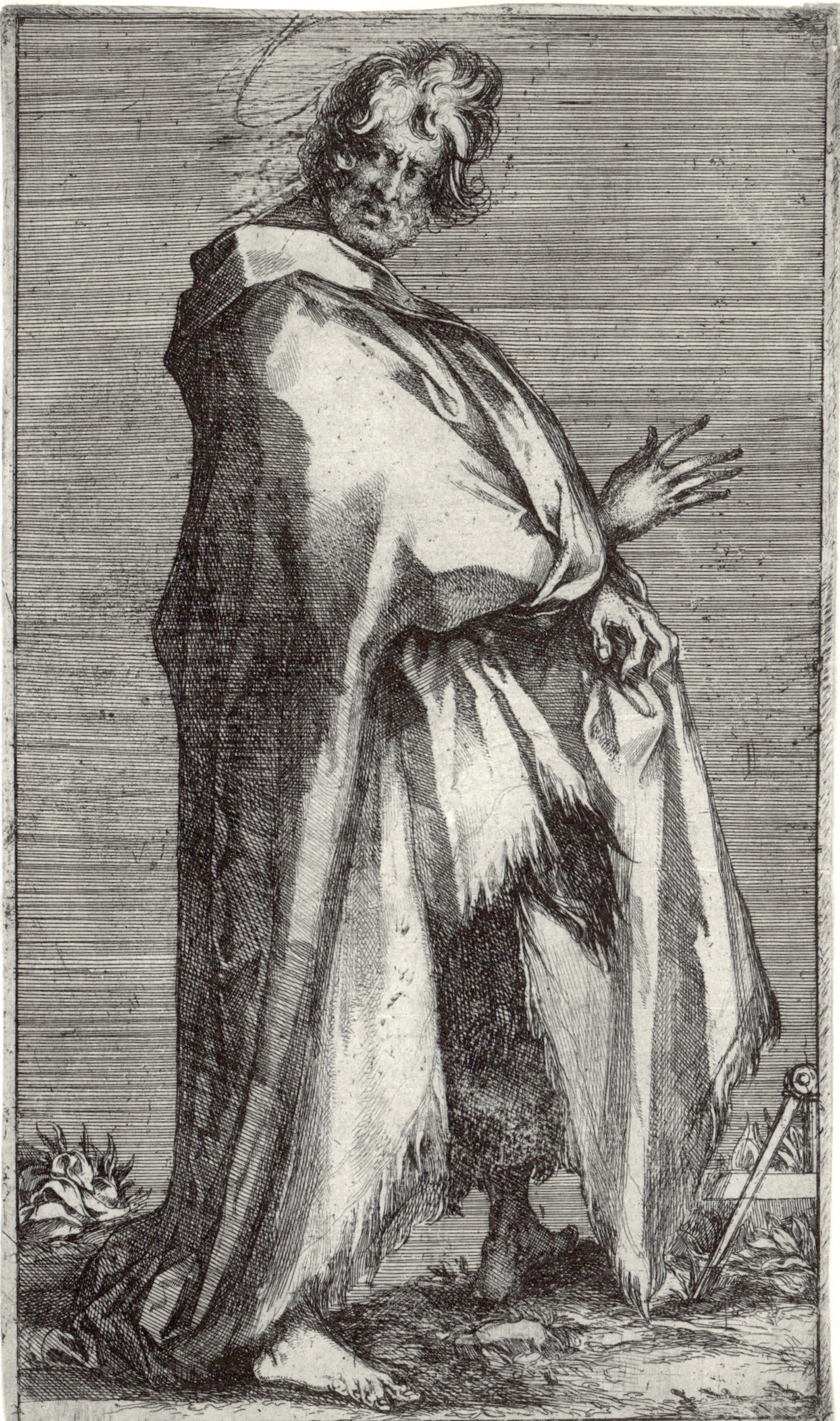

50

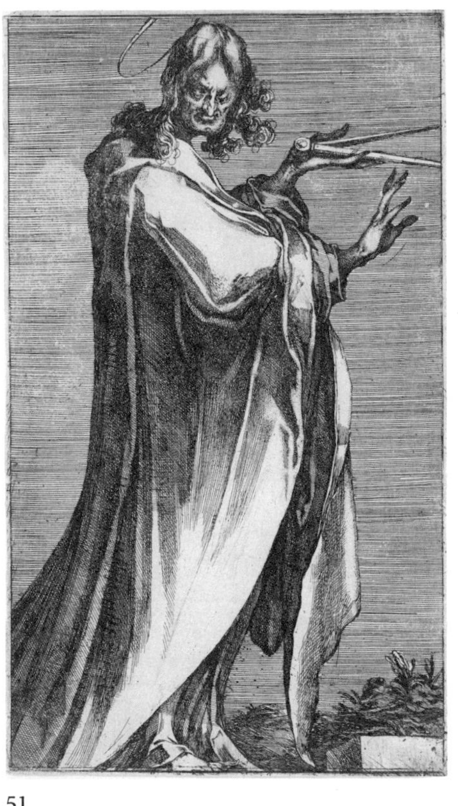
51

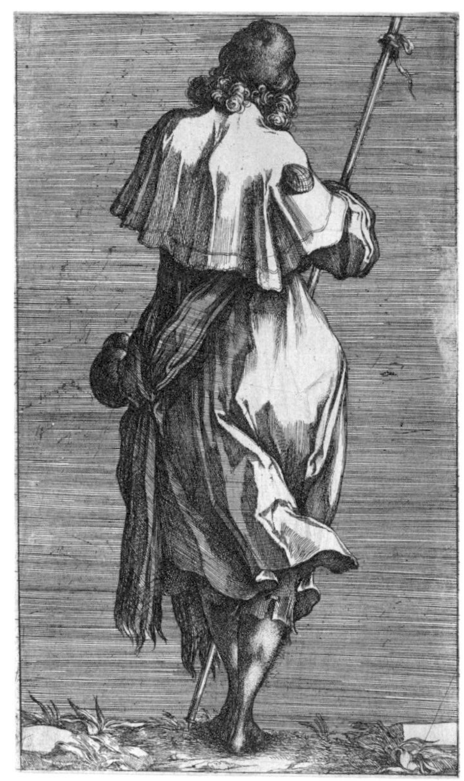
52

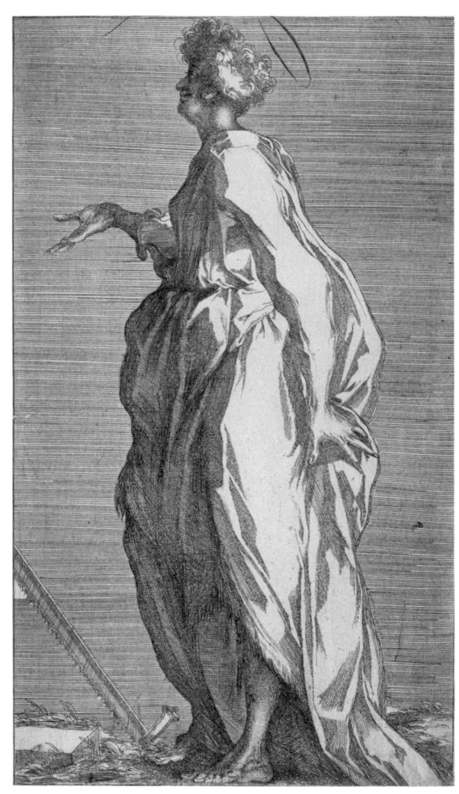
53

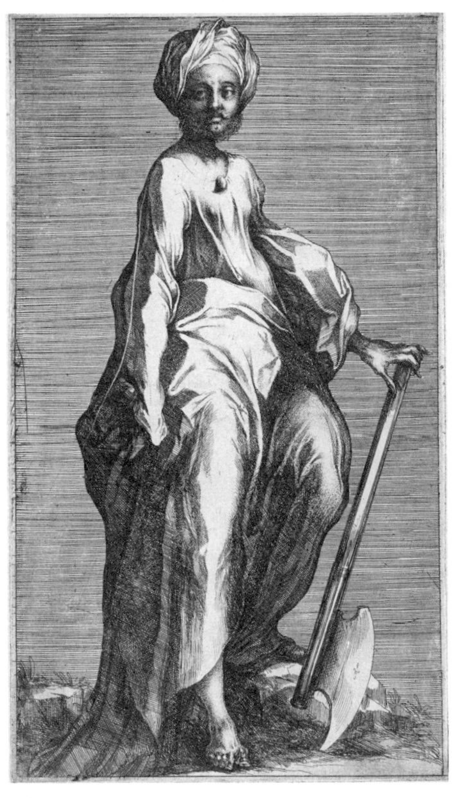
54

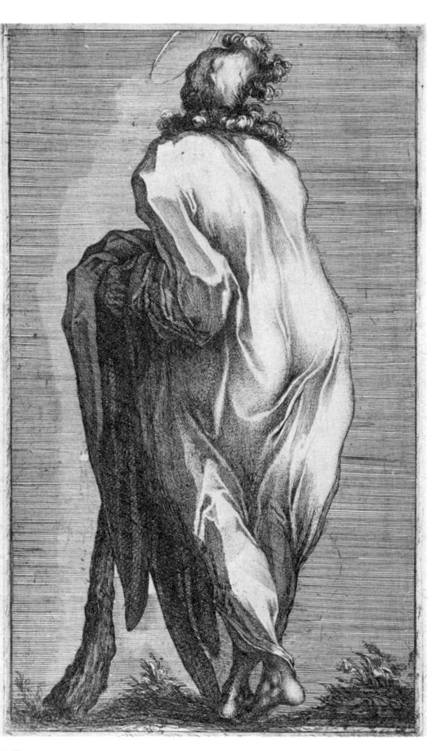
55

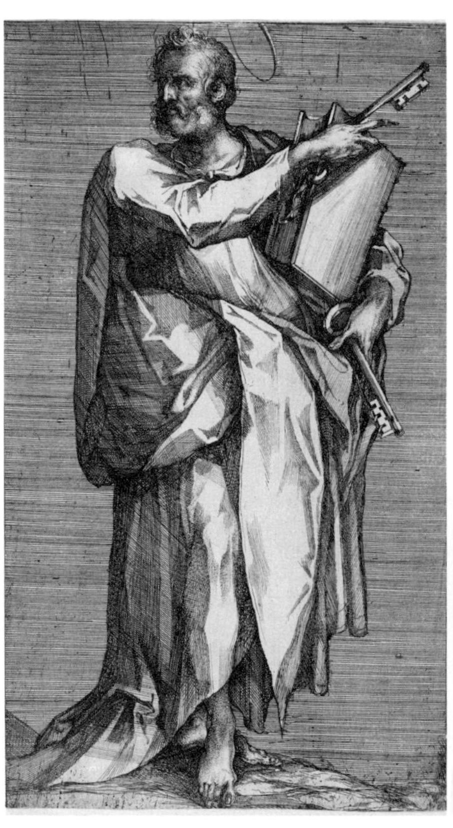
56

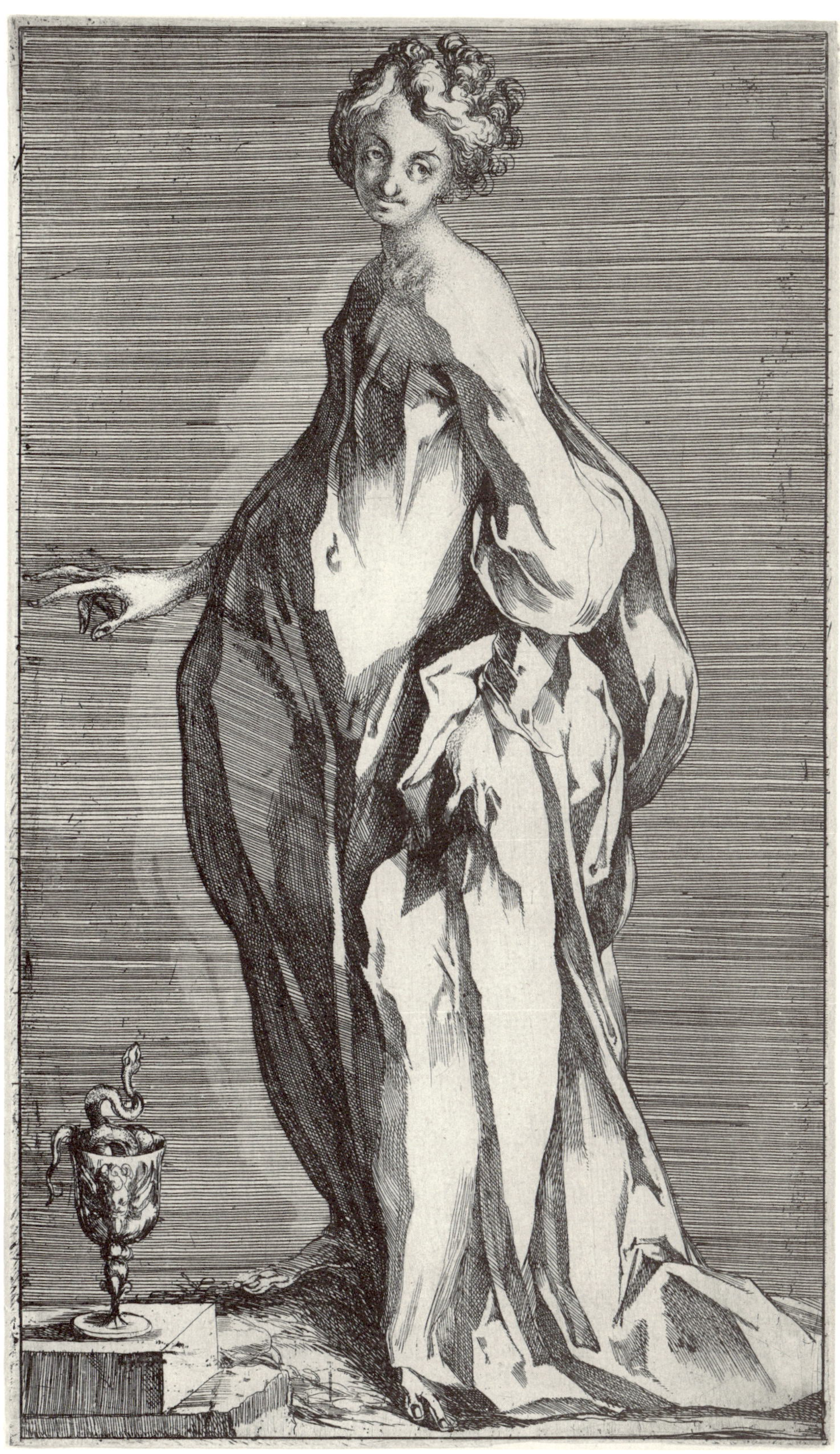

57

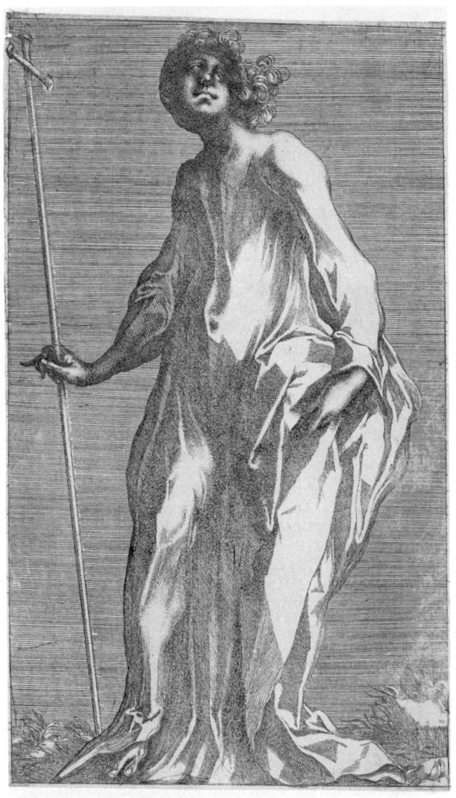

58

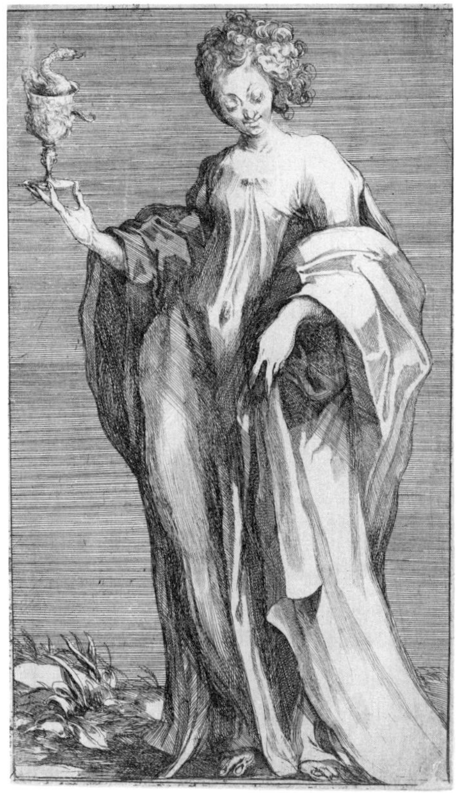

59

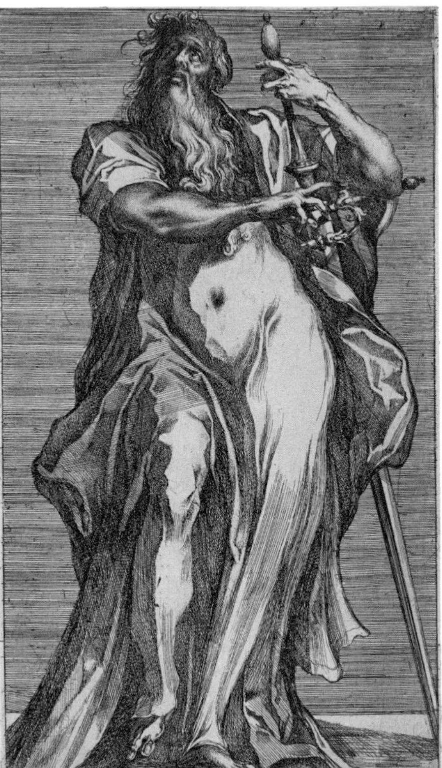

60

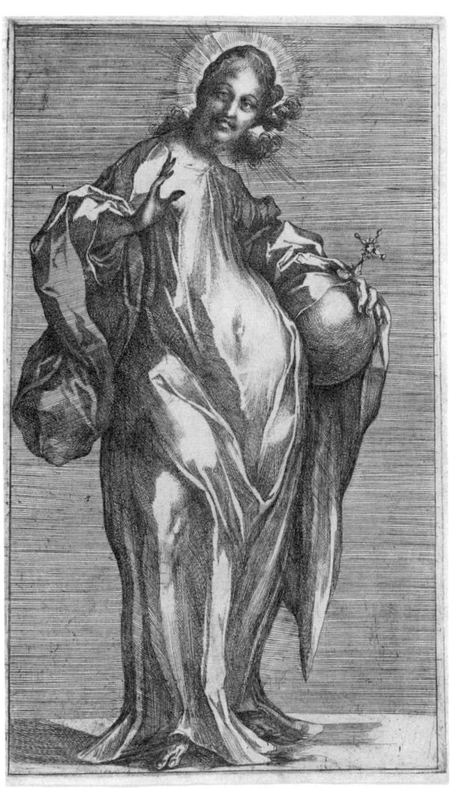

61

62
The Three Women at the Tomb
Etching, touched with burin
W. 46, R.-D. 9 (first state)
441 x 288 mm.
17¼ x 11⅜ in.
Watermark: crowned H of Duke Henri II (see Wiener Pl.11, no. 5)
Coll.: Robert-Dumesnil (Lugt 2200)
Museum of Fine Arts, Boston. Otis Norcross Fund. 40.119

63
Robert Willemsz
De Baudous
Netherlandish, ca. 1575-1644
The Finding of Erichthonius, plate from a set of 52 illustrating Ovid's *Metamorphoses*
After Hendrik Goltzius
Engraving
Hollstein vol. I, 16-67; vol. VIII, p. 130, 10-61
7 x 9¾ in.
Los Angeles County Museum of Art. Museum purchase with Graphic Arts Council Fund

The *Three Women at the Tomb* is probably Bellange's best-known etching. Often discussed and reproduced, it has been the basis of most people's familiarity and knowledge of Bellange's style. We do not intend here to take up the question of Bellange's religious sincerity, spirituality, neuroticism, decadence, or any of the other qualities often discussed in connection with this print. Rather, we accept the print as representing the moment when Bellange's dramatic and stylistic intentions, and his technical abilities came together in a most perfect meeting.

The four gospels each record differing accounts of the visit of disciples of Jesus to the tomb. Only Mark 16:1-8 corresponds with Bellange's image, with its one angel and three women, Mary Magdalen, Mary, mother of James, and Salome.[1] The women in Bellange's print do not carry jars of spices and ointments, as described by Mark (though had Bellange etched this scene several years earlier, one would have expected to see highly ornamental spice jars). The cave in the print is inspired by Mark's description, with its round entrance, and the "youth" in the white robe, sitting on the right-hand side of the tomb.

Blunt and Hauser have called attention to the pictorial device of the simultaneous representations of the women, seen

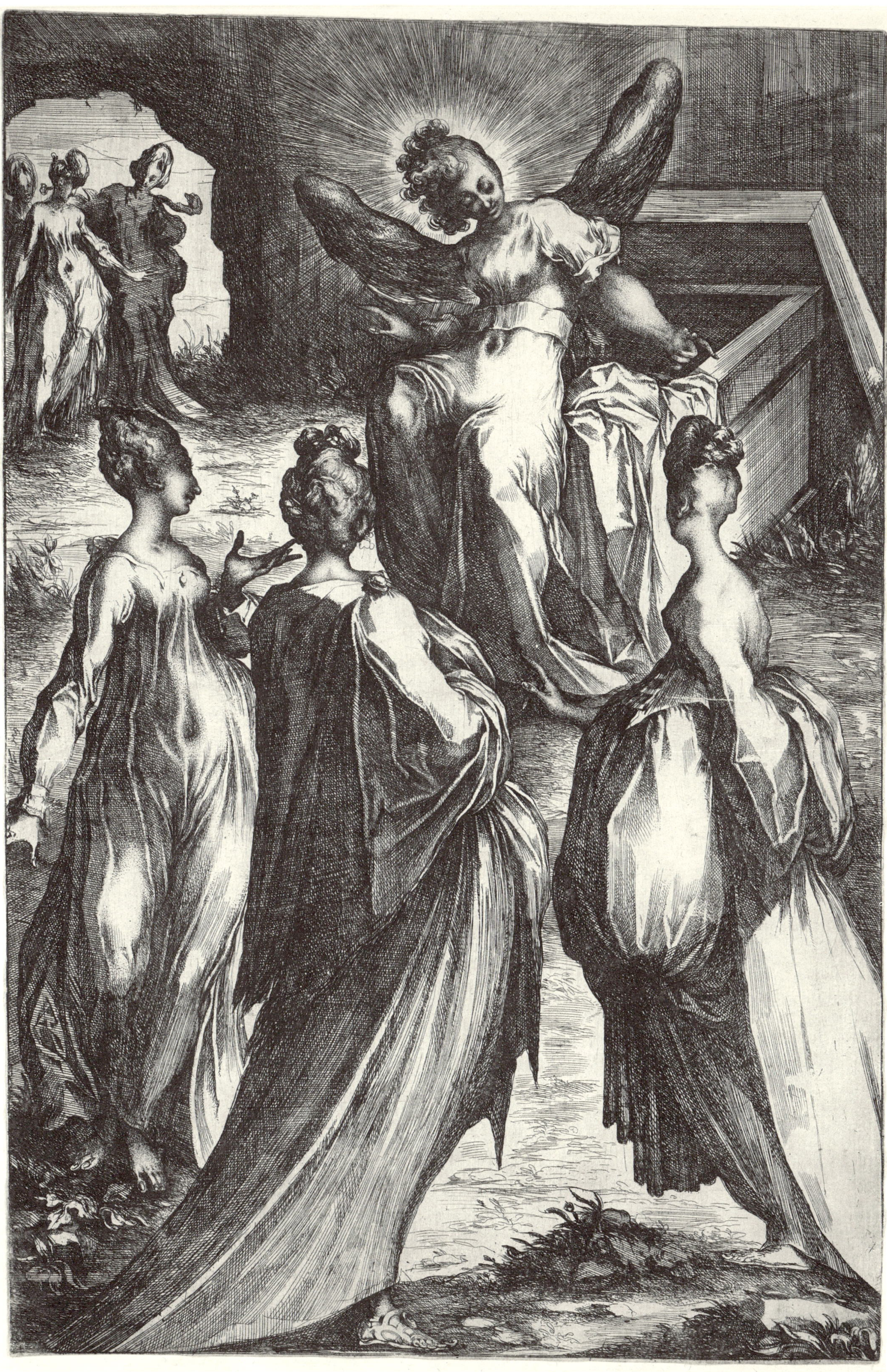

both at the entrance and within the tomb, a pre-Renaissance narrative device that never quite disappeared until the baroque period's insistence on the unity of time. Several writers have remarked on Bellange's dramatic depiction of space in this print. The tilt of the cave floor, with the three women almost below the viewer's eye level, and the swooping curves of the figures which direct the eye up to the angel, work to create a curious but functional space. Bellange uses the high horizon line in a number of his prints, including the *Adoration of the Magi* (cat. no. 31, 32), the *Martyrdom of Saint Lucy* (cat. no. 29), and the *Raising of Lazarus* (cat. no. 64), in all of which the high horizon creates space to crowd with figures, so that the device is less apparent and dramatic than in the *Three Women at the Tomb*.

Walch has shown that Bellange used two engravings by Goltzius as the source for figures in this print. The angel is derived from Goltzius' *Annunciation of the Birth of Simon to Manoah and His Wife*, B. 3; while the figures of the three women are derived from the daughters of Cecrops in Goltzius' *Finding of Erichthonius*, from his series of illustrations to Ovid's *Metamorphoses*.[2] We would add that it is possible that the general conception of Bellange's composition was derived from yet a third engraving by Goltzius, the *Resurrection*, B. 38,[3] where Bellange substituted the three women for Goltzius' soldiers inside the cave tomb. Bellange's very complicated and personal use of sources has been seen in a print like the *Martyrdom of Saint Lucy*, where he combined sections of at least two artists' prints with figures taken from one of his own prints. It is therefore conceivable that the *Three Women at the Tomb* was also constructed in this way. The image succeeds on the dramatic level because by this time Bellange's ability to pull together and personalize "borrowings" had become highly developed. Whereas he formerly tended to make a borrowing from another artist his own by dressing it up with some ornament, clothing, hairstyle, or facial expression, his now mature and distinctive sense of form takes the place of decoration. Ornamental details are almost entirely eliminated and are replaced by a powerful rendering of the human form through light. The ambivalent sexuality and affirmative sensuality of his figures are, if anything, more emphasized, giving them a far more expressive, less decorative value. Bellange's earlier, often distracting preoccupation with the difficulties of the etching technique, as in his stippling of flesh, is no longer noticeable. Now unconcerned with the description of local texture, but more interested in chiaroscuro, he uses his etching needle to build up rich darks, as along the contour of the women's gowns, which emphasizes the unnatural lighting. Thus, the successful union of drama, mystical content, technical ease, and a fully formulated style create a powerful image in the *Three Women at the Tomb*.

A.N.W.

1. None of the gospels mention by name three *Marys* at Christ's tomb, although an iconographic tradition does exist and such images are often entitled the *Three Marys*. This tradition can be explained by the presence of the Virgin Mary, when she is clearly identified as such.

2. Bellange may have been familiar with Goltzius' Ovid illustrations at the time he painted a series of Ovidian decorations for the ducal palace in 1611.

3. Reproduced in Hollstein, 31.

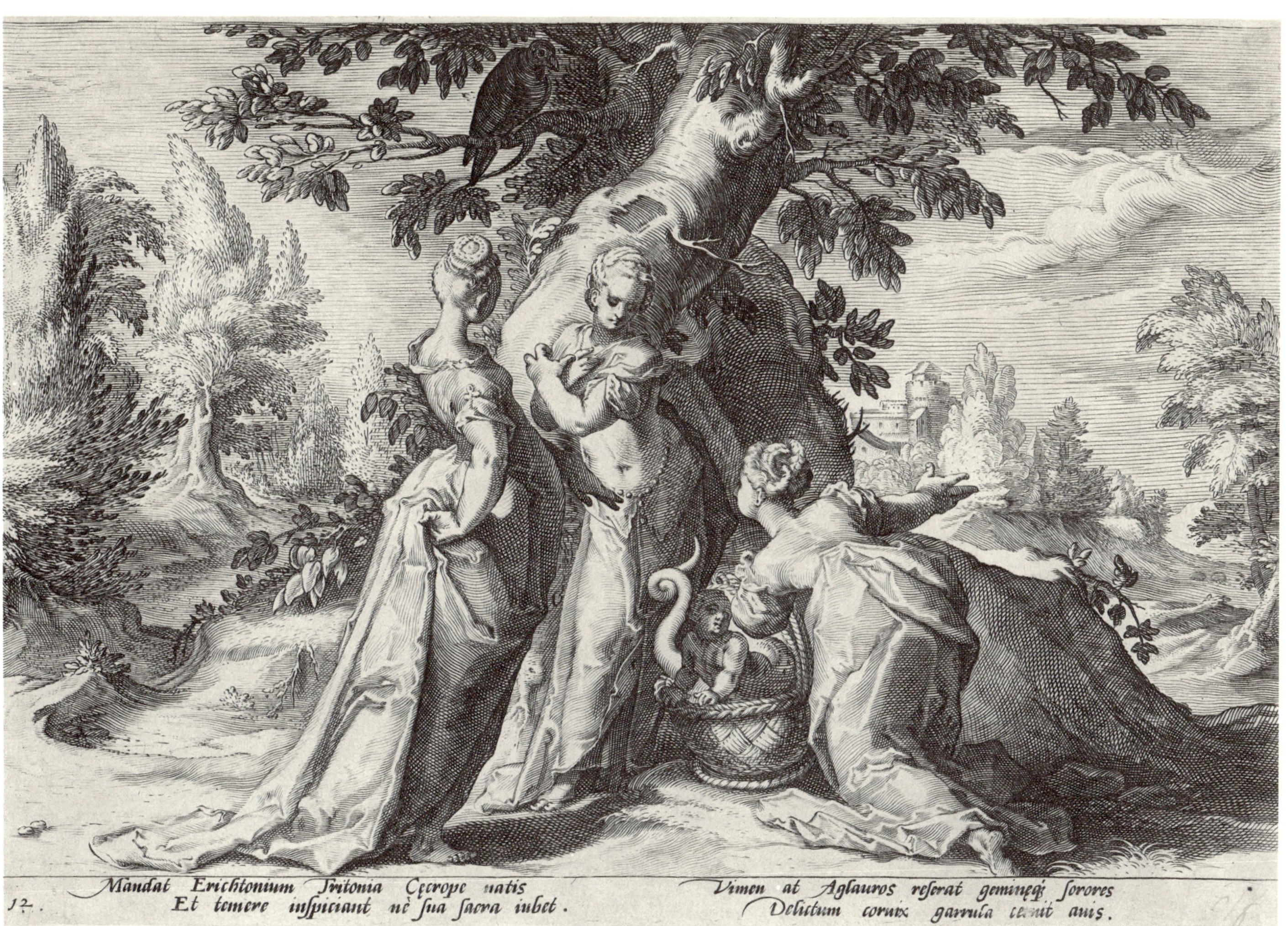
12.
Mandat Erichtonium Tritonia Cecrope natis
Et temere inspiciant nè sua sacra iubet.
Vimen at Aglauros reserat geminęq; sorores
Delictum coruix garrula tenuit auis.

63

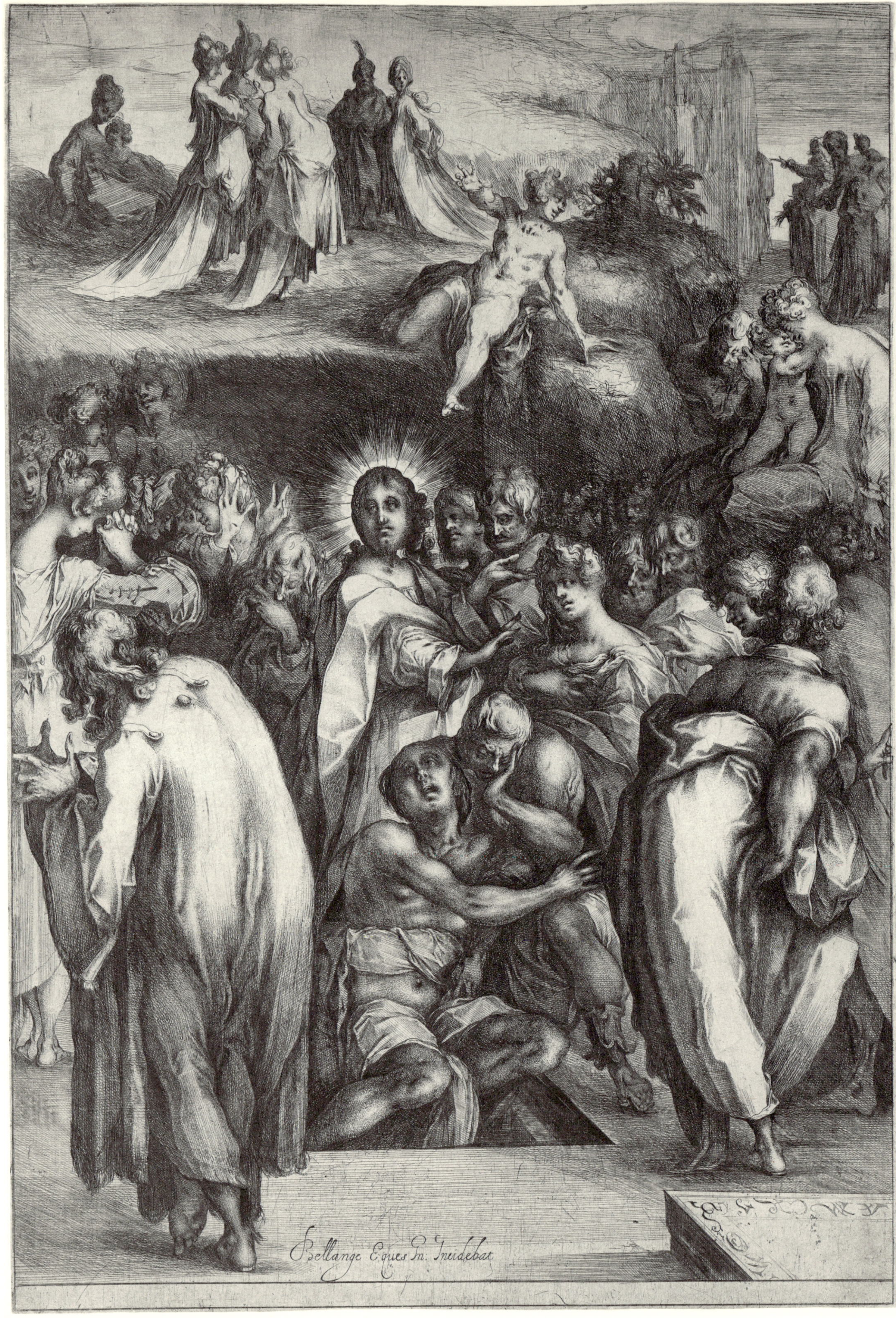
Bellange Eques In: Incidebat

64

The Raising of Lazarus

Etching and burin
W. 47, R.-D. 6
456-460 x 306-312 mm. (plate)
18⅛ x 12¼ in.
Watermark: large grapes (similar to Heawood 2107 except with 5 grapes on a side)
Museum of Fine Arts, Boston. Gift of Lydia Evans Tunnard in memory of W. G. Russell Allen. 63.2780

In this presumably last print by Bellange, the rich, muted tones of gray, achieved by the expert handling of the etching medium, are punctuated by spotlit forms. At first the image of Christ's miracle appears to have an aura of sobriety and rationality. However this is soon dispelled upon recognition of Bellange's capricious, personal vocabulary, so apparent in the surrounding spectators. Like giant flames, each of the two disciples who flank Lazarus balances tenuously on one foot, echoing the series of Apostles.

Compared with the *Martyrdom of Saint Lucy*, the *Raising of Lazarus* appears more sober and cohesive. This results from the selective use of light and shade, and to some extent from the more pertinent emotional responses of some spectators. The two-level composition is sophisticated and well wrought. The intricate design may be exemplified by the role of the youth seated on the edge of the cliff; his gaze and outstretched limbs connect the various groups of figures laterally, vertically, and in depth.[1]

Walch has suggested Jan Muller's engraving after Abraham Bloemaert's pen and wash *Raising of Lazarus* as a source for Bellange's print.[2] In Bloemaert's horizontal composition there are indeed arrangements and poses of figures that are recognizable in the Bellange.

The working out of design solutions to the problems inherent in the vertical presentation of the subject goes back to Sebastiano del Piombo's 1519 painting for the cathedral at Narbonne and seems to have been current in Bellange's time. An undated painting by Hendrik de Clerck (ca. 1570-ca. 1629), an Antwerp mannerist, closely resembles Bellange's design. The elements in common—vertical format, position of Christ behind Lazarus, and second level with a figure seated on it—appear in a number of Northern sixteenth and seventeenth century works, some of them mannerist.[3] The court style at Nancy is closely likened to Flemish mannerism, and it is probable that it was through these connections that Bellange chose to involve himself with the compositional problems and solve them in a personal and successful way. His rambling, episodic design is overlaid with a stylistically new element derived from Caravaggism—spotlighting to effect a dramatic focus.

S.W.R.

1. There is a pen study in the Louvre for the group at the upper left on the cliff.

2. Walch, pp. 97-98, illustrated.

3. See works by Aertsen, Finsonius, Pynas, Van Veen, and anonymous artists in the illustrated Decimal Index of the Art of the Low Countries (DIAL) under The Raising of Lazarus (73C52). The two-level composition with figures above may be seen in Lucas van Leyden's 1508 print of the same subject (H. 42).

65
Crispin De Passe
Netherlandish, ca. 1565-1637
(active Cologne, ca. 1594-1610)
Three Holy Women at the Tomb
Engraving
Hollstein 153
138 x 107 mm.
5 7/16 x 4 3/16 in.
On the edge of the tomb: *J. Bellange invent. Cr. d. Passe exc.*
Metropolitan Museum of Art, New York.
Elisha Whittelsey Fund, 1951

66
Crispin De Passe
Netherlandish, ca. 1565-1637
(active Cologne, ca. 1594-1610)
The Adoration of the Magi
Engraving
Hollstein 87
277 x 203 mm.
10 15/16 x 8 in.
At the right: *Mr. de Bellange inventor Crisp. de Passe fec. et exc.*
Bibliothèque Nationale, Paris

67
Crispin De Passe
Netherlandish, ca. 1565-1637
(active Cologne 1594-1610)
Jannette
Engraving
113 x 128 mm.
4 1/2 x 5 1/16 in.
Lower left: *J d Belange jnventor*
Plate 1 of *Mimicarum aliquot facetiarum icones ad habitum Italicum expressi; Abbildung etlicher Italianischer vermumbten bossen, der bluhender Jugendt zugefallen ausgangen durch Crysp d P* (Franken 1351)
Mr. and Mrs. Arthur E. Vershbow, Boston

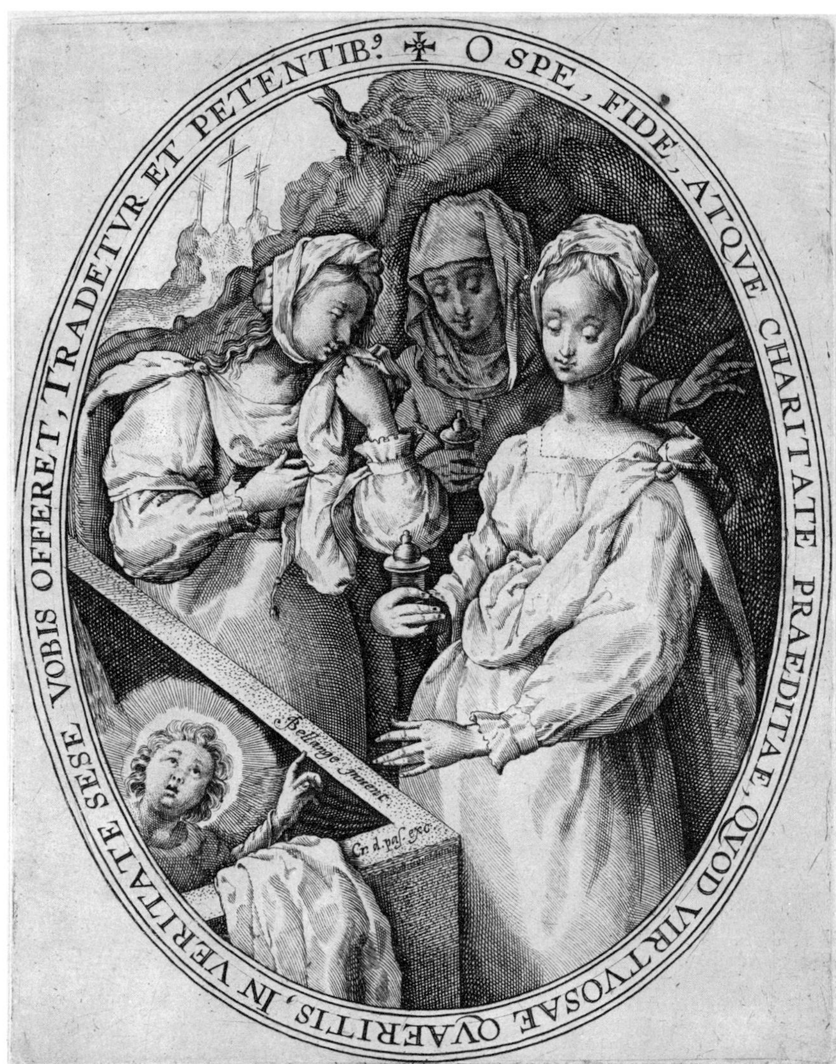

65

Jacques Bellange was apparently connected with printmaking activity about a decade before he himself began to etch, for eight prints after Bellange, four of which bear his name as the designer, were engraved and published by Crispin de Passe the Elder in Cologne before 1610.[1] Drawings related to two of the engravings exist,[2] but their attribution to Bellange is not unquestioned, and neither of the drawings represents the final engraved design. Whether or not Bellange was the draughtsman of these sheets in the Albertina, we should not necessarily reject his authorship of the final design of de Passe's engravings, with their additional figures and architecture.

The *Three Holy Women at the Tomb* (cat. no. 65), although undated, is part of a series of twenty oval engravings designed by various artists. Several of these engravings bear the dates 1600 or 1601. Bellange's design has been related to a red chalk drawing of the same subject, although the poses of the women are different, and the angel and the landscape do not appear in the drawing. Bellange's design must have been made about 1600, and it is the earliest known design by him.

The *Adoration of the Magi* (cat. no. 66) is close to another drawing, in pen and wash, whose design is attributable to Bellange. The drawing, in reverse of the print, includes the figures of the Virgin and Child, the three Kings, one of the serving women, and the half-length figure of a courtly youth. We are willing to accept the de Passe engraving as representing Bellange's final design, including the additional figures, and suggest that the woman in the far distance was later used again by Bellange in, for example, his Hortulana figure-types. The *Adoration of the Magi* is reminiscent of Bellange's later etching of the same subject (cat. no. 31), though here there are fewer figures in a somewhat more coherent space. The sunken area in the foreground, which is shallow in Bellange's own etching, is here quite deep and isolates a young man, who seems rather strange in a work of such a small scale. The device is better suited to a larger painting, where artists have, on occasion, inserted their own self-portrait.[3] It is possible that this engraving by de Passe reflects a lost, large-scale altarpiece by Bellange and that the man in the lower left corner is Bellange himself.[4] The lily he points to could conceivably identify his homeland.

No drawing has been associated with the *Beheading of John the Baptist* (fig. 5, not in exhibition), inscribed *Jacques de belange jnvet.* Nevertheless, the design of the figures, despite their translation

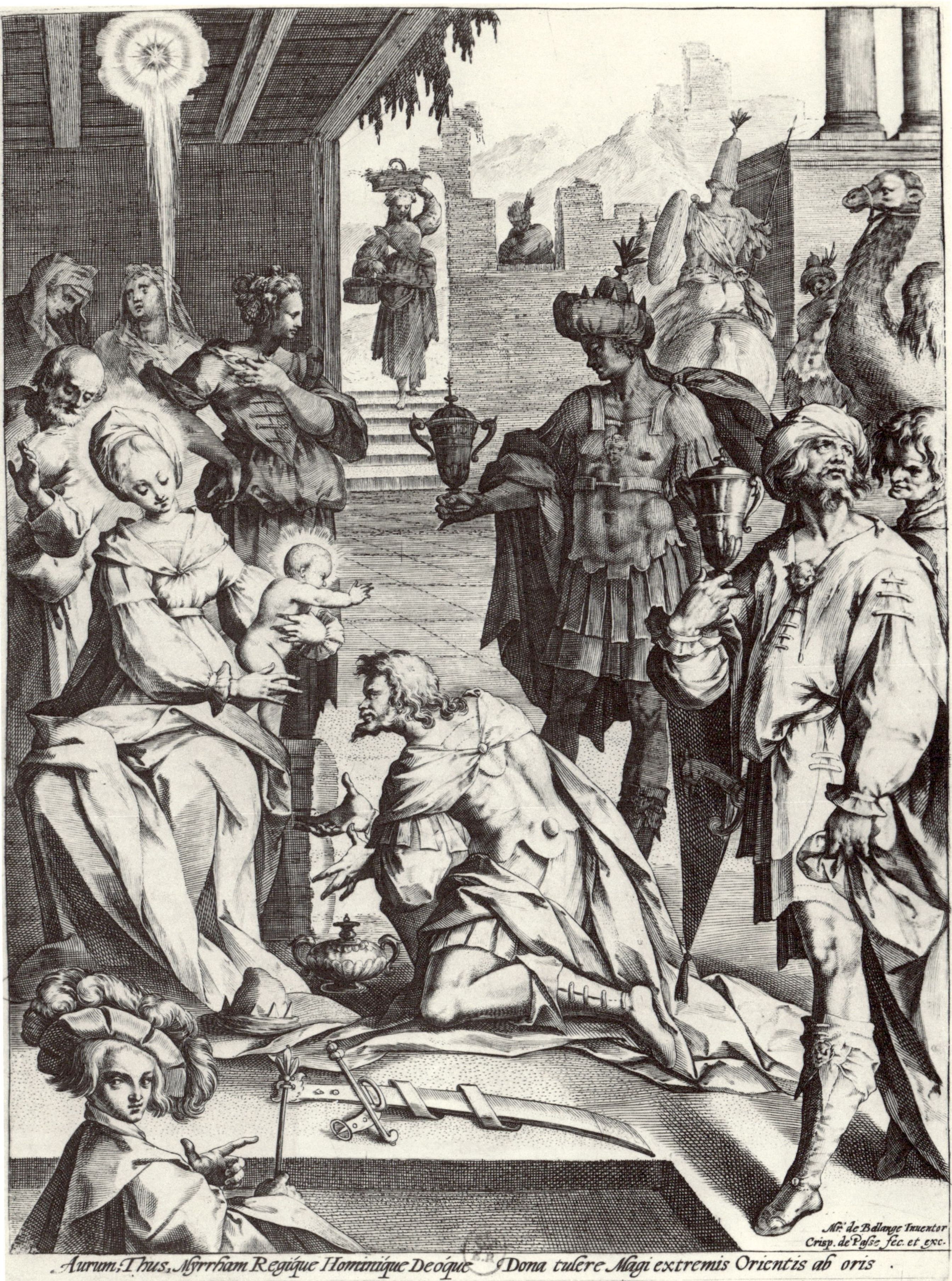
Mr. de Bellange Inuentor
Crisp. de Passe fec. et exc.
Aurum, Thus, Myrrham Regique Hominique Deoque Dona tulere Magi extremis Orientis ab oris .

66

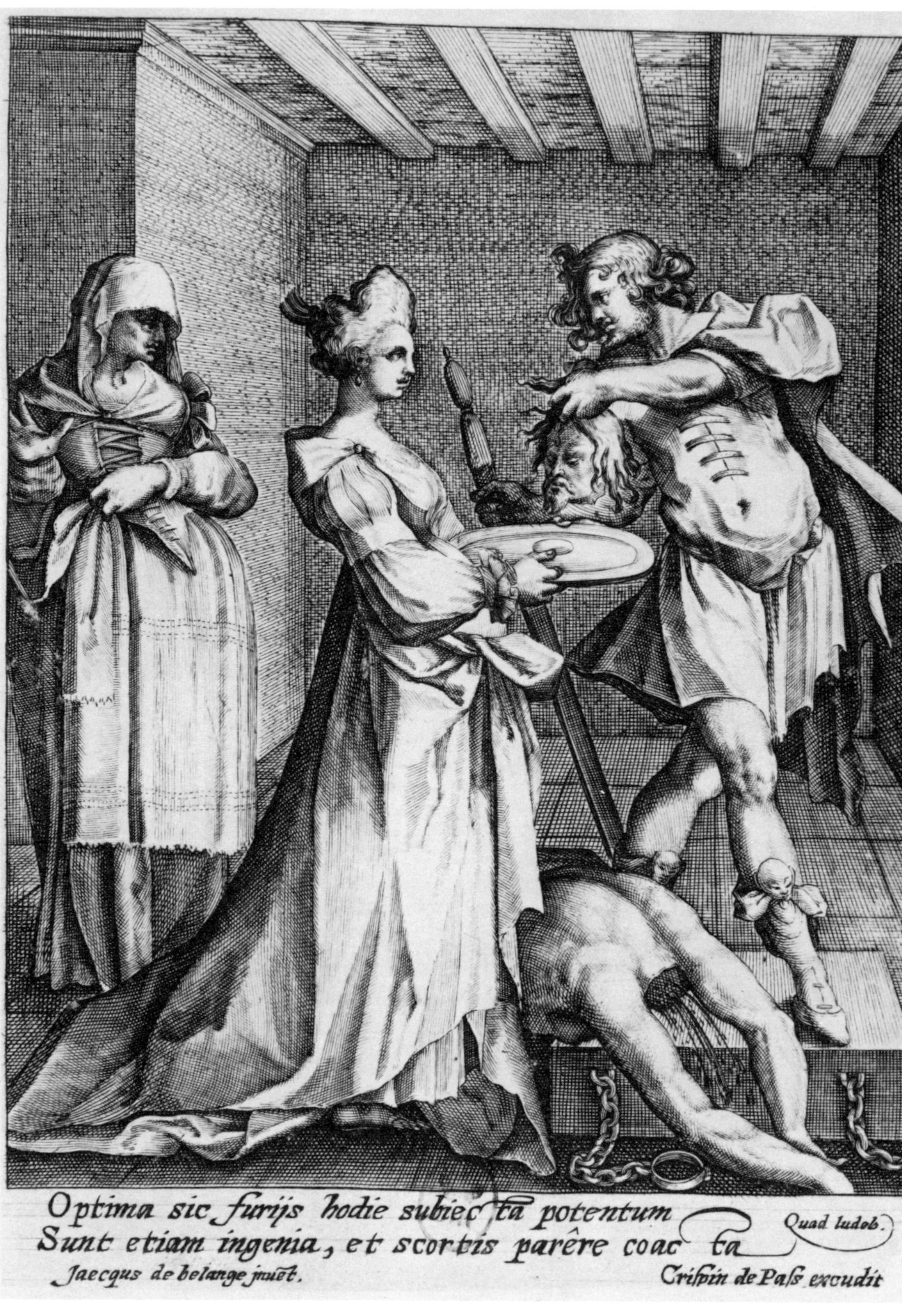

Fig. 6. De Passe, *The Beheading of John the Baptist*, engraving after De Passe, Bibliotheque Nationale, Paris

into a hard engraving style, is recognizably by Bellange.

There are no original etchings by Bellange, nor any known and accepted drawings by him that relate to the subject of Italian comedy. There is, however, an undated set of five engravings published by de Passe, plus a title page in Latin and German, which translates roughly as "Some farcical and witty images expressed in the Italian style."[5] The first engraving is inscribed with Bellange's name as the designer (cat. no. 67). Although the remaining four plates are unsigned, there are sufficient stylistic similarities to Bellange's figure types to attribute the designs to him. They show him involved in a type of subject matter that we would otherwise not know, the Italian comedy, then very much in vogue. They also provide a possible background for Bellange's later Hortulana and blind beggar etchings (also see cat. no. 68).

The eight subjects designed by Bellange and engraved by de Passe are among the earliest documents we have of Bellange. Because the *Three Holy Women at the Tomb* can be dated 1600-1601, and because Crispin de Passe had left Cologne by about 1610, an early dating for all eight seems likely. Moreover, de Passe was connected with the court of Lorraine during this period, for in 1599 and 1603 he published engraved portraits of members of the ducal family. Stylistically as well, the de Passe engravings appear to be quite early and thus are valuable documents that can help us understand Bellange's early development. The designs of these prints seem to be earlier than any of Bellange's etchings. The figures are rather more normative and solid, and their costumes are more clearly constructed, and are not so complex or inflated. The figures gesture and twist more moderately. Each character tends to be a rather isolated study and does not blend into dense massings. This is especially clear in a comparison between the etched and engraved versions of the *Adoration of the Magi* (cat. nos. 31 and 66). The engraver would certainly have dulled much of Bellange's spirit, but when all allowance is made for the hardness of the engraving, these prints still appear to antedate, say, the *Vision of Saint Norbert* (cat. no. 2) by a number of years.

Bellange's style was to become strange and most personal, and elements of it can be seen even in these early works; nevertheless these early engravings after Bellange indicate that his art grew rather naturally out of Northern late mannerist styles.

A.N.W.

1. He left Cologne in that year because of religious persecution.

2. The drawings are reproduced in F.-G. Pariset, "Jacques de Bellange: Examen de Quelques Gravures," *Archives alsaciennes d'histoire de l'art*, XII, 1933, p. 34 ff., figs. 9 and 12.

3. Salviati's *Visitation* in San Giovanni Decollato in Rome, for example.

4. The self-portrait in the *Entry of Henri II* (cat. no. 1) does not contradict this identification.

5. This series is reproduced in Pariset, "Jacques de Bellange," pp. 52-61, figs. 14-19.

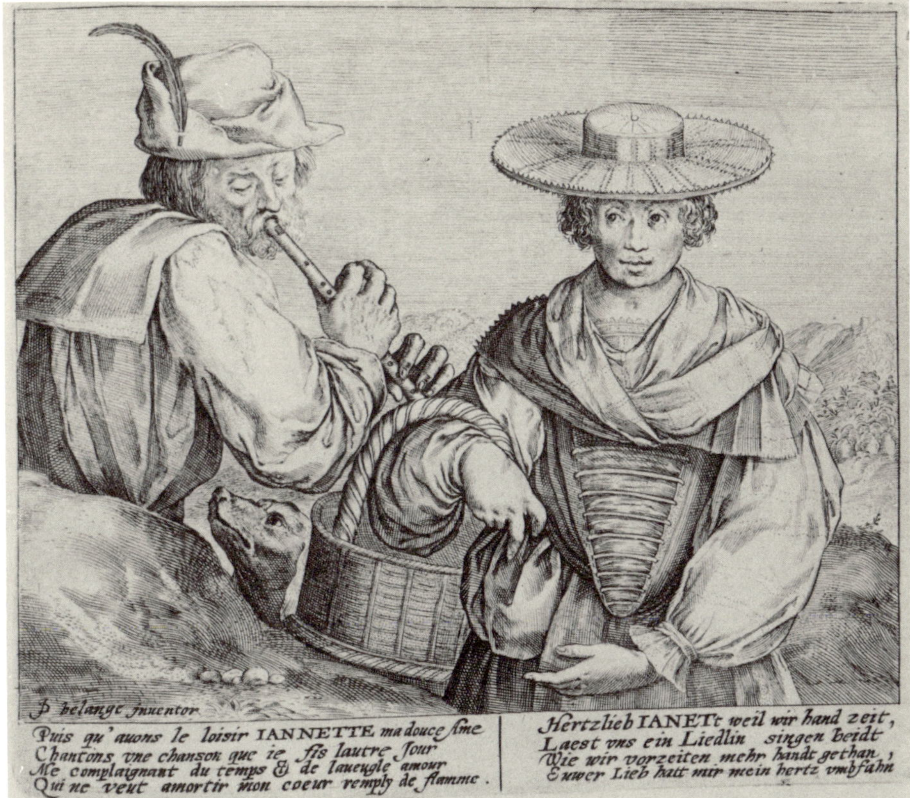

67

Fig. 7. De Passe, "Francisquine" (*Mimicarum* . . .), engraving after Bellange. Private collection

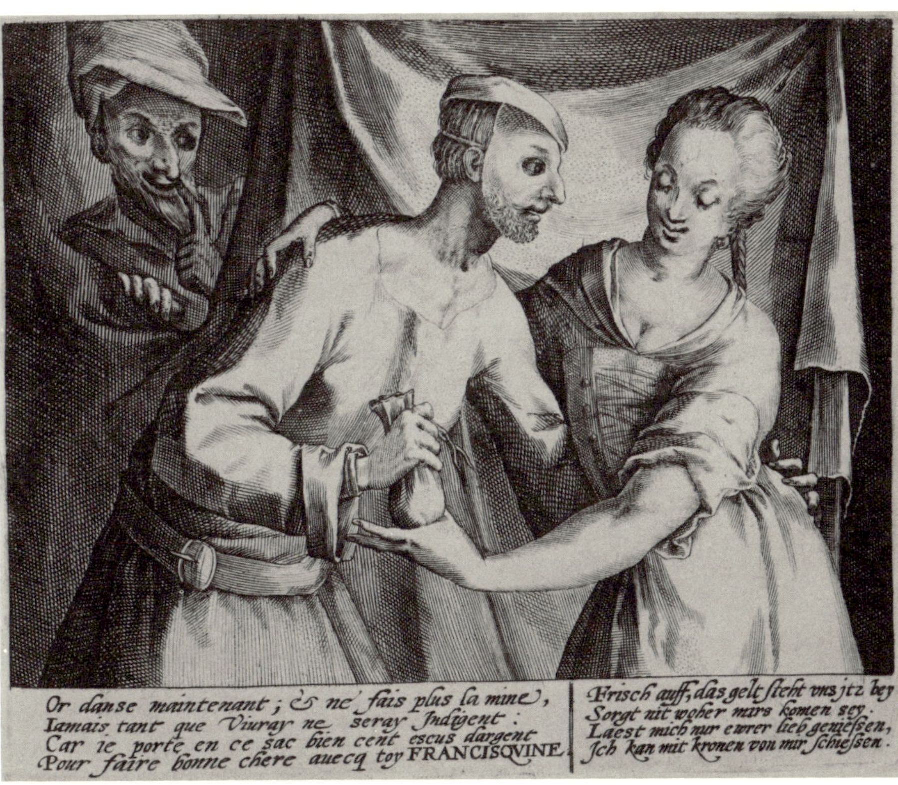

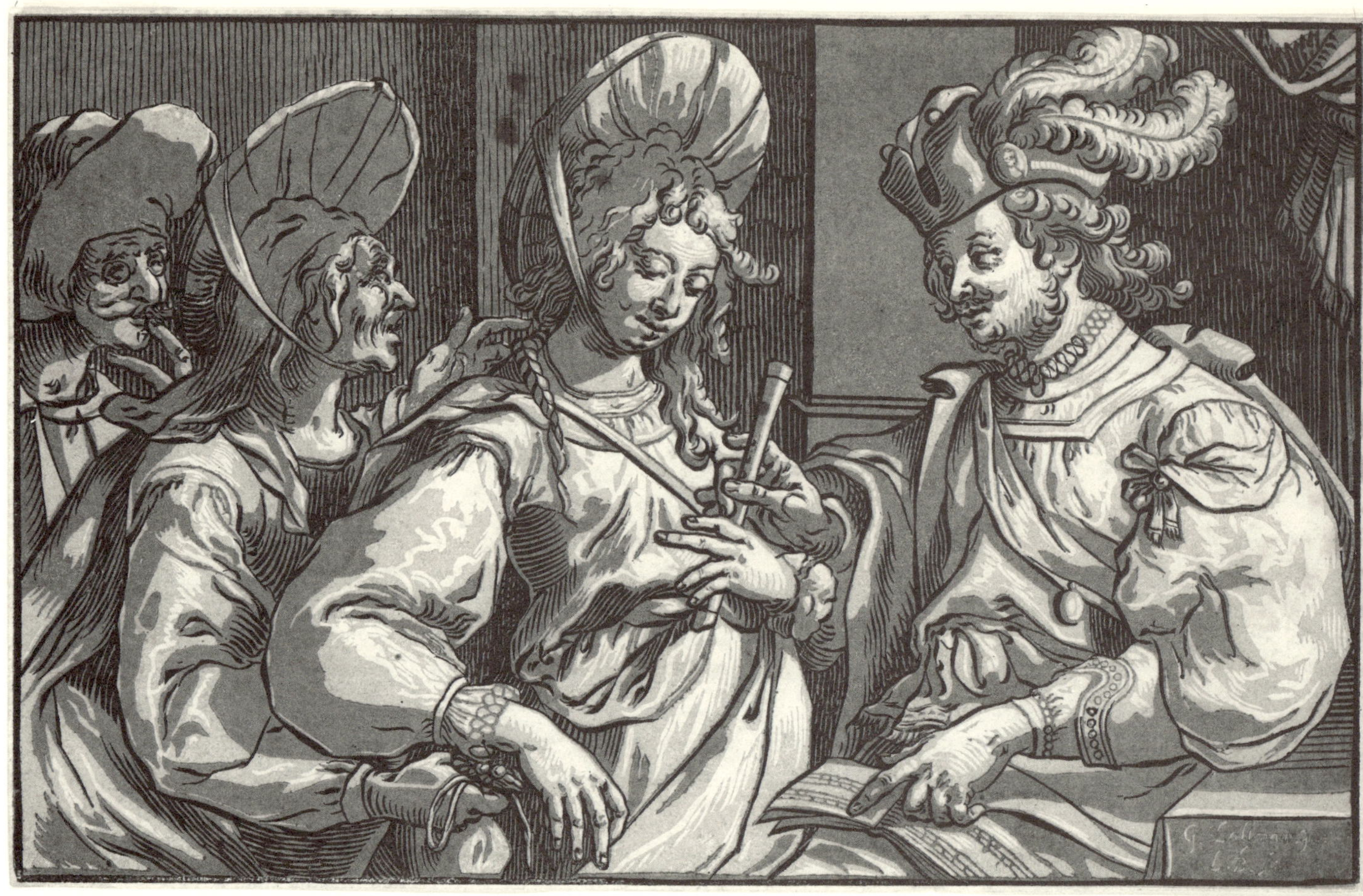

68

68
Ludolph Büsinck
German, 1599/1602-1669 (active France, ca. 1623-1630)
The Procuress
After Georges Lallemand
(1570-ca. 1635)
Chiaroscuro woodcut
3 blocks: black, brown, tan
Hollstein 24
219 x 336 mm.
8⅝ x 13¼ in.
Lower right: *G. Lalleman. In:/ L. B. sc.*
Museum of Fine Arts, Boston. Bequest of W. G. Russell Allen. 1975.353

The faces and attitudes in Lallemand's design for *The Procuress* are reminiscent of Bellange. The subject probably relates to the Italian comedy, and recalls Crispin de Passe's series on the subject after Bellange (cat. no. 67).[1] The old man at the left with his finger to his lips may derive from a similar figure in the *Francisquine* plate (fig. 7), and the old woman from *La Lettre*.[2] If the de Passe series dates from as early as 1600, Lallemand may have known the prints before he left Nancy for Paris in 1601.

A.N.W.

1. Wolfgang Stechow, "Ludolph Buesinck," *Print Collector's Quarterly*, 25 (1938), 393-419; 26 (1939), 348-359, "Catalogue of the Woodcuts by Ludolph Buesinck."
2. Repr. F.-G. Pariset, "Jacques de Bellange: examen de quelques gravures," *Archives alsaciennes d'histoire de l'art*, 13 (1934), 60, fig. 19.